CLUBLAND

CLUBLAND

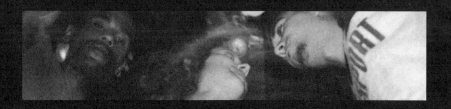

The Fabulous Rise and
Murderous Fall of Club Culture

FRANK OWEN

ST. MARTIN'S PRESS ❧ NEW YORK

www.stmartins.com

ISBN 0-312-28766-6

First Edition: May 2003

10 9 8 7 6 5 4 3 2 1

TO CHENE

CONTENTS

ACKNOWLEDGMENTS

I'd like to thank the following for their invaluable assistance: Todd Shuster of the Zachery, Shuster, Harmsworth Agency; my editors, George Witte at St. Martin's Press and Michael Denneny; Don Forst, Doug Simmons, Adamma Ince, and Tricia Romano at the *Village Voice*; society reporter Jacquelynn D. Powers, Joanne Rabin, and all the staff at the National Hotel in Miami Beach; nightlife impresario Rudolph; Brett Sokol and Tristram Korten at Miami's *New Times*; Bobbi Lauritsen and all the staff at the Ramada Inn in Elkhart, Indiana; and last but not least, Elke Alig.

CLUBLAND

PROLOGUE

New York City, Spring 1995

It began with a simple transaction inside a bustling nightclub, one of hundreds of comparable purchases that must have gone down on that drug-fogged night. In a dimly lit side room filled with vacant-eyed club kids, a crumpled twenty-dollar bill was surreptitiously tendered in exchange for a small packet of white powder. Overcoming my initial nervousness, I flipped forward my long hair as cover, bowed my head, emptied some of the contents onto the back of my hand, exhaled hard, and then snorted up the strange substance, which scratched the inside of my nose like ground-up glass.

On that Wednesday night in May, I was on assignment for the *Village Voice* researching an article on "Special K" (so named after the breakfast cereal), the animal anesthetic ketamine, which recently had migrated from the veterinarian's office to the dance floor, where it had been reappropriated by clubgoers as a mind-bending party favor. Fancying myself one of the last of the gonzo journalists and willing to do almost anything for a juicy headline, I intended to sample the psychedelic catnip that everyone in clubland was calling "the new Ecstasy" and then write about the powerful visions the drug supposedly caused.

I'd received conflicting reports from club goers who had tried the stuff. Some, especially novices who had ingested Special K thinking it was cocaine, said it was a deeply unpleasant and disorienting encounter, a vortex of delusional dreadfulness—the closest thing to dying without actually doing so. "I took so much K, I couldn't figure out if I was human anymore," a young sales manager from New Jersey said. "I had no meaning. I lost contact with reality. It was horrible." More adventurous hedonists, however, praised the drug as a shortcut to transcendence, a gateway to a magical kingdom that even Lewis Carroll or Tim Burton couldn't have imagined—a place where, if you took enough, you could meet yourself in an out-of-body experience, establish contact with space aliens, and glimpse God in a disco ball.

"K definitely gives you a sense of your own death," said habitual user Rusty, a twenty-year-old blue-haired fashion punk from the boondocks. "That's part of the fun. It's really neat as long as you don't have to walk around. You go on a little adventure in your mind. I close my eyes and imagine crawling through all sorts of tunnels—whether computer-electrical with lights everywhere or dark sewer tunnels with pipes everywhere."

His friend, twenty-year-old Betty, a self-confessed "hard-core K-whore" whose fingers came adorned with poison rings in which she stored the drug, told of one experience in which she turned into a wooden ABC block: "I was a big square, and when I looked down, my front was painted yellow with a giant A, my side was painted blue with a B, and my other side was painted red with a C. Another time I took K, I saw a man walking across a club turn into a papier-mâché figure with no eyes. The detail was so incredible that I could actually read the newsprint."

Yet another devotee was Jennytalia, a bald-headed, raccoon-eyed Calvin Klein fashion model, who sported what looked like a walrus tusk piercing her cheek. She trilled with barely concealed glee, "The most intense K experience I ever had was at a friend's apartment, where I fell on the floor and found myself looking at a table leg, which turned into the head of an alien that started talking to me."

While it all sounded strange and exciting, locating Special K to sample was easier said than done. Tramping purposefully from one club to the next, elbowing my way from one packed dance floor to another, I found that no one was holding. Everybody wanted K, but no one had it to sell. Scamming veterinarians with the "sick-cat excuse" or burglarizing their offices after hours did not provide nearly enough to keep up with the raging demand. The rumor was that desperate cat-owning night crawlers gripped by K-fever had resorted to deliberately breaking their pets' legs in order to secure a supply. My final port of call was the Limelight's Disco 2000 night, and if this notorious pills-and-powder circus failed to yield any ketamine, I was going to call it a night.

The Limelight in the mid-'90s was one of the most famous clubs in Manhattan and certainly the most distinctive. Once an Episcopal church with an imposing Gothic exterior and stained-glass windows, this gloomy labyrinth of dark corners and hidden nooks and crannies was a perfect setting in which to both sell and consume drugs. Approaching the velvet rope that marked the entranceway, I looked up and down the busy block. I wanted to make sure the shadowy cyclops who owned the Limelight wasn't at the front door. There was no need to worry; New York's most powerful nightclub magnate, Peter Gatien, nearly always stayed away on Wednesday nights. I was in a peculiar situation: At the same time I was engaged in reporting the K story, I was also writing a profile of the club's owner. If Gatien found out I was using the privileges he'd given me to roam his nocturnal domain in order to research a story about drugs, he'd have burst a blood vessel.

The red rope parted, and I made my way past the rabbit-costumed ticket taker and into an antechamber, where a gaggle of genderless figures sprawled sacrilegiously on the church pews that doubled as couches. They were lazily emptying a vial of white powder onto a small mirror and using a credit card to cut up the crystals. The nearby bouncers said nothing.

I stepped over the prostrate body of a comatose partygoer and followed the throng into a vast main hall, where I was met by a scene of shameless exhibitionism the likes of which New York hadn't seen since the pre-AIDS golden days of Studio 54. Beneath the fluted arches and wooden rafters, three thousand nocturnal freaks of a feather flocked together in various states of astonishment, inebriation, and erotic assembly. The club swarmed with side-show oddities; a pandemonium of dope fiends, gender benders, and all-purpose weirdos dressed to excess. If I couldn't find K here, then where else?

The theme for the night was gore. The king of the club kids, Michael

Alig, was celebrating his thirtieth birthday with a campy party called "Blood Feast," named after an obscure, particularly gory slasher movie in Alig's favorite cinematic genre. Many of the club kids came covered in raw liver and slabs of beef that turned rancid under the bright spotlights. I gingerly stepped around puddles of blood, trying to spare my new suit. The invitation to this messy affair was meant to be shocking, featuring the birthday boy lying dead, his skull shattered with a hammer beside him, as one of his sidekicks, Jennytalia, the wide-eyed wild girl who mistook a table leg for an extraterrestrial, ate a forkful of his brains. The blurb around the picture promised: "Legs cut off" and "Buckets of Blood" and "Skinned alive and melting in a bloodbath, slashed from ear to ear."

Emerging from the throng, I spied the party's host, the effects of too many late nights writ large on his sagging face. He was dressed like a cross between Shirley Temple and Boy George. Alig was surrounded by the usual cast of saucer-eyed hangers-on, who shrieked like overheated tea kettles at whatever witticism dropped from their leader's lips. Ever the good host, Alig, a thick wad of drink tickets in one hand, wobbled over on unsteady heels to greet me. His mascara was running and his lipstick was smeared. Spots of animal blood stained his shirt.

"Hello, Michael," I said.

"Hi, how ya doing?" he replied.

"Happy birthday. Nice party."

"Thanks. Here, make a fist." He screwed the top off a brown bottle.

"It's coke not K, right?"

"Or is it K not coke. I've forgotten. I think it's coke."

A jittery limb poured what looked like a full gram of powder onto the back of my hand. Most of it fell off the edge. "Never mind," said Alig. "There's plenty more where that came from."

I licked the edge of my hand. I could tell it was cocaine. "Where's Peter Gatien?" I asked.

"How the hell do I know—probably at the Four Seasons with a bunch of hookers."

"Listen I gotta go, Michael. I've got to find some K."

"If you see this guy with big fluffy wings walking around, ask him."

With renewed energy I traveled onward, climbing up metal staircases, down darkened corridors, scouring every corner of the mazelike club, pestering one known dealer after another, "Got any K, got any K," but to no avail. And then, as if in a vision, he appeared out of the crowd, a striking figure dressed in a white leather biker outfit with billowing theatrical wings sprouting out of his back, which dislodged a drag queen's wig as he passed.

Though he looked like a member of the Village People, he nonetheless radiated the regal arrogance that drug dealers who don't get high on their own supply reserve for their customers who do. My junkie escort for the evening, who claimed he was the master of the necessary protocol, introduced us: "This is Frank Owen from the *Village Voice*, he wants to try some Special K."

"I hope he has money," the winged man said with a scowl. "No discounts for journalists," he sternly told me, as I fumbled in my pocket, wondering how I was going to expense this without a receipt.

The dope peddler's name was Angel (nee Andre Meléndez), a twenty-six-year-old Colombian-born club kid who came to New York with dreams of becoming an actor and a filmmaker but fell in with a racy nightlife crowd of jaded pop culture junkies and became a full-time scene-maker instead. Angel was one of the Limelight's notorious "celebrity drug dealers," those flamboyantly attired figures—part party promoter, part pusher—who made no attempt to disguise their illegal vocation, indeed acted as if what they were doing was perfectly within the law. And tonight, he was my seraphic facilitator into the half-magical, half-terrible realm of the K-hole.

Special K was an odd substance to discover within the confines of a disco. After all, the last thing you could do on ketamine was move your body to the beat. Unlike cocaine, it didn't make you feel sexy and euphoric. Unlike Ecstasy, it didn't enhance music and movement. In fact, it was a downright antisocial high, an intensely personal experience that lent itself more to private reverie than communal celebration.

Two decades earlier, K had been known as vitamin K, a favorite drug among a select group of New Age psychic astronauts, among whom it earned a reputation as a potent tool for the exploration of inner space.

Ketamine's effect was summed up nicely by Jay Stevens in his classic history of psychedelics, *Storming Heaven: LSD and the American Dream*: "Ecstasy hinted at how powerful the mind could be, and once first gear was mastered, here was second gear, and a third. Compared to MDMA, Vitamin K was tenth gear."

K's usage in the '70s was much different than that of the '90s. Back then the drug was injected in liquid form, not snorted as powder, and was utilized for meditative purposes. Some users hooked themselves up to IV drips and floated in isolation tanks, increasing the intensity of the visions by shutting out distractions from the outside world.

Experts familiar with ketamine's previous incarnation as a hippie drug were surprised to learn that K had become prevalent in dance clubs. "To me it's mind-boggling that it's showed up in raves and clubs," remarked drug researcher Rick Doblin, president and founder of the Florida-based Multidisciplinary Association for Psychedelic Studies, "because I see it as a total out-of-body, consciousness-exploring drug."

By the mid-'90s, the rave generation that had discovered Ecstasy a few years previously, and in the process had birthed a global youth culture, was now tiring of the drug and looking for something fresh to replace it. The law of diminishing returns that affects any drug culture had kicked in. The initial flood of euphoric feelings that the drug unleashed—what British writer Matthew Collin called "the revelatory flash of the primal Ecstasy experience"—had faded to a trickle because of chronic overuse. Finally, the MDMA supply itself had become increasingly adulterated.

"K is the new high," one night crawler explained. "A lot of people are tired of Ecstasy because there is not enough good E around. Most of the initial users of K are stoned on E when somebody gives them a bump to prolong the high. They like that high, and they come back for more."

As I would soon find out, however, comparing Ecstasy to Special K was misleading. One may have been the gateway drug that allowed partygoers to try the other, but the effects of the two substances couldn't have been more different. Ecstasy works by flooding the brain with serotonin (which modulates mood and intensifies perception) and dopamine (which speeds up the metabolism and creates exhilaration) a combination that literally lights up the senses like a Christmas tree and makes anyone and everything appear wonderful without discrimination. Ketamine does something very different. It works by jamming neurotransmission—the flow of electrical information between brain cells, not unlike a pirate radio DJ or a computer hacker, except the network that's being disrupted is inside your head.

Ketamine was first synthesized in 1965 by pharmacologists at the University of Michigan. Two years previously, scientists had been looking for a safe general anesthetic when they discovered the phencyclidine PCP (later known on the street as "angel dust"). Their hopes for the new drug were dashed, however, when subsequent tests showed that PCP induced severe psychotic reactions among some human subjects. Further research led to the discovery of ketamine, which at first appeared to have none of the daunting side effects of its chemical kissing cousin.

Parke-Davis mass-produced the drug under the brand name Ketalar. The pharmaceutical giant marketed the product as a safe, nonnarcotic, rapidly acting analgesic. Unlike other anesthetics common at the time, ketamine could be used on the quick. There was no need to prep the patient—evacuate the bowels, empty the stomach, and so forth—in advance. And because ketamine caused only mild breathing depression, there was also no need for a respirator during medical procedures.

Ketamine was used extensively during battlefield surgery in the Vietnam War. But the human application proved to be problematic because of something called the "emergence phenomenon." Adding to the horror of the battlefield, injured soldiers coming out of operations complained about the hellish visions they'd experienced under the influence of the drug. "The large doses used on humans caused a full-fledged psychedelic experience among some people," explained Rick Doblin. "Patients coming out of operations weren't prepared for the hallucinations, so they panicked."

In the late '60s and early '70s, after LSD was made illegal, ketamine crossed over into the recreational sphere when it was discovered by New Age users, foremost among them the neuroscientist Dr. John Lilly—the Timothy Leary of ketamine. In the '50s, Lilly had invented the isolation tank; he was the model for the William Hurt character in the Ken Russell movie *Altered States*. His research on communication between dolphins and humans was the basis for another Hollywood film, *Day of the Dolphin*. In his autobiographical novel, *The Scientist*, Lilly described taking ketamine for the first time, after a doctor had given him the drug to cure his recurring headaches. From then on, Lilly became a daily consumer and ended up being hospitalized. A pioneer in many things, he was the world's first ketamine casualty.

One of Lilly's more outlandish claims was that ketamine could facilitate transspecies communication. At a Marine World in Redwood City, this latter day Doctor Doolittle went swimming with dolphins and afterward claimed that he had left his body and entered the mammals' group mind. Like many chronic users, he also said he had made repeated contact with extraterrestrials, whom he insisted managed something called ECCO (the Earth Coincidence Control Office). According to Lilly, these angelic creatures coordinated coincidence so as to push mankind along the evolutionary path to a higher consciousness.

No longer widely employed for adult humans, by the 1980s ketamine was still used to treat animals, burn trauma victims, and kids—who, for some reason not known to science, didn't experience the hallucinations grown-ups did. Ketamine was also used in Russia to treat alcoholics, and among a small group of psychotherapists in the United States to break down mental barriers in their patients.

"The way ketamine is used in psychotherapy is very different from the way it is used in rave clubs," said Doblin. "Ketamine jumps over the ego and gives patients a religious sense of eternity and timelessness. When you go beyond the ego, people have experiences that make them feel connected to basic primal energies. It's like going back to when you were a baby and you don't have words for anything and it's just sort of basic perceptions."

In itself, the separation of mind and body that ketamine induces isn't necessarily harmful and could be therapeutic. However, putative mental health benefits aside, studies also show that ketamine can be a very dangerous substance that heats up the brain to hazardous levels. Researchers discovered that animals given high doses of ketamine over a long period of time developed microscopic holes in the posterior cingulate cortex (the part of the brain important for understanding abstract thought) and retrosplenial cortex (a segment of the brain that plays a role in processing visual information). These became known as Olney's lesions or NAN (NMDA Antagonist Neurotoxicity).

While it was unlikely that Special K would kill the casual user like myself—after all, the doses consumed in clubs were far smaller than those administered in operations, which were considered safe—the psychological dependency that came with frequent use was another question. The first casualties of the new generation of K-heads were already starting to surface.

"There are now people who can't go out without it," said another Limelight drug dealer, this one dressed in snakeskin pants and a Marilyn Manson T-shirt that read "I Am the God of Fuck." "They do it so much that they can't communicate with others. It turns them into antisocial zombies."

The trip started out with a rubbery sensation. Walking across the dance floor was akin to wading through a river of molasses in a pair of marshmallow platform shoes. My whole frame felt woozy, the direct result of the drug starting to cut off the stream of nerve signals from the body to the brain. Yet, strangely, my thoughts became clearer and more vivid. The cloud of normal consciousness lifted from my mind, leaving my imagination free to roam.

As the drug took hold, familiar objects became alien, as if I were viewing them for the first time. I stared at my clunky shoes from Bergdorf Goodman and wondered what these concrete watermelons were doing at the ends of my legs. Inhibitions broke down, my working-class, chip-on-the-shoulder attitude started to dissolve. Anxieties disappeared. Pathways within the brain felt like they were being rerouted as I experienced a tremendous sense of vacant, carefree ease, ketamine's "gift of blankness" that I'd been told about in advance. I was gripped by a reaction I can only describe as eminent indifference. The person dancing next to me could have been choking the life out of his companion and the Limelight could have been going up in flames, and I wouldn't have cared a jot. Doctors refer to this as the drug's "dissociative" effect—the engendering in the user of a dispassionate sense of objectivity.

As I took more of the K, my sense of spatial perspective was turned on its head. A small room suddenly took on the dimensions of a sports arena. Time decelerated to a lethargic crawl: Seconds lasted for minutes; minutes went on for hours. Bodily movement became robotic. My feet seemed motorized. Walking required intense focus and a strong purpose. A short trip to the bar was like climbing Mount Everest. A journey to the toilet—baby steps all the way—was an odyssey worthy of Homer. And when I finally got there, I had to look down to check that I was really urinating, since I couldn't sense the piss coming out.

Speech was tricky. Summoning up all the concentration I could muster, I spoke to my companion in a machinelike monotone: "I think me needs to go sit down," I managed to say, sounding like a cyborg from a *Star Trek* movie. Who am I? What am I? Where am I? These were all difficult questions to answer.

For the next stage of the trip, I found a comfy couch to lounge on, knowing full well that soon my body would be totally numb. A giant generator—it sounded like a UFO in a movie—started buzzing over my head. Dangling on the edge that separates consciousness from oblivion, preparing to say good-bye to the physical world, I sensed the ground being whipped away from under my feet. Any tentative connection to my surroundings was slashed. A trapdoor had opened up in the fabric of reality, as I fell, like Alice into Wonderland, down a dark tunnel known to ketamine enthusiasts as "the K-hole."

I and I, as the Rastafarians would say, was divided and then multiplied, until I was no longer me. Completely oblivious to the material world, I'd left the fleshy precincts of my own body to become this disembodied pulse of pure energy. I, but not I, traveled at considerable speed through a gloomy industrial pipe, which was illuminated at regular intervals by flashing yellow beacons, toward a blinding white light ahead. Approaching the light, I found myself aghast, as I experienced what seemed like the propinquity of a higher being.

Coming down off the drug, I felt as if I'd died and gone to K-heaven, but it wasn't a frightening sensation in the slightest. Quite the contrary, it was deeply comforting; I had the distinct sense that death was not an end but a new beginning—I was convinced my spirit would live on beyond my physical demise. I didn't get to communicate with aliens or the spirits of the dead, a frequently reported hallucination, but I did get a taste of my own mortality, the soul beneath the skull beneath the skin. Staggering out of the Limelight into the bracing night air, the whole event reminded me of the near-death religious experiences that some terminally ill hospital patients report.

The Limelight was the center of a world of clubland hedonism that had its roots in the psychedelic happenings of the '60s and the disco dance halls of the '70s, but by the mid-'90s had morphed into something darker. By this point, the glitter was peeling from the disco ball, the superficial veil of fun and fabulousness had slipped, leaving the mood on the dance floor hovering somewhere between nihilism and decadence. Omens of the bad things to come were everywhere that season . . . in the music, in the drugs, and on the blank faces of the partygoers, many of them desperate people too callow to know when enough was enough. Nocturnal society had made a decisive move away from the innocent love-and-peace ethos of the late '80s and early '90s toward a fascination with scary trips and weird scenarios.

No one could have predicted just how tragic a turn events would soon take, but right from the outset of what would become a five-year-long journey into a dangerous underworld of drugs, murder, and corruption stretching from Manhattan to Miami Beach, the fact was becoming increasingly obvious that something was rotten in the state of clubland.

Limelight doorman Kenny Kenny summed up this appetite for self-destruction that gripped the scene: "It's much more hard core these days," he warned. "There's not enough fabulousness. It's like people are looking for beauty in horror."

1 THE ONE-EYED DON

New York City, Early October 1995

It was one of those brilliant autumn days in New York, the city radiant with luminous color. While the soothing afternoon light skipped gaily across the surface of the Hudson River, Peter Gatien's world was all grim turmoil. A couple of nights ago, in the early hours, the stony-faced Gatien saw his flagship venue in Chelsea, the Limelight, padlocked by the NYPD. Friday evening, just at the peak of business, and his temple of thump-thump-thump—located at the corner of Twentieth Street and Sixth Avenue in a weathered Victorian pile that once housed St. Peter's Episcopal church, then later a drug treatment center—was packed to the vaulted rafters with gyrating penitents hanging off the two tiers of metal balconies that surrounded the cavernous main floor. The irony wasn't lost on the revelers, who seemed to take a perverse delight in frolicking on the altar or sniffing blow in the pulpit. Out on the churning dance floor, the atmosphere was like the pagan party scene in some Hollywood biblical epic, the last fling of a primitive tribe threatened with extinction by powerful social trends few of its members could fully comprehend.

Meanwhile, a string of stretch limousines idled impatiently outside the noisy nightclub, which was fast becoming a stone monument to an era of all-out licentiousness, now vanishing under the puritanical political regime that had taken over the city. Nonetheless, a long procession of young party people, all eager to pay the twenty-dollar admittance, shuffled along the avenue. A drag queen with a clipboard and a bad attitude inspected the line for the undesirable or the unfashionable.

All of a sudden, the block was filled with police cars and paddy wagons, their flashing blue lights illuminating the bulky brown façade and soaring bell tower. A team of undercover detectives—men and women who had been busy buying drugs in the Limelight since early August—was already in position inside the club, when a phalanx of fifty uniformed cops, wearing nylon NYPD windbreakers and carrying high-powered flashlights, stormed through the narrow front entrance of the edifice, rushed up the spiral staircase and through the lobby, which was filled with the obligatory video monitors and bad art installations. Their senses assaulted on all flanks, some of the police wore earplugs to protect themselves against the cacophony emanating from the colossal speakers. Above their heads, half-naked girls writhed in cages. Barreling down the dark corridors, pushing their way through the startled crowd, and peering into murky recesses, the cops fanned out through the labyrinthine club, each of them carrying a list with the names and photos of thirty known drug dealers.

The Limelight was a huge space. The ceiling stretched four stories high over the main dance floor. Five staircases from the main chamber led to numerous lounges, alcoves, VIP rooms, and the chapel area (sometimes known as the Shampoo Bar), all of which were decorated in different themes (the TV Room, the Peacock Room, the Topiary Room, the Opium Den, the Arcadia Room). No wonder the cops became disoriented and had trouble finding their way around.

The paramilitary seizure did not go according to plan. The police were puzzled that none of Gatien's employees seemed particularly surprised by the bombshell assault. As the animated night dwellers filed out of the club, the cops also wondered why twenty-six of the intended targets were absent that night. They'd received numerous reports about the furious drug action at the club. They'd heard about the special rooms, designated as hard-core drug spots, where guards stood outside and permitted only trusted patrons to enter. But, that night, the place was cleaner than the manicured grounds of Disney World.

In the end, the bust was a nonevent. An embarrassed NYPD only managed to make three minor arrests of small-time marijuana peddlers.

The cops suspected that someone had tipped off Gatien in advance about the raid. While the Limelight was temporarily padlocked as a public nuisance, within a week Gatien was back in business, having paid a $30,000 fine and posted a $160,000 bond. He also filed a list of nightclub employees with city hall and agreed to forfeit the bond in the event that anybody on the list was involved in peddling drugs on the premises.

The raid was the disappointing culmination of a two-month investigation into Gatien's operation, fueled by the demise earlier in the year of eighteen-year-old Nicholas Mariniello, who died at his parents' New Jersey home after a night of partying at the Limelight. His heartbroken parents suspected their son had died of an overdose of the designer drug Ecstasy—a commonly used social lubricant among the young ravers and club kids who flocked to the Chelsea hot spot. For years, the local precinct had been deluged with angry and tearful calls from ordinary suburban moms and dads saying their kids, some as young as fifteen or sixteen, had come home stoned or had gone missing after a visit to the Limelight. But the Mariniello family was politically connected. They knew important people. They phoned former New Jersey Governor Tom Kean, who supposedly put in a personal call to New York Mayor Rudolph Giuliani. Manhattan District Attorney Robert Morgenthau began to probe Gatien's finances. Major behind-the-scenes cogs whirred into action, even though the Morris County, New Jersey medical examiner, after conducting an external examination (Mariniello's parents nixed the idea of an autopsy), revealed the cause of death not as chemical overindulgence but instead "asphyxia due to hanging" and the manner of death as "suicide."

Special narcotics prosecutor Robert Silbering, the city's top drug enforcement official, whose office assisted in the raid, defended the police action: "It's not as if we targeted the club without good reason," he commented. "According to the information that the police department received, the drug dealing at the Limelight was both open and substantial."

Pacing up and down in his spacious office at the Tunnel, another one of his lucrative Manhattan dance halls, the normally unflappable Peter

Gatien was scalding mad. Not that you could easily tell. Red-faced fury was not Gatien's style.

Like its owner, the Tunnel had a decidedly spooky quality. Situated right by the West Side Highway, the gigantic club was housed in a former railway depot—40,000 square feet of enveloping blackness—that was said to be haunted by the ghosts of the homeless people who used to live there. When the place was empty, employees swore you could hear the sounds of crying children.

Gatien was dressed like he had just come from the gym. A framed photograph of the club owner posing with the Staten Island rap group Wu-Tang Clan sat on his desk. Expensive-looking art prints with a nautical theme hung on the walls. A rack of silver weights gathered dust in the corner. From the next room came the sharp sound of a shredding machine hungrily eating up documents.

The forty-four-year-old Gatien, who was passably handsome in a gaunt sort of way, looked like he was nursing a hangover. His lips were dry and cracked; his thin, short hair plastered to his skull. He appeared both edgy and exhausted. His pallid skin looked like it hasn't seen sunshine in ages.

In the wake of the raid, the club owner had spent the morning meeting with his lawyers and fielding phone calls from anxious investors and landlords worried about the stability of his nighttime kingdom. He was afraid those months of delicate negotiations with the Forty-Second Street Business Improvement District—regarding a new club to replace his former Times Square hangout, Club USA—were now ruined. He also feared that because of the bad publicity, the Atlanta Olympic Committee would withdraw its recent invitation to build the official disco in the athletes' village.

Sitting back in a tall leather chair, Gatien exuded the humanity of a dial tone. The vacant presence at the heart of clubland struck up a Marlboro with a quick flick of his lighter and then flipped up his trademark black eye patch—the result of a teenage ice hockey accident. He massaged the circumference of the scarred and empty socket. He refused to wear a glass eye because it felt so uncomfortable.

"So much for having the police in my pocket," cracked Gatien, after letting out a long sigh of smoke. "I guess the drag queen must have kept the money." The joke was a reference to a rumor I brought up at our last meeting that a transvestite in his employ was regularly dispatched to the local precinct with a bag full of payoff cash for the cops.

The common perception among Gatien's rivals was that the Canadian businessman used his wealth to purchase political favors. Certainly, he knew how to grease the wheels of the big city machine. He employed lawyer Susan Wagner, a former official in Mayor Ed Koch's administration, to smooth over neighborhood opposition at community board meetings. He retained Geto & DeMilly, a well-known lobbying firm, under whose auspices he made substantial donations to such local politicians as public advocate Mark Green, Manhattan Borough President Ruth Messinger, and Mayor Rudy Giuliani. Gatien regularly hired off-duty New York City police officers to patrol his parties. Each year, he threw a big Christmas bash at the Limelight for the local firefighters, who got drunk all night for free. But his detractors went further, saying that he had effectively bought himself immunity from the illegal goings-on at his clubs.

For the record, Gatien denied he bribed anybody. "You don't have to buy people off to operate a successful nightclub in New York as long as it's legitimate," he said without inflection, his flat, deep monotone perfectly matching his gray personality. "The whole thing could have been solved with a phone call. I thought we had a good relationship with them. I meet with precinct captains on a monthly basis and talk to police officers several times a week. All they had to do was tell me there was a problem with drugs at the Limelight, and I would have done something about it."

Gatien's exasperation about the closing of the Limelight was only semiauthentic. According to one of the Limelight's executive directors, Steven Lewis, an NYPD detective with showbiz dreams named Mitch Kolpan allegedly tipped off the club owner about the raid in advance. Brash, gregarious, ruddy-faced, Kolpan stood six feet, three inches in his bad haircut and terrible suits and had a predilection for telling corny jokes. Instead of bagging bad guys, Kolpan seemed to spend most of his time hanging around Peter Gatien's office. Gatien put Kolpan on his payroll after meeting him on the set of the Robert De Niro movie *A Bronx Tale*, which the club owner helped finance (and for which he received credit as executive producer). Kolpan, who had never acted in his life, finagled an audition with De Niro after using his gold shield to breeze past the security guards. "I'm not even an actor," Kolpan supposedly told the star, "but I'd make a great gangster." De Niro laughed and cast him in a small role as a cop.

Lewis claimed that two weeks prior to the raid, Gatien had a closed-door meeting with Kolpan at the Tunnel. Following the sit-down, the club owner supposedly informed several managers that the Limelight was going to be busted. The night before the bust, Gatien's employees circulated a list of names around the club. Any drug dealer on that list was told to disappear pronto. Instead, many of the dope peddlers simply decamped for the evening to the Gatien-owned Palladium on Fourteenth Street, where they continued doing business. (Kolpan was never charged with any wrongdoing.)

Sex, drugs, and up-to-the-minute dance music were the unbeatable recipe that made Gatien a wealthy man in the '90s. His pleasure domes—the Tunnel, the Palladium, the Limelight—were packed every night, pulling in about fifty thousand paying customers a week. On a good weekend, he claimed he raked in as much as a million dollars in combined revenues. In the fickle world of New York nightlife, he exhibited a remarkable staying power, keeping the Limelight open and cost-effective for twelve years.

No one had more profitably ridden the dramatic changes that had affected New York nightlife since the late '80s. Back then, Gatien owned only one club in New York, the Limelight, which the hip elite regarded as a tacky meeting place for the so-called "bridge-and-tunnel set" from New Jersey, Brooklyn, and Queens. At the same time, there was a recession going on. AIDS also seemed to signal an end to the festivities. And the clubgoers who made legendary establishments like Area and Danceteria happen in the '80s had grown older and stopped going out every night.

But paradoxically, all these negatives worked in Gatien's favor. The retirement of the '80s generation from active duty cleared the way for a new, less elitist contingent of partiers who cheerfully paid for their own drinks. Economic constraints ensured that people who no longer could afford big-ticket items like holidays abroad spent their disposable cash closer to home, taking mini vacations at dance halls. The fear of AIDS meant that voyeurism, pornography, and fetishism suddenly took on a new appeal—a trend exploited in all of Gatien's clubs, most famously at Club USA, an $8-million homage to kinky sex that opened in 1992 but closed two years later when the landlord who owned the Times Square building went bankrupt despite Gatien's booming business.

Gatien's democratic door policy—catering not just to club kids and ravers but also to smartly dressed yuppies from the outer boroughs who came to gawk at the freakily attired flotsam and jetsam of the demi-monde—also led to his fantastic success. At his clubs, downtown trendies and the boys from Brooklyn dressed so much alike as to be sometimes indistinguishable. Gatien courted out-of-towners, too, recognizing that the local nightlife was a major tourist attraction. Young Japanese tourists regularly lined up outside to take photos of the world-famous Limelight.

But Gatien's runaway success bred resentment among his biggest rivals. They claimed Gatien was an evil emperor who used dirty tricks to shut down their clubs. They said that he utilized corrupt police department contacts to harass them and sent club kids into their competing venues to set off fire alarms. In the cutthroat world of nightlife, for one club owner to drop a quarter on a competitor was not uncommon.

Gatien adamantly denied he used such hardball tactics: "I do fourteen or fifteen nights a week," he said, fixing me with his glimmerless stare. "So I'm more vulnerable to that type of underhanded behavior than anybody else. I get fire trucks coming to my places on phony calls all the time. I get the police coming, saying that they've had a report someone was shot when everything is peaceful. I get all that, and I never blame competitors. It's a game I've never played."

The club owner suspected that the shuttering of the Limelight was the opening volley in a much larger war. He thought it heralded a broader crackdown on local nightlife. Before the Limelight opened in 1982, the surrounding area had been a dangerous dump where it was unsafe to walk after dark. But within years, the same area had grown into a thriving commercial and residential district with a buoyant mix of small businesses and large-scale retailers. Nonetheless, in its quest to clean up Gotham, the administration of the self-righteous former federal prosecutor Rudolph Giuliani decided to go after nightclub owners, just as it had gone after the squeegee men and Times Square hookers before them. Giuliani thought of nightclubs not as pop culture playgrounds that brought significant economic benefits to the city—not as important social safety valves where young people went to release the stress of urban living or as valuable incubators of musical movements (house, hip-hop, punk) that had swept the globe—but rather as wholly sinister venues that promoted rampant antisocial behavior. Nightclubs had helped spearhead the revival of previously derelict downtown neighborhoods. But under Giuliani, these venues were far more likely to be regarded as spawning criminality than curbing it.

As the best-known nightclub owner in the city, Gatien suspected he was about to become a high-profile scapegoat for the ills affecting nightlife in general. "I'm the most successful nightclub operator in the city because I'm the most responsible nightclub operator in the city," the impresario insisted, his face twitching with barely concealed anger. "Why pick on me? There are more drugs on Wall Street or in Madison Square Garden or at the Port Authority Bus Station. My organization is the only one in New York nightlife that has any staying power, and that's because we operate as a business, not as a bunch of party people. I worked very hard to dispel the stereotypical image of the New York club owner as someone who's a big womanizer, drug taker, and drinker who stiffs everybody and then goes into Chapter 11 after eighteen months."

In the press, Gatien liked to present himself as a respectable entrepreneur and clean-living family man. He regularly took the kids to Disney World and went sailing at his country estate in Ontario on the weekends. He resided comfortably with his now-common-law wife, Alessandra (or "Alex") Kobayashi, and their infant son, Xander, in a five-story town house on the Upper East Side, which they shared with Gatien's two teenage daughters from his first marriage, Jennifer and Amanda, and his other son, Chandler, from his second marriage. Partly out of concern for his kids, Gatien tried to distance himself from the often-seedy milieu from which he made his loot. His public relations people pushed the image of Gatien as a moneyman who bankrolled the scene but didn't partake of the nighttime pleasures his clubs offered.

Gatien was usually absent from the frenzied partying at the Limelight. When he did turn up, he walked through the club unrecognized, his profile lower than a limbo dancer's, his stiff body language standing out in sharp contrast to the undulating silhouettes surrounding his wraithlike presence. He knew that people said he was a cold fish. Gatien didn't care. He claimed to be acutely aware of what happened to club owners who mixed business and pleasure.

"The reality of operating a successful nightclub is that you can't be a party animal and function as a businessman at the same time," he said, stubbing out another cigarette in a big glass ashtray already overflowing with butts smoked down to the filter. "Most of the important work that goes into a nightclub is done during the day. We wouldn't have been able to support a scene for over a decade if I didn't get up in the morning and pay the bills."

At that moment, Alessandra, dressed all in white, appeared in the doorway of her husband's work space. The atmosphere crackled with negative electricity. I'd heard Alex's name mentioned often during the four months since the Special K article came out, usually in association with the words *bitch* and *dragon*. But this was the first time I'd actually seen the trim and attractive young woman—the proverbial tough cookie laced with arsenic straight from the pages of a hard-boiled novel, or so I was told. Dictatorial, arrogant, and ruthless, she had a rep in clubland as Gatien's Lady Macbeth, the power behind the throne, unafraid to use her clout to strike fear into the hearts of any of her husband's employees who displeased her imperial highness. Gatien's staff complained endlessly that she regarded them as lower than dirt. "She's a quintessential power bitch," said one. She despised the party people Gatien surrounded himself with. She was also said to be something of a surveillance buff—she tape-recorded her phone conversations and was rumored to have installed a hidden camera in her home to catch her cheating husband, who liked a bit of slap and tickle on the side. Even Gatien's publicist warned me, "She's a lean, mean, bean counter. Be very careful what you say around her."

The Gatien relationship was an odd mixture of romance and finance.

The two met in 1991 at the Limelight, when the then twenty-two-year-old woman, who had an eye for rich and powerful men, came in to apply for a job. Despite his usual demeanor, Gatien was smitten. Here was a girl after his glacial heart. She started out as the club's ticket taker and ended up marrying the owner. In 1993, their relationship was cemented when they had a child together. Now, tough-minded businesswoman Alex pulled the purse strings of the corporation. She was the chief financial officer, who controlled the payroll of Gatien's thousand-strong staff. Her name appeared on the checks. She made sure her husband stayed on a strict budget and had tried to place a mostly cash business on paper. Gatien claimed she'd put his up-to-that-time muddled finances on a much sounder basis.

"She makes this a very legitimate organization," Gatien had insisted, prior to his wife's unexpected interruption. "Most nightclubs are run in a fiscally irresponsible manner, but we're not. Financially, we're a very organized company thanks to Alessandra."

Contrary to his claims of financial rectitude, Gatien's operation was far more chaotic than he described. Organization insiders painted a portrait of behind-the-scenes pandemonium. Paper-shredding machines buzzed and sliced around the clock. Employees said that cash register receipts recorded by door clickers and bartenders at each of the clubs were taken over to the Palladium at the end of each night and then disposed of the next morning. Promoters and DJs were still paid under the table. Certain transactions weren't recorded in the books. Money moved through the organization via mysterious methods. What Gatien took in was not necessarily what he reported to the authorities. "The clubs make a lot of money, but they don't make a lot of money, if you catch my drift," one source familiar with Gatien's accounting practices claimed.

A favorite topic among Gatien's top people was "Where does all the money go?" Waste and employee theft were rampant in his organization. "The clubs are taking in buckets full of cash, but there are always problems getting bills paid," said another key player who worked in the office. Employees talked openly about the possibility of corruption at the very apex of the management structure.

If Gatien was something of a mystery man, Alessandra seemed even more aloof. She shied away from the press and was notoriously touchy about revealing details from her past. She claimed to be a former Wilhelmina model and a graduate of Columbia University, though neither institution had ever heard of her. For a long time, she had everybody in the office, including Gatien, believing she was Japanese. Gatien said that she was the daughter of the Benihana restaurant chain's Rocky Aoki (Kobayashi, the surname she used when she met Gatien, is Rocky Aoki's first wife's maiden name), though Aoki's publicist denied any blood relationship. However, she had worked for the restauranteur as one of his helpers. "My sister [Grace Kana Aoki] brought Alex to our house in New Jersey to sleep over for the night," explained Kevin Aoki, Rocky's son. "She started flirting with my father, and not long after, he hired her as an assistant and to take care of the house."

Said the Limelight's executive director, Steven Lewis: "Kevin Aoki told me to watch out for Alex."

Jennifer Gatien, the club owner's blonde-haired, blue-eyed teenage daughter, also didn't trust Alex. As was common belief in the office, she strongly felt that Alex wasn't who she said she was, and without initially telling her father, she hired a private eye to dig up dirt on her stepmother.

In the course of his investigation, the private eye obtained a letter—that the Aoki family subsequently confirmed to me as authentic—from a Detective F. Engel of the 19th Precinct Detectives Unit concerning an alleged robbery in 1986 at the Manhattan home of a woman named Susan Mald. In the letter, a follow-up communication that was addressed to Rocky's daughter, Grace Kana Aoki, Engel wrote: "You state in your telephone call that you had contacted and spoken to Mrs. Susan Mald who had hired [Alex] as a child-care helper, and during the time she was employed and at the residence of Mrs. Mald, a large amount of personal belongings of Mrs. Mald, such as jewelry, was missing from the residence. Be advised that the information you supplied above is correct. [Alex] was subsequently terminated from employment by Mrs. Mald, who strongly felt she was responsible for her loss, although the matter could not be criminally prosecuted due to two other employees having access to complainant's apartment during this time." Half the jewelry from the alleged robbery was later returned in an anonymous package decorated—like in the movies—with cut-up letters from a magazine.

The investigator also spoke directly to Grace Aoki, who claimed that Alex had run up $27,000 in charges at Bergdorf Goodman on her father's credit card. Grace also accused Alex of slashing some of her clothing and leaving the garments in a trash can. (Alex was never charged with any wrongdoing.)

"Running up my dad's credit card was the least of it," Kevin Aoki would tell me later. "She made my sister's life into a nightmare."

"She turned my life upside down," corroborated Grace. "I was the one who introduced her to everybody, so I got the blame for bringing this con artist into my family."

The investigator also found out from Grace that Alex wasn't really Alex, and she wasn't Rocky's offspring, either. Her real name was Susan Koe, and she wasn't even Japanese. She was born of Korean and Caucasian parentage in exotic Flushing, Queens, and her actual father was a typewriter salesman for Olivetti, not a CIA agent as she sometimes claimed. Alex had fooled everybody, including her own husband. ("Jennifer Gatien called me up, and I put her in touch with my father, who confirmed to Peter that Alex wasn't his daughter," Grace said. "She told Jenny that she was my dad's illegitimate daughter.")

One morning not long after the big discovery that Alex was an imposter, when the employees came to work, they were told she was no longer with the organization. There'd been a major blow-up. She was out. A new management team was coming in to take over. But days later, Alex walked back in and resumed her position, as if nothing had happened.

Gatien's publicist claimed: "The belief in the office is that Alex has Peter by the balls. Whatever he has on her, she has twice as much on him. It figures heavily in their relationship."

For his part, Gatien claimed he was unfazed by what the private eye dug up. "I don't care," he said. "I love the woman. She's been really good for me. I couldn't give a shit who her father is."

After she barged into her spouse's office, Alex acted like there wasn't a reporter in the room. When Gatien objected to her making phone calls at his desk while he was in the middle of an interview, she shotgunned him a dirty look, flipped back her long brown hair, and then stormed out. The harshness of her gaze could have peeled skin.

"Where were we?" Gatien continued on his well-rehearsed rant, seemingly unabashed by his wife's rudeness. He persisted in sounding like a politician reading from a prepared script. "Our industry is under-appreciated as far as what it does economically for New York. New York is no longer a manufacturing town. What we do well here is enter-tainment. Nightclubs employ people, pay taxes, attract tourist dollars, and are a breeding ground for new ideas that begin at clubs like the Limelight and the Tunnel and end up on Madison Avenue. We operate a responsible business, but we often become the target for broader social problems. Drugs are everywhere in society, not just in discos. A police captain once said to me that he liked having nightclubs in his precinct because when he needed to make arrests, the clubs were an easy, nonmoving target."

Gatien took a sip from a bottle of water, then got up and walked over to the window to admire the panoramic view of the Hudson River. I asked him if he would have problems when it came time to renew the various licenses he needed to operate his establishments. He fell silent for a moment. Through the open door came the distant hammering sounds of workmen renovating his club. Gatien turned and then answered "I'm sure I'm going to have a lot of explaining to do."

But if the club owner thought he could insulate himself from the unlawful behavior at his clubs by smooth public relations, he was in for a rude awakening. Unbeknownst to both of us as we spoke, two federal Drug Enforcement Administration agents were surveying his office through a one-way window from the third floor of a warehouse directly across the narrow cobblestoned street.

2   TWO STONE STALLIONS

Delta 35 was one of the most hardworking and suc-cessful groups within the U.S. Drug Enforcement Administration. A hard-core, no-holds-barred field unit made up of handpicked go-getters, Delta 35, like the Canadian Mounties, had a reputation for always snaring their man. "A very, very forceful group of guys," a former law enforcement officer described them.

Among the Delta 35 team in 1995 were Robert Gagne and Mathew Germanowski, who for years had worked the New Jersey Turnpike, looking to catch drug couriers on the way up from Florida. It was dangerous but exciting work. Gagne and Germanowski were used to winning and winning large.

This pair of pumped-up young stallions soon found themselves deep into an investigation of what they thought was a major Israeli connection to the burgeoning New York Ecstasy trade. In recent years, Jerusalem and Tel Aviv had come to rival Amsterdam as distribution centers for the drug. In the United States, the Russian mob even used young Hasidim as religious cover to smuggle consignments of the drug into the country via JFK and Miami International airports.

Two months before the Limelight was raided, on a stifling hot afternoon in August, Germanowski was parked at the corner of Ninety-seventh Street and Queens Boulevard. He was behind the wheel of a dusty four-door sedan with Pennsylvania license plates—the sort of bland ride beloved of undercover operatives. The sun beat down through the brutal humidity, turning the sidewalk into a giant tandoor oven. Under his sweaty T-shirt, Germanowski was wearing a Nagra body transmitter. The traffic was so heavy that the noise of honking cars threatened to spoil the transmission. At a nearby pay phone, an informant who had promised to introduce the DEA agents to a major Israeli E dealer was punching in a numeric code to the target's pager. Germanowski checked his watch.

Within minutes, a Mediterranean-looking male, with a medium build, standing about six feet, one inch tall, came trotting down the street, his eyes darting left, right, and center. He was dressed in a white T-shirt, red-and-blue–checkered shorts, and flip-flops. He strolled over to the car, leaned his head in through the window, and introduced himself: "How ya' doing, man. My name is Ghel. I hear you need to speak to me." His real name was Israel Hazut, a twenty-seven-year-old low-level supplier who was trying to break into the big leagues by passing himself off as an important Ecstasy trafficker.

Germanowski introduced himself as "Jimmy G." He said he was a nightclub owner from Pittsburgh, and he and his partner were in town to score some high-grade party favors. "I'm looking for the strong stuff," Germanowski emphasized, as his trained eye made a mental note of the suspect's appearance for the field report he would type up later.

"I've got the stuff you want," Hazut assured him. Somehow, the unsuspecting Israeli didn't notice how much Jimmy G—with his trainers and tight jeans, military-style haircut, and overdeveloped upper body—positively reeked of undercover heat.

"Everybody loves these," continued Hazut, as he reached into his pocket. "This is the best stuff in the city. The market is booming right now. I supply these pills to all the big Manhattan clubs."

"Oh, yeah, which clubs?"

"Like the Limelight."

The agent's ears pricked up. "Isn't that owned by Peter Gatien?"

"That's right. I supply E to people at all of his clubs."

Germanowski's interest was seriously piqued. He played it casual, but internally he was bursting with anticipation at the prospect of bag-

ging such an illustrious target. If he could bring down a high-profile figure like Gatien, think of the kudos to come.

Hazut handed him two small white capsules in a see-through plastic
bag. The twin highs were intended as a trailer for the main attraction.
Germanowski inspected them for a moment and then handed over a
pair of twenty-dollar bills. Hazut said that if he liked them, he could get
a lot more. "I can put together an order of any size, but I need at least
five days' advance notice." Hazut further informed Germanowski he
would bring the price down on orders of 6,000 or more. Germanowski
disclosed he was pondering the possibility of ordering 15,000 to 20,000
hits. Hazut retorted that he would have no problem getting hold of that
amount. The foreigner seemed eager to cut a deal. What the DEA agent
didn't know was that Hazut, despite his boasting, had never put
together a trade involving more than a few hundred pills. This was
going to be the biggest score of his life.

Hazut went on to express concern about dealing with capsules rather
than pills, because with capsules, you can open the casing and adulter-
ate the powder. "I don't want my product diluted, you know. I have my
reputation as a businessman to think of."

"Don't worry," assured Germanowski. "I'm not going to step on the
stuff. I'll sell them as is."

"You seem like a good guy," said Hazut. "You seem like somebody I
can trust."

"If the stuff is any good, I'll be back in touch." Germanowski replied.
"Maybe, we can do a lot of business together in the future."

"Don't worry, it's slamming stuff. You'll like it, trust me," Hazut
assured the undercover agent.

The topic then changed to additional banned substances. Germanowski said he had some other "packages" to pick up.

"What are you picking up, coke?"

"Nah, heroin."

"What are you paying for it?"

"Eighty-seven thousand dollars a key."

"Get out of here, I could get you a much better price."

"Oh, yeah. Come up with a figure and get back to me."

"My people only put big deals together. How much you after?"

"I'd start with three-quarters of a key and take it from there."

"That should be enough to get them interested."

Hazut then gave Germanowski the code 018 to identify each other when they communicated via beeper. Before walking away from the car and disappearing down one of the side streets, Hazut told G he'd love to come and party at his club in Pittsburgh.

On the afternoon of September 12, 1995, Germanowski and Hazut met once again on Queens Boulevard. This time, Matt's partner, Bob Gagne, was waiting in the sedan.

Hazut approached carrying a black bag over his left shoulder and asked, "Can we do this in the car?"

"There's someone in there you haven't met," Germanowski warned.

Hazut said he didn't want to meet anybody new. "It's OK," said the undercover agent. "He works for me. He's safe. You've got nothing to worry about."

Germanowski slipped into the front of the car while Hazut got in the back and sat next to Gagne. Gagne was dressed in his signature golf shirt, open at the neck, showing off the brown hairs on his ample chest. He tried to put Hazut at ease by offering a Cheshire cat grin. The Israeli opened his carryall and removed a clear plastic baggie with a large number of white capsules and handed them to Germanowski. There were 179 pills, all that Hazut could get for the moment. The negotiated price was $22 a hit—a little steep considering the amount of the order. Not that the covert operatives cared to bargain. After all, it wasn't their money.

After inspecting the merchandise, Germanowski immediately wanted to know, "Are they as good as the sample?"

"Don't worry about it. They're the same, they're 100 percent, they're the best." The DEA lab had already tested the sample Ecstasy capsules and found them to contain over 90 percent pure MDMA. They were, indeed, the authentic goods that Hazut had promised.

Germanowski asked Hazut again, "Are you *sure* they're as good as the sample?"

"My friend, they are 100 percent MDMA; you are going to love them. Try them out and let me know if you want a bigger order. Make sure you give me five days' notice."

Germanowski also inquired about the heroin. Hazut didn't have a price yet but promised he would get back to him.

The Israeli started to look nervous. His brow furrowed with worry, and he kept shooting glances over his shoulder. Germanowski asked what was the matter. "I'm not sure, can you just drive around the block? I don't like the look of those four guys sitting in that car across the street." Hazut had inadvertently spotted the DEA backup team lurking in the shadows. As they slowly circled the block, Gagne removed $4,000 from a green duffle bag and handed it to Hazut. Gagne asked him if he wanted to count the money. Hazut shrugged and said, "No, I trust you guys; you're good business people." The car turned back onto Queens Boulevard and stopped. They all shook hands. Hazut got out and left.

Their next encounter was at the end of September outside the Tower Diner, a Greek coffee shop on Queens Boulevard. Even though the location was directly across the street from his apartment, Hazut pulled up in a blue Pontiac Grand Am. Hazut jumped out of the car and immediately apologized for not being to able to get the heroin but promised he would have a sample from his source in Los Angeles by the end of the next week. He asked Germanowski if he liked the E and wanted to order some more. Germanowski said he loved them and would like to purchase twenty thousand capsules right away. Hazut replied it would take some time because his brother was having trouble getting the powder from his other brother in Miami. Germanowski suggested that if Hazut got the powder, he could put it in the capsules himself. Hazut reiterated his concerns about buyers ruining the potency of his product. He said he didn't like to sell only the powder, because buyers might dilute the drugs, which would hurt Hazut's rep as the best source of E in the city. Germanowski once again promised Hazut that he wouldn't take the edge off the product and further assured him that he would give all the credit to Hazut. Hazut said he might have 250 capsules by next week and would call G when he was ready to sell.

Germanowski then tried to pump Hazut for information about the "brothers." He asked him how many so-called brothers he had. Hazut said three, "One brother in Los Angeles with the heroin, one brother in Miami with the MDMA, and one brother up in the apartment." Germanowski had previously talked on the phone to Hazut's roommate and business partner, Michael El. Suddenly, El appeared at the window of the apartment and motioned for Hazut to come home. "Listen, I gotta go and run some errands."

Before leaving, Hazut asked Germanowski if he was interested in cocaine. "Why do you always mention cocaine?" Germanowski asked.

"The brother in LA with the heroin can also get coke in quantity."

"I'd like to meet this brother. I'd like to place an order for a large batch."

Hazut signed off. "We can get as much as you want."

On October 17, around 5:00 P.M. Gagne and Germanowski squeezed themselves into a booth inside the Tower Diner, where they drank coffee and picked impatiently at stodgy food. This would be the final meeting between the two parties. A few days earlier, over the phone, Hazut told Germanowski to forget about the capsules. He had "some other stuff" coming in from Amsterdam. They were called "apples." And they were just as potent as the capsules.

Michael El arrived, all breathless regrets. He apologized to the agents for Hazut's absence. His "brother" had another appointment to keep. El said that the reason Hazut wasn't there was because he was delivering five hundred "apples" to someone who worked at the Limelight. He didn't specify a name.

Germanowski asked when the twenty thousand capsules would be delivered. El again said he was sorry, but he couldn't get the capsules. His source with the powder in Miami had dried up. But he had a good sources for "apples." El palmed a plastic packet (which contained two small white pills) to Germanowski under the Formica table. Both pills had the imprint of an apple on one side. "They're the best E that anybody can get anywhere," El claimed. "They come from Amsterdam, from an old friend from the motherland, who can supply any amount you need." El said he would have no problem shipping twenty thousand pills because his friend owned a legitimate business in Holland and was constantly sending packages to the United States. The price was $20 a pill up to a thousand. Over a thousand the price dropped to $18 a pill. Over ten thousand, the price dropped to $15 a pill. El bragged that the best E in the world came from Holland and Israel and he had access to it. The agents had heard this story before.

A waiter in a dirty apron brought the check. The conversation finally turned back to the Limelight. El stated that there was a booming market for Ecstasy right now in the clubs around the New York area, particularly at the Limelight, where demand far outstripped supply. When the supply of good E ran low, El would supply the club with a weaker version known as "blue-and-whites"—named after the color of the capsules. They seemed to be fairly popular, despite being inferior to the apples, El claimed. The next time Gagne and Germanowski came to town, he'd take them to the Limelight so they could see for themselves.

By now, Gagne and Germanowski were fed up with the Israeli duo's excuses. It was going on three months since they first met, and they still hadn't managed to seal the major deal. They hid their irritation but strongly suspected that Hazut and El were not the drug trade movers and shakers they posed as. They talked a good game but lacked follow-through.

Then on December 11, while the feds listened at the other end, the Miami brother called Hazut to tell him that he had just Fed-Ex-ed 4,400 pills (called "playboys" because of the bunny logo imprinted on them) due to arrive in New York later that day. He hadn't had time to try the new shipment but intended to do so over the weekend. The Florida connection was worried about his money: "When am I gonna get paid?" Hazut told him he had a string of customers lined up. He reassured him that he would be reimbursed as soon as he off-loaded the merchandise. Later the same day, the Miami brother called back in a panic. Instead of reaching Hazut, he spoke to Michael El and warned El that the shipment was "hot." By some means, he had figured out that the DEA was on to them. When the shipment came El should not sign for it and claim no such person lived at the address. He also instructed El to remove any incriminating evidence from his apartment.

Gagne and Germanowski decided to pounce. Within hours, Hazut and El were arrested and transported to the DEA offices. Once there, Hazut claimed he was only a minor dealer: One of the largest deals he'd ever put together was the stuff he'd sold to Germanowski for $4,000. In the end, it didn't matter that Hazut and El weren't big-shot dope peddlers, or that the 4,400 "playboys" when tested turned out to contain nothing but salt and caffeine. In the agents' eyes, the Israeli duo was merely the initial stepping stone on the road to eventually bringing down someone far more evil and corrupt.

The Drug Enforcement Administration's New York headquarters stood under a rusty railway bridge at the corner of Seventeenth Street and Tenth Avenue, directly across from the Roxy dance hall, another notorious drug spot (which, as it happened, was not owned by Peter Gatien). A windswept parking lot filled with luxury automobiles confiscated from well-heeled dope peddlers separated the two locations. Nearby stood the Red Rock Saloon, a former hangout for the Irish gangsters who used to control the area, now a biker bar. At first sight, there was nothing on the outside to indicate that this bland, yellow-brick warehouse contained such a commanding organization. But if you looked closer, you noticed the video cameras at every corner of the building, the cluster of satellite dishes and antennas on the roof, and the large tinted bulletproof windows draped with bomb-retardant curtains that made it impossible to see into the lobby. The safety measures were installed after the front entrance had been sprayed with machine gun-fire during a drive-by.

In January 1996, three months after the unsuccessful raid on the Limelight, Sean Bradley walked under the red canvas awning and into the nondescript lobby of the DEA building, carrying several bags full of fashionable threads from a West Village boutique. The attendants sat like bank tellers behind Plexiglas windows. Behind them, the DEA logo and portraits of Bill Clinton and Janet Reno decorated the wall. To the side were two high-tech rotating doors that operated when government credentials were slid through an electronic reader. Bradley asked one of the bored-looking receptionists for Special Agent Mathew Germanowski. The receptionist told him to take a seat. Bradley, a drug dealer who stood five feet, four inches and sported bleached-blond hair, baggy jeans, and gang tattoos on his arms, looked out of place in such a bland setting. Germanowski came downstairs and warmly greeted Bradley before inviting him up to the office to confer with his partner, Bob Gagne.

The floor was divided into cubicles. Cheap government-issue furniture cluttered the space. Matt's cube was next to Bob's. Matt had a picture of his wife and son on his desk. His area was tidy. Bob's was cluttered with knickknacks and sporting memorabilia. He had the infamous "Blood Feast" poster of fashion model Jennytalia eating Michael Alig's brains pinned up on the wall next to another poster of the heavily made-up club kid with a dart in his right eye. Propped up in the corner of the cubicle was a bag of golf clubs custom made for Gagne. Both were avid players of what they referred to as "the sport of kings." Bob lived in Queens, Matt in New Jersey. The duo—agents since the early '90s—regarded themselves as experts in physical surveillance and at conducting undercover stings, debriefing informants, and interpreting the veiled lingo that drug dealers use to communicate with each other.

A disgruntled teenage raver and Limelight habitué, Sean Bradley had hooked up with the dynamic crime-fighting duo after Secret Service agents arrested him in November 1995 for trying to pass funny money amidst the plastic palm trees at the Woodbridge Shopping Mall in New Jersey. Bradley had gone to the mall, a popular rendezvous for local kids, on a spending spree using counterfeit fifty-dollar bills. He first stopped at Foot Locker to buy a pair of sneakers for his statuesque stripper girlfriend, who loomed over her tiny escort. At another store he bought her a dress. But at Sam Goody, when he attempted to purchase a Genesis CD for a relative with criminal taste in music, the vigilant shop assistant spotted the bogus bill. Mall security rushed over. They called the police, who escorted Bradley to the Woodbridge jail. The local cops buzzed the Secret Service, the government agency that probes counterfeit money. When the feds arrived, Bradley nearly urinated in his pants. They threatened to charge not only him but also his girlfriend if he didn't give up the name of the Bensonhurst wise guy who had furnished him with the bills. But the fast-on-his-feet nineteen-year-old soon formulated a plan to get out of trouble. He was too scared to give up the name of the Brooklyn mobster. But, in exchange for leniency, Bradley offered to give authorities inside dope about the Ecstasy distribution network at Peter Gatien's nightclubs, where he himself sold drugs. Ratting out club kids and ravers seemed like a far less hazardous course of action than turning in a member of the mob.

After the DEA was contacted, Bradley was shuttled off to meet Germanowski and Gagne. What he told the agents made their eyes bulge in astonishment. Bradley claimed that Gatien knew all about and gave his personal stamp of approval to the extensive drug trafficking that went on at his clubs. He told them that drug dealers made regular payments to the Canadian businessman for permission to be allowed to do business in his establishments. He recounted how one Tunnel drug dealer, Bernard Poltevien, a Haitian who sold cocaine in front of the upstairs unisex bathroom, supposedly became angry when a friend was banned from the club. "As much as I pay Peter, I'll bring whoever I want into this club," the snitch claimed Poltevien told him. Bradley also estimated that Gatien earned $6 to $7 million a year from the sale of illegal narcotics at his various discos, though how he came up with that probably fictitious figure was unclear.

Bradley further claimed that Gatien cultivated corrupt contacts within the NYPD, who alerted him to upcoming police raids. He said that Limelight management warned him two weeks prior to the famous stymied drug sweep to steer clear of the club that weekend, or if he did come, to make sure "not to have anything on you." Bradley alleged that in the wake of the raid, Gatien was extremely paranoid and had tried to limit the sale of Ecstasy, but once the heat was off in a few weeks, the customary drug activities were supposed to resume. In addition, he maintained that Gatien had openly discussed his concerns about drug dealing in his clubs at meetings that Bradley said he attended. He told the engrossed agents, who were frantically scribbling notes, that Gatien specifically warned drug dealers at these get-togethers, "Use caution when working."

Bradley then went on to explain how the Limelight and the Tunnel operated under a "chain of command." According to Bradley, Gatien shielded himself from responsibility for the illegal activities at his clubs by employing people below him to oversee the drug distribution. At the top of the hierachy stood Gatien, of course, while directly under him were the three executive directors: club kid king Michael Alig, rave pioneer Michael "Lord Michael" Caruso, and downtown Manhattan mainstay Steven Lewis. Bradley specifically fingered Alig and Caruso, who each ran their own separate narcotics crews, as the leading supervisors of the furious drug action. He also said that Caruso's dealers regularly carried guns into the Limelight. Steven Lewis's job, said Bradley, was to stand at the front door and ensure the entry of house dealers into the club while keeping out the freelancers.

Below the executive directors, the next rank consisted of the promoters, who were the hosts for the night. As well as providing the right music and ambience, Bradley claimed that part of the promoter's job was to ensure an adequate supply of good-quality chemicals, since his or her paycheck was determined in part by how many people attended the club on the particular night, and the number of people who attended the club was directly related to the availability of mind-altering goodies. Bradley also said that promoters hired so-called runners to move throughout the club hawking Ecstasy. He finished off by outlining where the drugs consumed at Gatien's clubs came from and how they got into the country. He described how traffickers, including his girlfriend Jessica, would smuggle tens of thousands of Ecstasy hits from Amsterdam in false-bottomed suitcases and within days those very same drugs would end up being sold on the dance floors at the Limelight and the Tunnel.

Gagne and Germanowski were astonished at their good luck. If only half true, this was still startling stuff. Only a few months into the investigation, and already it seemed like they had the key to the entire case. Bradley's offer of cooperation was especially opportune because a month earlier, the Limelight had been briefly shuttered following the stymied drug raid. After weeks of physical surveillance of Gatien's establishments, the duo was delighted to have someone who not only could make supervised drug buys in the clubs but also could give them a behind-the-scenes look at the narcotics trafficking that went on there. An agent is only as good as his informants. Drug cases are mostly built on the information provided by snitches. Even though he was a minor figure on the scene, the agents thought they had a prize rat in Bradley, someone who could help them infiltrate and topple Peter Gatien's empire.

Bradley was the original snitch in the Gatien investigation, but he was a long way from the last. In this country, the use of paid informers by law enforcement has skyrocketed in recent years, as the War on Drugs has transformed the American criminal justice system into a literal rattrap. Law enforcement has grown dependent on anonymous snitches to such a disturbing extent that the DEA today employs as many informants as it does agents. The agency also spends millions for the purchase of evidence, so-called buy money, which the informant, instead of using to buy drugs, often keeps.

Subsidized by the taxpayer, confidential informants frequently earn a second income by continuing to commit crimes while working for law enforcement. Sammy "The Bull" Gravano, John Gotti's accuser, was busted for running an Ecstasy ring in Arizona not long after he got out of the witness protection program.

The *National Law Journal* wrote in 1995: "Today's criminal justice system is addicted to informants. Law enforcement's reliance on informants has grown to almost Orwellian proportions. . . . New forfeiture laws have made drug busts a law enforcement prize, generating lots of cash both to pay informants and increase their own operating budgets. Even more important, perhaps, mandatory sentencing laws and crushing prison terms adopted in the 1980's have created powerful incentives for criminals to go to any lengths to avoid jail."

One of those lengths is to lie or exaggerate in order to impress their handlers. Few informants fib all the time. Outright fabrications are too easy to spot. What they do, instead, is to mix fact and fiction, just as their handlers tell them to do, in order to construct a believable cover. Given that they're paid by results, the informant's own financial interest is to come up with deep dirt on targets, whether or not that information is accurate.

Police and prosecutors say informants are a necessary evil. As a practical matter, the justice system would grind to a halt without them. But what happens when the informers are bigger criminals than the defendants on trial, and how do you distinguish between truth and drug-induced fantasy—the real deal and a profitable hustle—in this shadowy underworld, where disinformation is routine currency?

After he signed the requisite paperwork, Sean Bradley was immediately "activated" as a paid government informant. He was given a computer printout with a set of rules for making undercover drug purchases (so-called controlled buys) in nightclubs. He was told to observe if the buy was "open and notorious" or "quick and quiet." He was instructed to pay attention to what was going on around him—were any club staff nearby, for instance? He was ordered to purchase as wide a variety of drugs as he could. And, if at all possible, he was told to make the buy in the presence of an undercover agent. He was also told that he could sell drugs to protect his cover but was warned to limit the transactions to five hits of Ecstasy and two vials of Special K a night. He was also advised that it was permissable to personally ingest small amounts of drugs for the same reason.

The agents trained Bradley and taught him all about surveillance techniques. They took him into the tech room—the secured area where they keep all the wiretaps. The agents also schooled him on the topic of interviewing methods—how to interrogate people without them knowing that they're being interrogated. They would tell Sean how proud they were that he was learning the ropes of the rodent racket so quickly.

In return for his services, Bradley was paid a modest weekly stipend, but the real payday, the agents said, would come later, after Gatien was arrested and all his clubs were seized and then auctioned off. Then, Bradley would get the usual quarter share of forfeiture—up to a maximum of $250,000—routinely offered as bounty to snitches in important drug cases. The reward money was a significant incentive to tell his handlers what they wanted to hear. To Bradley, who had quit college and was unable to hold a real job for more than a short period of time and who usually supported himself by selling Ecstasy and Special K, this was a significant sum of money. The young man also got a lenient deal on the counterfeiting charges: six months of unsupervised probation, which left him free to continue dealing drugs while he helped the DEA.

Bradley relished his role as an undercover informant. "It was like I was a little fucking agent," he confessed. He was thrilled to hook up with such an all-powerful organization. The cloak-and-dagger stuff gave him a sense of prestige previously lacking in his life. The punk-ass zero whom nobody respected turned into a regular junior G-man. Deficient in stature and status, the little squirt was now a clandestine big shot.

When he sold out Peter Gatien to the feds, the ill-tempered Bradley—whom an acquaintance compared to the Joe Pesci character in *Casino*—had more complicated motives than simply avoiding jail time. Bradley worked both as a house dealer and supplier for the twenty-year-old Baby Joe Uzzardi, a key figure in the Ecstasy scene at Gatien's clubs. Baby Joe was one of Gatien's top promoters. The New York University student was being groomed to take over Michael Alig's position as executive director, because Alig had turned into such a druggy mess. Bradley met Uzzardi at the Tunnel in 1994, and they quickly established a business relationship. Baby Joe would give Bradley a heads-up concerning forthcoming events, and Bradley would make sure enough drugs were available. Despite their mutual business interests, Bradley harbored a deep resentment toward his theoretical friend, because he believed that the more fashionable and in-the-know Baby Joe had gone back on an agreement to hire him as a promoter. He felt slighted. "He doesn't give a shit about me," he told the DEA agents.

Bradley's association with Uzzardi provided the drug agents with a doorway into the narcotics distribution at the Limelight and Tunnel. Bradley wore a hidden microphone to meetings with Uzzardi's cronies and taped his telephone calls with Baby Joe, in which they discussed drug deals in detail. He introduced agents to targets as "my friends from New Jersey." He made controlled buys from one of Uzzardi's drug dealers. He surreptitiously took photos of potential targets doing drugs inside the Limelight and the Tunnel. He even smuggled a camcorder into the Limelight, but the ambience was too dark to capture anything. The bulk of the evidence allowed the DEA to obtain a court order from a judge to wiretap Uzzardi's NYU dormitory phone. The agents were thrilled when the arrogant and flamboyant Uzzardi was caught blabbing about numerous drug transactions at both the Tunnel and the Limelight. He crowed that he had "really good drug dealers who deliver a quality product." He boasted about the tens of thousands of dollars he made selling drugs at Gatien's clubs. He said he sold upward of 1,200 hits of Ecstasy a night.

Bradley clearly enjoyed targeting the well-liked Uzzardi. Once, Bradley gloated about getting Uzzardi to peddle eight hits of high-grade Ecstasy directly to the agents. "That's fucking incredible because Joe hardly ever does hand-to-hands," he marveled.

The animosity that Bradley felt toward Uzzardi was rooted in the disparities between ravers and club kids. While the two subcultures coexisted under the same roof at the Limelight, united by their common interest in Ecstasy and techno music, there were important differences between the lifestyles. Baby Joe was a fashionable figure from an affluent family who sported fabulous outfits tailor-made by his art school girlfriend. Bradley, the product of a troubled home, was a saggy jean–wearing raver, the heterosexual alternative to club kids. Music, more than fashion, was his passion.

"The truth about drug dealers is the bigger you are, the more modest you are," Baby Joe said about his subordinate. "Sean is like this little explosive firecracker that just like basically reveals that he's not a big dealer; he's a punk, you know."

Bradley also didn't get along with agent Bob Gagne. "Gagne thought I was just a stupid kid and he was a big, bad federal agent," Bradley would say afterward. By contrast, Bradley looked up to Germanowski and thought of him as a friend. He called him "Gee" as a sign of affection. "He seemed really concerned about me, not just the case, but with me and my girlfriend. He was like the older brother I never had. If I had a problem with Jessica, I would call him for advice. He once took me to his home. He helped me with all my legal problems. He also promised that when the case was over that he would move me to a safe place, and I could start a new life with the award money."

By early in the New Year, Germanowski was so confident that Bradley's stories had the chime of authenticity that he sat down and punched out a report—based on Sean's information—that would explain to his bosses the hierarchy at Gatien's clubs and go some way to illuminating the unusual sociology of clubland.

In the DEA Report of Investigation, dated January 5, 1996, Germanowski adopted a paradoxically Marxist analysis:

> The three nightclubs [Limelight, Tunnel, and the Palladium] are considered among the elite nightclubs in New York City's "underground" community. The underground community is made up of three classes of people. The classes are ranked by order of importance, according to club management. The first class is the hardcore homosexuals. This class includes gays, lesbians, transvestites, cross dressers, and bisexuals. The main promoter for this class is Michael Alig. The second class is made up of "ravers". This group consists of those people with multi-colored hair, pierced body parts (other than ears), and any sort of radical appearance. The main promoter to handle this class is Lord Michael [Caruso]. The third class consists of the arts and entertainment community, such as actors, singers, and record producers. This class is represented by Steve Lewis. Dependent on which class of crowd is anticipated, determines what type of drug the club will have available on a particular night.
>
> Prior to the raid on the Limelight, there was a room (one of approximately fifteen) that was called "the bedroom." This room was extremely popular with the homosexuals and ravers. Both would go into this room and purchase drugs, usually from a runner posted at the door where one enters, and then go into one of the four beds and participate in group sex. To gain access to this room, one would have to go past a doorman. If the person entering was not a regular, or appeared not to be openly homosexual, one would not be able to get into this room. . . .
>
> Behind the bars in both the Limelight and Tunnel there are several flashing lights. The bartenders have a signal with the promoters and runners. If undercover officers were inside the club or a police raid was suspected, the bartenders would activate a series of lights that would all be red. If the runners saw red lights spin-

ning behind the bar, they would know to leave the club immediately via a pre-arranged exit and also to immediately stop selling any and all narcotics that they may have on them.

The next stage of the investigation required a radical transformation. Bradley wanted to take Matt and Bob directly into the belly of the beast, by ensuring the DEA agents gained access to the exclusive VIP lounges at the Limelight and the Tunnel, where much of the hard-core drug activity took place. After the straight-looking Gagne and Germanowski were rebuffed by door people, Bradley decided to dress them up as club kids so he would have no hassle getting them past the Tunnel's velvet rope. The bleached-blond raver took the two decidedly unfashionable undercover agents shopping for clothes at Pat Fields in the West Village. Finding outfits to fit the oversized muscle men was no easy task. With the help of drag queen shop assistants, the duo finally found the appropriate look.

Later, sashaying limp-wristed around the DEA headquarters, the six-foot one-inch Germanowski fluttered his eyelashes and blew kisses through black lipstick as he modeled a long black dress with a slit down one side that showed off a recently shaven leg. He'd also just cropped his hair, dying the remaining stubble platinum, and had his ears pierced. He flung a silk wrap around his ample shoulders. Germanowski decided that he liked all the dressing up. He began to understand the attraction of the club kids. Gagne, the less fashion forward of the two, went for a more subdued suburban punk look: black shirt and trousers with a dog collar around his neck. Germanowski attached a chain to the collar and led his partner around the squad room to the hoots of colleagues. Together, they looked like a couple of gay, Gothic longshoremen under the influence of some as yet undiscovered mind-bending chemical. That evening the two beefcakes headed out for what would be their third or fourth foray into Peter Gatien's Ecstasy underworld.

On a freezing Saturday night in late February 1996, with snow banked up six feet high on the sidewalks, the dolled-up DEA agents entered the Tunnel. It was just after 1:00 A.M. The place was half empty. The snowiest winter of the century had hit Gatien's clubs like an icy blast to his bank balance. Sixteen back-to-back storms that deposited a record ninety inches of snow kept customers away in hordes.

All three—Gagne, Germanowski, and Bradley—headed toward the Police Room, a special alcove wallpapered with "Closed by the NYPD" notices and festooned with yellow "Do Not Cross" tape. Instead of a velvet rope, wooden police barricades brought over from the Limelight kept out the hoi polloi. The room was created and named following the NYPD raid on the Tunnel's sister club five months ago and was meant as a deliberate provocation—an attempt to poke fun at the authorities and their ongoing crackdown on clubland.

This space was Baby Joe's domain—a smoke-filled VIP section where drug deals among the favored few could be transacted in relative privacy. A svelte drag queen named Gravity was the door person. Gravity recognized Gagne and Germanowski from a previous visit and promptly admitted them. Straight away, the agents noticed drug activity taking place out in the open. Some patrons passed around marijuana joints, while others inhaled white powder off their fingernails.

Baby Joe came across the room to greet Bradley and his thickset buddies. Sean had introduced Uzzardi to Gagne and Germanowski a few weeks ago at the Limelight as his "two friends from New Jersey . . . G Man and Bob." Sean had been away for months, and all of a sudden he reappeared with these two bruisers. The stylishly attired Baby Joe tried not to snigger, but Sean's friends looked comical—like overgrown frat boys auditioning for a bit part in *Velvet Goldmine*. Trying to be gracious, he asked them if they were having a good time and gave them some drink tickets.

Uzzardi also had a warning for the peculiar trio: "Be careful," he cautioned. The word was out that undercover cops were at the Limelight that night looking to bust anyone caught doing or selling drugs. Baby Joe thought they might also pay a visit to the Tunnel. But he reassured Germanowski and Gagne that even if the cops did turn up, they would be safe, as long as they stayed within the confines of the Police Room.

A couple of hours later, at about 3:30 A.M., Germanowski and Gagne reentered the Police Room with Bradley. Bradley and Germanowski informed Baby Joe that they wanted to buy three hits of Ecstasy. Baby

Joe told them, "Talk to Mike," and pointed to one of his runners, a six-foot, one-inch male with dark hair and a pierced nose. "Come to the front of the room with me," Mike instructed. "How many do you need? Hang on a minute." Mike walked away. About sixty seconds later, Mike returned with a man who was wearing a floor-length maroon dress. Mike asked for the money. Germanowski gave him $90. The guy in the dress handed Germanowski a small plastic bag containing three blue-and-white capsules. He immediately recognized them as "blue-and-whites"—the inferior Ecstasy that Israel Hazut had tried to sell him at the Queens Diner. Gagne and Germanowski went back into the Police Room and thanked Baby Joe for the E. "No problem," said Joe. "If you need any more, let me know."

Around 4:00 A.M., Gagne saw Executive Director Steven Lewis enter the Police Room, approach Baby Joe, and whisper something in his ear. After Lewis left, Baby Joe then motioned to Bradley to come over. Joe told Bradley that people had been arrested at the Limelight, and that Lewis wanted Bradley and his friends to leave right now. Joe said he stood up for Bradley, supposedly telling Lewis that Bradley was in the place as his guest, not to sell drugs, but Lewis insisted. They all had to go. The undercover agents became incensed. Words were exchanged. Security was called.

"I remember these two huge guys, one of them with horns," an employee who witnessed the confrontation told *New York* magazine. "They were pissed off, and they kept trying to get back into the Police Room. The bouncers wouldn't let them in. They got so irate we had to throw them out. At that point, they were swearing at us, and they didn't sound much like club kids then."

3 COMING TO AMERICA

Ontario, Canada, 1952

Peter Gatien's troubled hot spots were a long way from his humble provincial roots in Cornwall, Ontario, a weather-beaten backwater of approximately 47,000 people on the U.S.-Canadian border. Originally founded by English loyalists on the St. Lawrence River, Cornwall, when Gatien grew up there, was a mill town, notable for its lack of distinguished landmarks or points of outstanding beauty. Many of its streets were named after famous European battles such as Dieppe and Dunkirk.

Gatien claimed you could smell Cornwall in the distance long before you actually saw the place. As you headed across the Seaway International Bridge and down Highway 401, past the Indian reservation and toward the industrial town, a sour stench assaulted the nostrils. The atmosphere was redolent with sulfur emanating from a large paper mill, Cornwall's most important employer. Such was the poisonous smell that on her first visit, Gatien's wife, Alex, almost threw up in the street.

Located only sixty miles west of Montreal, Cornwall was evenly split down sectarian lines. It was like Belfast without the gunmen: Half of the population was Anglo-Canadian; half was French-Canadian. The vast majority of the French also spoke English. The vast majority of the English didn't bother to learn French. The Anglos tended to vote conservative and practice Protestantism, while the French Catholics were generally more liberal. Gatien spoke French at home and at school until his teens. English was his second language.

"Cornwall was the type of town where your career opportunities were limited," the entrepreneur recalled. "If you finished high school, you went to work in the post office or the local factory. If you finished college, the most you could hope for was to become an accountant or lawyer. There was a subtle inferiority to being French and Catholic. At the local mill, the English had all the white-collar jobs while the French did the grunt work."

Born Jean Pierre Gatien in 1952, Peter was the middle son of five strapping brothers. Big families were the norm in their part of town. The next-door neighbors, also Catholics, had twelve children. Peter was a shy kid who rarely said much, the ugly duckling of the clan; his more vigorous and academically proficient brothers took the limelight, while he remained in the shadows.

Peter's father was a postman, his mother an elementary school-teacher who mended furs on the side to make ends meet. The Gatiens lived in a gray, three-bedroom, stucco-covered house—one of the many identical prefabricated structures thrown up after World War II to shelter the homecoming troops. His parents bought the 650-square-foot home for a cost of $4,000 in the same year Gatien was born. Theirs was a frugal, but not necessarily unhappy, lower-middle-class existence. The family had hot water once a week. Their devoutly religious mother made all their clothes, down to their socks, until they were teenagers. Both the boy's parents taught Gatien that he had to work hard to get ahead in life. In the summer, he helped his dad at the post office, standing in front of a big box for eight hours sorting mail. "It was mind-numbing. I don't know how my father did it for all those years," recalled the club owner.

There was nothing glamorous or decadent about Peter Gatien's upbringing. In this rigidly circumscribed world dominated by sports, religion, and work, everybody toiled, without exception. Slackers were unheard of in Cornwall, as were atheistic, pointy-headed intellectuals who didn't believe in the holy trinity of local sport—ice hockey in the winter, touch football in the autumn, and baseball in the summer.

Faith, too, was a huge part of Gatien's early life. A dedicated altar boy, he would get up at 5:30 every morning to help serve masses at 6:45 and 7:30. He was paid seventy-five cents a week for his duties. During Lent, he went to mass every day, fearing God would punish him if he didn't. He went to confession every Saturday and was instructed that impure thoughts were a sin. He wondered how any thought could be immoral and learned to develop a finely tuned sense of guilt. For a couple of years, he attended a Jesuit school, College Classique de Cornwall, where he had to wear a black blazer, a burgundy tie, and gray woolen pants that made his legs itch. He bent his knee toward Rome so many times, he seriously considered becoming a priest.

Ice hockey, which he first played at age five, was his real passion— skating effortlessly down the ice, with a frigid wind smacking him in the face, was when he felt most alive. In the winter, the Gatien brothers would hose down the backyard and turn it into a makeshift ice rink. A Montreal Canadians fan, Peter fantasized that one day he might play for the National Hockey League. "Ice hockey was like a religion in Cornwall," he said.

Peter's dreams of playing professional sports were dashed when, at the age of sixteen, he lost his left eye in a hockey accident, a misfortune that he assessed, only half-jokingly, as "probably the best thing that ever happened to me." Gatien described the life-changing incident as if it had happened to another person. "I remember turning around to skate up the ice, and I didn't see it coming, but a stick caught me in the eye," he said, betraying not a flicker of emotion in his voice. "The nail at the bottom of the stick designed to keep it together must have been out. I just remember feeling something on my nose. It's funny, the guys I used to play with, a couple of them made it to the NHL, but most ended up working in insurance offices."

Did his personality alter after the accident? "Not really, I was always the quiet type," he said. "It was painful at the time, but to tell you the truth, I never regarded it as much of a handicap."

In 1969, at the age of seventeen, Gatien started to get into the hippie counterculture. He experimented with pot and LSD. He listened to the Rolling Stones, Grand Funk Railroad, and Iron Butterfly. His introspective nature became even more apparent. He would sit for hours outside his parents' home in a little Austin Mini, outfitted with an eight-track sound system too big for the compact vehicle, blasting out "Satisfaction" and "Gimme Shelter" while dreaming of any life other than the one he was currently living. He got into arguments with his father over the length of his hair. The Vietnam War was raging—one of his teachers was a draft dodger who had fled to Canada. Gatien was vaguely aware of the social and political tumult going on just across the border, even if it seemed like a million miles away from his prosaic existence.

Against his father's objections, Gatien decided to go to college. His dad believed he was acting above his social station, even though his two older brothers already were on their way to becoming a doctor and a lawyer. He thought Peter should join him down at the local post office. "My father had an inferiority complex," Gatien claimed. "He didn't put a lot of expectations on us. He thought that in Cornwall, you don't need a college degree to survive."

Gatien went to Carlton University in Ottawa to study psychology. But after only two semesters, he grew bored and returned to Cornwall. Since he'd been away, his high school principal, who used to ban blue jeans and tie-dyes in the classroom, had relented, removing the dress code. Students craved this hippie wear, which couldn't be found anywhere in town. Gatien sensed an opportunity. Using the $17,000 insurance settlement he had won following the hockey accident, he swiftly opened a clothing boutique opposite his old high school. The "Pants Loft" was decorated with bits of barn wood he'd scavenged from surrounding farms. It was such a success that he opened up a second one in nearby Smiths Falls, but Gatien claims he closed it after an investor ran off with the money.

The same year he opened Pants Loft, Gatien got married—the first of three times—to his childhood sweetheart, Sheila, a common scenario in his town, where couples frequently wed at an early age. "There weren't a lot of pretty girls to chase around in Cornwall. There wasn't a whole lot to do, so you got married," explained Gatien matter-of-factly. They had two children together—Amanda and Jennifer.

Gatien soon realized that flogging discount jeans was no clear pathway to riches. The profit margin was too small. Selling booze, he thought, was the way to go. The markup was tremendous. "If you bought a pint of beer for 25 cents, you sold it for $1.25. When I was in the jeans business, I bought a pair of jeans for $4 and sold them for $8. So it was five times the markup," he once told *The New York Times*. Even in those days, his business mind was working overtime. He sold Pants Loft to another budding hippie entrepreneur (who later turned it into a national chain) and began to scout sites for a local saloon.

Within weeks, Gatien came across a dilapidated country-and-western bar called the Lafayette House, the roughest spot in Cornwall, patronized by shit-kicking farmers and head-butting mill workers. The first day Gatien took it over, he had to evict a set of grizzled barflies and nearly got into a fight with them. "You have to go," he told them. "We're going after a different crowd."

Over the next weekend, he transformed the place. He painted the walls black, put in a mirror ball, and constructed three new bars. He called the joint the Aardvark Hotel and immediately booked the Canadian pomp-rockers Rush as the opening act for a meager $1,000. The five-hundred-person joint was packed with working-class youngsters eager to experience the first club of its type in Cornwall.

Claude McIntosh, editor of the *Cornwall Standard Freeholder*, told *New York* magazine, "Peter had brought in these disco balls and painted the whole place black. They put up this rope in front and made all these burly bouncers dress in tuxedo shirts and bow ties. People said the Aardvark was a place where you could get hooked up. It wasn't much of a town for cocaine or that, but you'd hear you could go to the washroom and buy all the magic mushrooms or hash that you'd want."

A year later, after a visit to a Montreal disco, and sensing the sea change in popular culture about to happen, Gatien reinvented the place once again, fashioning it into a dance club. He installed a new lighting system. He cut his hair. He dropped the hippie look in favor of three-piece polyester suits. His parents, who stressed self-sufficiency, were proud. Only twenty, he was making big money for a small town.

In 1974, at the age of twenty-two, Gatien packed his bell-bottoms and his gold medallion, and crossed the border to New York to attend the world's first-ever disco convention, which had been organized by *Billboard* magazine at the Roosevelt Hotel. He was intimidated, if energized, by the big shots he met there. When he saw a real estate ad in *The New York Times* for a Florida nightclub, Gatien seriously weighed the opportunity. The listing described a bankrupt supper club that was being sold in Hollywood, Florida, for $290,000. Gatien did some quick calculations in his head and figured out that the sound system and lights were worth more than the asking price. After borrowing some money from his brothers, he flew to Florida to meet the owners and bought the club on the spot, even though he didn't know what Chapter 11 meant. "I was twenty-two and I had bought one of the largest nightclubs in America almost by default," he recalled. He transformed the place—with neon, chrome, and spinning wheels—into one of the most popular nightlife attractions in the South and the first of five Limelights to bear the name. "People loved going out in those days," he remembered. "It was easy to get people to come out. There were no promoters and no drink tickets. It was the best business to be in. You could do no wrong. It was all profit."

After three years, he sold the club for $900,000 and moved to Atlanta. It was 1979, the disco era was drawing to a close, and Gatien recalls the "stress clinics" that dotted the city. Someone would hire a Third World doctor, set him up in a storefront, and get him to hand out prescriptions for Quaaludes. The scheme was legal at the time. Gatien remembers driving through the city streets and seeing lines outside the clinics.

In an affluent suburban section of Atlanta called Buckhead, Gatien came across another bankrupt club, this one in a shopping mall, where he planned to open a second Limelight, using the same winning design formula that he'd employed in Florida. The surrounding neighborhood was smack in the middle of the Bible Belt and looked like something from *Gone With the Wind* before the Yankees invaded. Gatien rented one of the antebellum mansions and set about gathering the necessary permits needed to debut his new establishment. The city fathers aired the usual grievances about noise and public morals, but they were easy enough to placate.

When the club opened, Georgia had never seen anything like the Limelight, with its glass dance floor suspended over a pool full of live sharks, which Gatien got from an aquarium in Florida. Nearby, a black panther prowled in a cage. There was a movie theater in the club. The walls of one room were completely covered with peacock feathers. Whirling lights and glitter balls illuminated the mob of dancing good old boys and drag queens. When minor celebrities passed through Atlanta for a show, they would often pop in to the club to shake a tail feather. Major stars like Tom Cruise and Ali McGraw were specially flown in from New York to boost the club's profile. Gatien had created the right place at the right time.

Devoted hedonists drove fourteen hours from as far afield as Tennessee, Alabama, and Florida just to attend the famous Limelight theme parties. Every Wednesday night, two thousand people would pack the club dressed like Fred and Pebbles Flintstone or wearing nothing but bath towels. "In those days," Gatien claimed, "you didn't have to pay women to dance topless on the bar. They did it for free out of sheer exuberance." It was all good, clean, innocent fun. The club did feature a minor drug scene, though. Cocaine was available. But Gatien didn't touch drugs. During this period, his only indulgence was the occasional glass of white wine.

"The club put Atlanta on the map as a party town," said Claire O'Connor, who worked for Gatien for over ten years, first as his publicist, then as a director. "The thing about the people who came to the club was that they weren't jaded like New Yorkers. They had no inhibitions. They were determined to have fun, and they didn't care what anybody thought about them."

Even though Gatien was raking in the money, he remained dissatisfied and restless. Something was still missing. He had created Atlanta's answer to Studio 54, with all the provincialism that the title implied. From Canada to Florida to Georgia, every three years or so, he felt the need to pick up stumps and move elsewhere. In those days, New York was the undisputed center of the club world, and Gatien needed a new challenge.

"Canadians must have this thing they learn in high school," said Claire O'Connor. "If you make it in New York, you're the biggest thing in the world."

Ready for the big time, in 1983, Gatien arrived in New York City, carting a bag full of money and determined to become a major player in a town that had broken stronger men than he. To him, Gotham was synonymous with success. He had ambitious plans. In those days clubs like Studio 54 and Xenon set the tone. Though disco as a national phenomenon had crashed spectacularly, in New York, people still loved to go out to dance en masse. The problem, as Gatien saw it, was that club owners, such as Studio 54's Steve Rubell, were basically giving away the scene for free.

Gatien wanted to create an epic disco like Studio 54 but one where patrons would not be subjected to intense door scrutiny and where everybody coughed up admission. He sought celebrities in his club, sure, but only to the extent they attracted paying customers. He had no interest in being the life of the party or hobnobbing with pretentious air-kissing phonies. He was Canadian, after all. He could count his real friends on the fingers of one hand. He wanted to wield real power but—unlike Steve Rubell—strictly from behind the scenes. He was smart enough to know that seen-it-all New Yorkers were unlikely to be impressed by another gigantic chrome-and-mirror palace. Obviously, he couldn't just replicate the same old formula. Instead, he came up with an idea to open a club in a landmark building, maybe a mansion or an old library or, best of all, a house of worship.

Gatien was looking for a property when he was tipped off about a deconsecrated Episcopalian church at the corner of Sixth Avenue and Twentieth Street that was owned by Odyssey House, a drug treatment center, which could no longer afford to keep up the landmark building. The surrounding area was shabby in the day and desolate after dark. One of the few signs of commercial activity was a row of photo processing stores. There were hardly any shops or restaurants nearby. Inside the shell of a structure, few of the original ecclesiastical features remained. Row after row of cot beds and the general air of brownish gloom that hung over the place made it look more like a homeless shelter than a former house of God. But decades of neglect could not hide the soaring architecture and the spectacular, intricately colored windows—designed by Tiffany rival John La Farge—one of which memorialized John Jacob Astor, who died on the *Titanic*. Clearly, the church had once catered to a very wealthy congregation.

Even though he had been raised as a staunch Catholic, Peter dismissed concerns that a church was not a proper setting for a nightclub.

"I wanted to create a club that made an architectural statement," he claimed. "So the church was perfect, because not only was it a breathtaking structure, but it had been built for public assembly, which made it easier to transform into a club."

Gatien took over the property in January 1983 and poured millions into creating the Limelight. Cost overruns nearly caused him to go bankrupt before the club even opened. He had to sell his car and other possessions to pay the architect. Gatien also had a falling out over money with his brother, Maurice, a lawyer, who was supposed to be an investor in the new venture. "There were a lot of problems with his brother," claimed Claire O'Connor. "He thought he was a partner. But Peter kicked him out, because he wanted to create something all on his own."

Finally, the club was set to open. The buzz preceding the debut was deafening. For months, back page advertisements in local magazines promised "A Blessing in Disguise." Opening dates came and went, which only served to heighten the anticipation. The Right Reverend Paul Moore, the Episcopal bishop of New York, wrote a letter to *The New York Times* expressing "horror" that a former house of worship was being turned into a disco. Then, finally, the invitations went out: "Andy Warhol and *Interview* invite you to the grand opening of the Limelight."

The opening of the Limelight on November 9, 1983, was madness on a mass scale. An estimated ten thousand potential patrons showed up, less than a third of whom would actually gain admittance. A sea of glittering humanity clogged the width of Sixth Avenue all the way down to Fourteenth Street. Celebrities—Jacqueline Smith, Valerie Perrine, Karen Allen, Billy Idol, Andy Warhol, Cornelia Guest, all big names back then—were hoisted by security guards over the heads of the mob and literally carried into the club. Some partygoers came dressed as Biblical figures. One Jesus impersonator came hoisted aloft on a full-size cross. The club thought it was too extreme; management refused to let him in. They wanted to play up the spiritual angle of the new venture but not to the point of offensiveness. There were also a handful of religious protestors who held a vigil outside, protesting the use of a church as a nightclub. One of them held aloft a sign that caused much mirth: "If you want to get down, get down on your knees."

Gatien was on the steps of the church directing the chaos. Nobody in the throng had the foggiest idea who he was, this slightly pudgy, baby-faced Canadian with the black eye patch. The provincial outsider, with few discernible social graces and even fewer notable vices, was now the toast of downtown Manhattan, or at least his disco was.

The next day, the Limelight phones rang off the hook. Claire O'Connor recalled, "There were a lot of people who were pissed off that they didn't get in. Tons of apology letters had to be written by us and Andy Warhol's people."

The first few years, the Limelight was a press to print money. Using the proceeds from the profits, Gatien began making plans to open two other Limelights, one in Chicago, in a former museum, and the other in London, in another church. He dreamed of creating a global chain . . . McClubland.

"Many times when I was there, people would offer to buy the club for as much as $10 million," remembered O'Connor. "But Peter always turned them down. It wasn't worth it. He was making that in a year."

Then, in the middle of the decade, two catastrophic events sent Gatien's world spinning off its axis. The first occurred in May 1985, when Steve Rubell debuted his new dance hall, the Palladium. Rubell's cavernous culture club on Fourteenth Street famously featured the work of such leading downtown artists as Keith Haring, Francesco Clemente, and Kenny Scharf. More popular than the artwork, however, were the generous open bars and free admission on the weekends. The Limelight was used to playing host to two thousand paying customers every Friday and Saturday night. Who was going to pay to come to the Limelight when you could go over to the Palladium and get in and drink for free? As a result, business plummeted. All of a sudden, the Limelight was stale toast. You couldn't pay the glitterati to visit. The fabulous few stayed away in droves. Gatien was reduced to courting the after-work crowd, throwing glorified office parties for tipsy secretaries, or renting out the club to the Hell's Angels or Al Goldstein's *Screw* magazine, for private bashes. The one bright spot was Sunday night's rock-and-roll jams, where practically ever major young rock band of the time, from the Red Hot Chili Peppers to Guns N' Roses, graced the stage.

The second very bad thing that happened to Peter Gatien in the mid-'80s was that he discovered the joys of smoking crack cocaine with hookers in a turn of events that was completely out of character for this normally sober operator. No one saw it coming. Up to that time, Gatien really was that rare bloom, a club owner who didn't do drugs. At first, close friends thought that he had contracted a mysterious illness. He lost weight, and his hands trembled. His baby-fat cheeks started to grow hollow. The usually punctual businessman began missing appointments. He wouldn't turn up to work, sometimes for as long as a month. After being alerted by a close friend that something was seriously wrong with the club owner and furthermore that he was refusing to seek medical assistance, one of his brothers, Raymond the doctor, rushed across the border to examine him. Gatien told his sibling he had a bad case of the flu. Raymond could find nothing wrong. The last thing anybody suspected was that the buttoned-down entrepreneur and family man was sneaking off to hotel suites for marathon benders, where he would cavort naked with a harem of call girls and light up mountains of white rock.

Claire O'Connor was shocked when she found out about the parties. Gatien made her swear an oath of secrecy. "Peter was always deeply ashamed of the hotel parties," she said. "He didn't want people to know. He hid it from his family. It was very ugly. He did it once and that was the beginning of the end."

"I covered for him as best I could," continued O'Connor. "I tried to keep it together, but he put me through hell. I had every story in the book ready to explain why Peter wasn't around."

Though voices in his head castigated him for his weakness, Gatien's hunger for crack was boundless. He found refuge in a furtive world governed by appetite alone. Anyone who has ever taken crack in significant amounts will tell you about the extreme and ultimately frustrating sexual effect the drug has on the user. Crack's powerful embrace is like living inside a never-ending orgasm, chained to a relentless treadmill of desire that can never really be satisfied, except perhaps by death. Gatien's mind raced with fast-cut pornographic images that now seemed more significant to him than the business he'd spent years building, or even his own family. The drug unleashed in the previously repressed Gatien a frenzied and insatiable sexual drive that became more vital to him than life itself.

The darkness that he'd kept at bay for years by erecting a protective façade of normalcy, now finally welled up inside him. The bonds of common morality were now completely loosed. The emotional numbness he'd felt his whole life gave way to a surge of frenzied pleasure that bought him to his knees. With the help of crack cocaine, he fell headlong into the void of guilt and self-hatred that had always threatened to engulf him, and he liked the sensation. Sitting spookily mute in the corner, twitching in nightmarish ecstasy, while worried prostitutes looked on wondering whether their wealthy client was about to expire from a heart attack, Gatien had finally found his true self. And it wasn't a pretty picture.

"It was very frightening to be around Peter when he was freebasing," said one of the paid escorts who attended the dissolute bashes. "He was always threatening to jump out of windows. He had this party demon inside of him that no amount of cocaine could exorcise."

As the decade closed, Gatien's flagship venue was hemorrhaging cash. After the initial success, Limelight had turned into a gigantic white elephant. The disco was decidedly un-hip. Gatien turned to club kid chief Michael Alig to boost his flagging fortunes.

Rudolph, the Argentinean club director who masterminded the famous downtown hot spot Danceteria and who had set the creative pace in downtown nightlife for a decade, had made a blunder. At the urging of his business partner, who hated Alig, he decided that the club-kid thing was past its sell-by date and sent them all packing from their then home base at the Tunnel. (This was before Gatien owned the venue.) The club kids were too high maintenance. They expected everything gratis. Some nights the bar receipts were practically zero.

Alig's traveling freak show needed new quarters. Gatien offered Alig carte blanche—complete creative control and all the money he could want. "And so Peter inherited Alig's club-kid kit, ready assembled," said Rudolph, "and installed it in the Limelight." The first weeks the club was half empty, as only a handful of club kids and drag queens turned out to support Alig's new venture. But by the end of 1990, Alig's Disco 2000 parties—"the nightclub of the future and a place where adults could be children again" according to Alig—had a reputation as the most outrageous in town. All of a sudden, the Limelight was once again cool. "I bring people into the club that a year ago, wouldn't even come within a block of the Limelight," Alig told the *Wall Street Journal*.

A typical night at Michael Alig's Disco 2000 was akin to stumbling across a secret society devoted to vice, where elaborately costumed, rouged, and wig-topped pleasure seekers engaged in a triumphal procession of shocking acts that scorned law and morality's very existence.

Here, hedonism was a religion, transgression was celebrated as a consecrated rite, and intoxication was manifold, induced not just by the apparently infinite supply of chemicals available but by the pounding music, the extravagant clothing, the erotic displays, the playful games, the dazzling light shows.

Even though Disco 2000 felt like a gay bar scene in some as-yet unmade episode of *Star Wars*, half the audience was heterosexual. There were models and actors and artists, gym rats and transvestites, voyeurs and fetishists, pimply street scum and blue-faced aliens in chiffon dresses, trust fund brats squandering the family fortune, grown men in diapers looking for their inner child, and underage kids stumbling around so stoned they needed a map to find their way to the bathroom.

"We've been forerunners in mixing gay, and straight, and the in-between under one roof," said Alig, explaining Disco 2000's sociological significance. "Here a straight boy can walk around feeling comfortable in eyeliner and platforms."

At Disco 2000, you met outrageous exhibitionists with names that succinctly described their particular party trick: Clara the Carefree Chicken. George the Pee-Drinker. Woody the Dancing Amputee. Danny the Wonder Pony, who, for a small fee, allowed patrons to ride him around the venue, not to be confused with Dan Dan the Naked Man, a Westchester antiques dealer, who wore a blond wig and dressed up in his wife's fishnets and negligee. And Queerdonna, the super-sized drag queen who lip-synced to Madonna tunes.

Everybody was a potential performance artist. Ida Slapter was just another drag queen in the crowd, until one night she got up on stage, laid out a plastic sheet, stuck a finger down her throat, and proceeded to puke, much to the audience's delight. The next week, she gave herself a champagne enema and squirted it into the fleeing multitude. During a follow-up appearance, she inserted a string of Christmas lights up her butt, and had somebody slowly pull the lit bulbs out one by one, to the strains of Gloria Estefan's "Coming Out of the Dark." The story was that she kept the battery pack that powered the lights wedged in her lower intestine.

Disco 2000 could be a cathartic experience, a place where sexual identity wasn't fixed but malleable and negotiable, something to be invented on a weekly basis. But observers and participants knew that this frenzied partying, this orgiastic exhibit of illegal and semilegal acts could end in tears at any minute. Disco 2000 would be targeted sooner or later by local or federal authorities.

Pouty-lipped Irishman Kenny Kenny worked the door at Disco 2000 for seven years and wistfully recollected: "A lot of it was liberating. If you came from a repressed background like I did, Disco 2000 was very exciting. You felt like you couldn't be judged by anybody for anything. It was perfectly OK to walk ￼round naked, for instance. Basically, any kind of sexual behavior was OK; any variation on sexuality was OK. In retrospect, it was destined to become a nightmare. But at the time, at least for a while, it felt beautiful. It was kind of like the hippie thing. We were lost children who had found this surrogate family."

For many, the highlight of Disco 2000's out-of-control festivities came at 3:00 A.M., when an erotic frenzy shook the room. The Hot Body contest was about to begin. Dressed like a catamite Vegas Elvis, Larry Tee—the man who wrote proto–club kid Ru-Paul's worldwide smash

"Supermodel"—invited the audience members up on stage to compete for a meager fifty-dollar prize by stripping for the crowd, which howled with laughter at the erect penises and pierced labia on display. Nubile women with heaving bosoms and trimmed pubes, obese men with protuberant paunches, courting couples on a dare, chiseled muscle males showing off their six-packs, a scrawny man in a cowboy hat who rode a three-hundred-pound naked woman across the stage, and a hard-core masochist who tugged angrily at his huge nipples and stubbed out lit cigarettes on his genitals.

The lascivious movement of the dancers won lustful cries from the audience. "Show us your pussy!" The sexed-up crowd became increasingly unruly. Grasping hands clawed at the bare bodies. An Italian gangster whipped out a wad of hundred-dollar bills and proceeded to slap the money onto the strippers' skin. The performers were too stoned on Special K to notice.

"Hey! Behave yourself. This is a family show," pleaded the contest's helium-voiced host. "Do you like what you see? Do you want to see more? Well, stop manhandling the talent." With this, Larry Tee picked up some of the big dollar bills that had fallen on the stage, stuffed them in his sock, and made a quick exit.

Finally there were the infamous Emergency Room parties, "featuring attending anesthesiologists," the invitation promised. A Red Cross medical tent was erected in the chapel area of the club, where patrons were examined on gurneys by drag queens dressed as sexy nurses and then handed prescriptions for illegal drugs, which they then took to another part of the room where club kids in white coats and stethoscopes filled them.

Michael Alig—the center of attention, as always—would run around the club with a little prescription pad diagnosing partygoers and handing out scripts, as a throng of acolytes chased after him, begging for the socialized medicine.

"The Emergency Room parties summed up the whole experience of the time," said Larry Tee. "It was Michael heading into the abyss, dragging everybody with him. He took people who didn't get high and got them to hand out drugs. Michael had a great ability to drag other people into his obsessions."

A few years into Disco 2000, the nightclub had become a full-service drug supermarket. "You couldn't not notice the lines of dealers in the club going 'K, K, K,' or 'coke, coke, coke,' or the people clutching the walls or passed out on the floor," said Larry Tee. "It was like Zombie Land. Peter must have known what was going on. Peter ignored this, because his clubs were making lots of money. People came to the Limelight to score. Even in the state I was in at the time, it was obvious to me that they couldn't possibly get away with this for much longer."

Alig, the artisan of illusion, presided over this scene. But Gatien, the one-eyed voyeur, was the one who financed the Limelight. Gatien loved the haggard and hollow-eyed Alig like a father loves his son, partly because Alig's irreverent antics were playing such a key role in turning the club into a roaring success by drawing downtown trendsetters to what might otherwise have become an obsolete '90s-style discotheque. But the relationship went deeper than that. Peter came alive in Michael's company. His normally granite face would develop cracks. Gatien, who had to sneak off to hotel rooms to get high, secretly envied the life of freedom, creativity, and excess that Alig had created for himself. To Gatien, Alig represented everything his Catholic upbringing and business responsibilities prevented him from becoming.

Party promoters such as Michael Alig occupied a uniquely fortunate position in '90s New York nightlife. They were a privileged nocturnal caste that wielded considerable power without responsibility. The role of promoters, even more so than that of the DJ or club owner, was fundamental. The promoter was the one who organized the party, decided on a sexy theme, and filled the dance floor week after week. Promoters enjoyed all the trappings of fame and success—money, groupies, drugs, and rank—without many of the drawbacks. While his peers were sweating their way through college or in low-paying jobs, Alig lived a life characterized by, in his own words, "an unending supply of drugs and an almost limitless amount of money." Combine that with his burgeoning fame, the most bittersweet narcotic of all, and you had a heady brew that would have floored most people long before it finally did Alig.

"Twenty years ago," Alig summed up, "a kid would go 'Hey, Mom, look at that guy with long hair. Isn't he cool?' Today he'd say 'Hey

Mom, look at that man, he drinks his own pee and sleeps with dead transsexuals. Not *that* again.' "

In 1991, at Alig's suggestion, Gatien hired an unknown Staten Island party promoter called Lord Michael, a.k.a. Michael Caruso, who pioneered a groundbreaking new sound called "techno" that was said to be all the rage in Europe. Caruso brought in hordes of outer-borough ravers and quickly turned the club into New York's premier platform for the best techno acts from around the globe. The Limelight was not only fashionable again; the venue also enjoyed serious musical credibility.

Gatien now embarked on a campaign to control the local nightlife. He bought the club kid magazine *Project X* from Rudolph and started a techno record label called Vortex. In December 1992, he opened Club USA in a former Minsky's burlesque theater on Forty-seventh Street, near Times Square. Inside, the decor was *Blade Runner* meets *Pee-wee's Playhouse* reimagined by the Marquis de Sade. The disco featured a giant tubular slide and a peep-show hallway; a VIP room created by French fashion designer Thièrry Mugler that looked like a padded cell; S&M mannequins in glass tubes, in the manner of British pop artist Allen Jones; and a giant neon sign depicting a hand flipping an Ecstasy pill into a mouth that recalled Studio 54's infamous coke spoon suspended over the dance floor. In the same year, Gatien also bought the Palladium from Steve Rubell. In 1993, he took control of yet another vast club, the Tunnel. For a while, in the first half of the '90s, Peter Gatien seemed to own New York after dark.

4 THE ECSTASY BANDITS

New York City, 1991

The air was thick with the smell of clammy chemistry.
The depth of feeling among the electrified crowd was palpable. As the
lasers bounced eerily off the yellow-and-orange stained-glass windows,
a nervous impulse passed from one neuron to another. The drugs were
beginning to take effect.

Percussion rolls ricocheted in the gloom of the dance floor, even as
the blinking mechanical strobes strafed the dancers, making them look
as though they were in the grip of a mass epileptic fit. On an overhead
screen, images culled from old cartoons and movies changed with the
brusqueness of a TV remote control. The music grew louder, blaring
out of the giant speakers like syncopated claps of thunder, some bastard
progeny of disco and heavy metal howling in the mechanical night. The
faster and harder the rhythm, the more frenzied became the crowd of
young bare-chested delinquents.

Every week, they traveled via subway or car service from unfashionable districts like Bay Ridge, Bensonhurst, Ozone Park, and Coney
Island to the deconsecrated church that housed the Limelight. Here,
their muscles oiled by their own sweat, thousands of them slam-danced
to rumbling, industrial-strength techno records imported from Europe.
With all the flailing arms, crashing bodies, and pumping fists, this
elated churning looked more like a soccer riot than a rave. These tat-

tooed kids—these Vinnies and Frankies, Michaels and Sals, with their slicked-back black hair, cutoff jeans, and Doc Martens shoes, these territorial gladiators who would normally be brawling in the streets—were instead giving each other big hugs on the dance floor, their natural-born bravado melting under the influence of the drug, as if a nonaggression pact had been secretly negotiated. The kid you savagely beat up two years ago was now your best friend. "I love you, man," was the night's most frequently heard refrain. Even though they had grown up in a masculine world where sharing one's innermost emotions was thought to be the hallmark of a sissy, bursts of joy—the sort of feelings no self-respecting tough guy would normally admit to—came gushing to the surface and circled the room. The raging bulls had discovered a pleasure even more intense than violence.

"This shit is amazing," one out-of-breath hooligan shouted to another.

"Un-fuckin'-believable," his buddy retorted, the Ecstasy having worked its wondrous therapy, if only for a time.

In the early '90s, Limelight's Future Shock parties were among the most viscerally thrilling events in town. The brainchild of Michael Caruso, better known in the club world as "Lord Michael," the short, stocky, techno promoter was a key figure in the dissemination of rave culture in America. This musical trailblazer created the careers of a number of now-prominent DJs and transformed the Limelight into Manhattan's primary platform for electronic acts from around the globe. He—and the sociopathic *goodfellas* with whom he worked—also pushed huge quantities of Ecstasy on the outer-borough patrons who horded to the Limelight for his events. Future Shock quickly became the macho, heterosexual alternative to Disco 2000 and the other side of the nightclub's crime-to-drugs-to-pop culture equation.

Michael Caruso was born and raised in Staten Island's Port Richmond section, a nondescript, somewhat run-down neighborhood of simple wooden-frame houses, body-repair shops, and unhygienic-looking delicatessens; all under the shadow of the Bayonne Bridge. Here, crabgrass grew between the cracks in the pavement, and the taverns had names like Oogie's and Beer Bellies. It was the sort of area that during the day appeared calm and peaceful on the surface, where every second male you saw had his head under the hood of a car and where the automobiles were better tended to than the domiciles. But once nightfall came, the respectable folks retreated behind their Kmart curtains, and drug dealers and hookers infested every corner.

Caruso had an unexceptional upbringing. He was an average student who punted for the high school football team and hooked hoops in the local park. He lived the jock life for a while before he got into drugs and music. He was one of the first white kids on Staten Island to discover hip-hop. He used to hang out at the Mariner's Harbor projects, where he met future associates of the rap group Wu-Tang Clan. His parents were one of the many blue-collar Italian families that moved from Brooklyn to Staten Island after the Verrazano Bridge opened in the '60s. Caruso's father owned a garage, while his mother was a high-school substance abuse counselor, who lectured her son about the dangers of drugs and unprotected sex. By his late teens, Caruso was cruising around Staten Island in a white Mercedes 190E, getting blow jobs in the backseat, and dealing cocaine and angel dust, which he purchased from the Port Richmond Crew, one of the Staten Island arms of the Lucchesi crime family.

During this period Caruso got up close and personal with hard-core criminals for the first time. Caruso was no tough guy ("geeky and chubby" was how one acquaintance described him), but he had a high regard for gangsters. He would often drive over to the verdant Todt Hill section, Staten Island's wealthiest neighborhood, to admire the marble mansions that mob bosses lived in, dreaming of the day he would have his own palatial pad on these elegant tree-lined streets. Staten Island had a well-deserved reputation as the place where wannabes became wise guys; the borough's vast, scrubby expanses were a proving ground for the criminally minded.

The Port Richmond Crew was not your typical cluster of neighborhood hooligans. Their office was a local laundromat, from where they controlled half the cocaine traffic on the island. Kilo weights were shipped in directly from the Caribbean to the crack dens and whorehouses that in those days infested the North Shore. To join the gang, you had to commit at least two serious felonies. Extortion, murder, arson, narcotics trafficking, loan sharking, and money laundering were all in a day's work. Caruso particularly admired the group's tight organ-ization. Through a network of street contacts—crooked cops, petty boosters, prostitutes, and dope fiends—they knew about every crime that went down in the area. And the gang always took a cut.

Being an informant against the formidable Port Richmond Crew was a mistake you only made once. In 1990, they wasted crew member George Van Name, who had testified about their drug-dealing activities before a secret grand jury. He was lured to a remote spot where he was shot four times in the head and once in the mouth, the last bullet a warning sign to other potential snitches.

Caruso became tight with members of the Port Richmond Crew. He was awestruck in their presence. Drugs, guns, money—this was the life. Caruso could literally feel the authority they wielded, the way the pave-ment shook when Tony Bones, Rocky Pops, Frankie Flash, Fats, Skip, and Smurf swaggered down local streets, swinging stones of steel between their thick legs; the way that even law-abiding residents both feared and admired them in equal measure. They were everything Caruso didn't have the heart to become.

"We were young, well-connected, street-smart hustlers with a no-nonsense approach to business," boasted former Port Richmond Crew member Brendan Schlitz, who was later incarcerated for obtaining Van Name's probation file from a corrupt law enforcement source and pass-ing it on to the killers. "We did what had to be done. You could tell that Caruso looked up to us."

The same year that the Port Richmond Crew clipped Van Name, Michael Caruso experienced an epiphany of sorts on his first trip abroad. In 1990, while recovering from a traffic accident, the then twenty-year-old started his nightlife career by throwing parties at a tacky Staten Island disco called Wave Street. The Wave was cement-head central—a club full of warring, liquored-up, nut-grabbing toughs almost exclusively from the lily-white South Shore. Cops frequently vis-ited to break up fights. Like many local Italian kids at the time, Caruso was into *freestyle*, the sentimental Latino-derived pop disco that was all the rage in late '80s New York. But he soon grew disillusioned with this musical direction, rejecting it as too corny, too much like the stale and familiar rituals that *Saturday Night Fever* depicted. At the Red Spot, a more bohemian club just around the corner, he happened to hook up with local DJ Lenny D, who told him he was going to the UK to check out this burgeoning scene where kids stayed up all night dancing at illegal parties to this exhilarating new sound called "techno" or "acid house."

Caruso accompanied Lenny D to Britain, where he acted as the DJ's tour manager. What he saw there made an indelible impression. Britain at the beginning of the '90s was a country transformed by the combination of music, drugs, and technology. In terms of youth culture the place was a zany, colorful paradise. House music and techno had originated in America but were confined largely to obscure black gay underground dance clubs. In the UK, however the culture had become a mass movement practically overnight. Ecstasy and raving had woven its way into the fabric of British life to such an extent that pubs—the traditional venues where most Brits distract themselves from living in such a gray, rainy, depressing country—reported an alarming drop-off in business.

During this trip Caruso earned his honorific title "Lord Michael," when the Brits teased him about the flash roll of cash he carried on his person. (Later, Caruso would boast to friends, the real reason he crossed the Atlantic was to launder $750,000 in drug money with a crooked British accountant, though he may just have been saying that to impress his gangster buddies.) In a club in London's West End, Caruso also eagerly gobbled down his first hit of Ecstasy, supplied by an older dealer named Meru, a '60s throwback who became Lord Michael's major drug connection when he got back to Staten Island. "It was like all your worst enemies were now your best friends," Caruso said about Ecstasy's initial effect on him.

After he came down from the drug, Meru told Caruso, "You should pursue the techno thing, bring it into New York, and really make it happen." That way, Meru could visit him and hook him up with pills to sell.

It was an odd alliance. Together, Meru and Caruso represented the twin poles of rave culture. Meru was a stringy-haired middle-class dropout who dressed in raggedy tie-dye clothes and rejected the trappings of consumer society. He was a so-called zippie—half-hippie, half-raver. He carried a guitar with him everywhere he went, and he saw raves as latter-day hippie festivals, weekly Woodstocks.

Caruso, on the other hand, was a child of the streets. Totally apolitical, he didn't care about spiritual revolution or overthrowing the establishment. To him raving was a leisure activity, pure and simple, the escapist pursuit of pleasure for pleasure's sake. Fiercely ambitious and competitive, he was out for a good time, to make a name for himself, and to meet pretty women. Ecstasy wasn't a gift from God but a great way to acquire riches and get blitzed out of your head on the weekends.

An excited Caruso returned from the UK with a bag full of acid house T-shirts and a crateload of twelve-inch singles. He distributed the records to other DJs on the island. One of those DJs was Pete Repete, who played records at the Red Spot. The response to Repete's selections was immediate and enthusiastic. At the Wave and Red Spot, this basic, hyperkinetic, anthemic sound caught the fancy of a new generation of Italian-American males, who formed Caruso's core constituency when he transferred to the Limelight. "It was something different," recalled Repete. "They liked the aggressive feel of the music immediately. The music became a substitute for fighting." They liked it even more when, after a visit from Meru, Caruso started handing out free Ecstasy tasters.

Until Lord Michael turned Staten Island on to Ecstasy, the combination of smoking angel dust, snorting cocaine, and drinking alcohol in amounts that would have stunned a full-grown elephant was the way to get high. That which would have immobilized most normal people, only seemed to further dissolve the few inhibitions Staten Island tough guys had against violence. And like their more famous Brooklyn counterparts, they loved to fight long, to fight often, and to fight hard.

They would brawl over girls and turf. They would tussle over respect or the lack thereof. They would rumble with "the moolies" and "the PRs." They would trade punches over short baggies of drugs. They would scrap because they didn't like the music the DJ played. Raging through the night, starting fights in one club after another, they would smack you in the face first and ask you "What the fuck you looking at?" later. Such was their reputation that doormen in Manhattan clubs checking identification would automatically turn away any young male with an Italian last name and a Staten Island address.

Nonetheless, Caruso sensed that raving was the next big thing, and he was determined to capitalize on it. Beckoning from across the harbor was downtown's dazzling nightlife. Strobe-lit dreams of trendy parties and designer drugs reverberated in his head. He had a strong sense he was destined for something other than outer-borough anonymity. And he was right. Pumped up on music and chemicals, Caruso and his army were now ready to invade Manhattan.

Caruso got his big break when Michael Alig and his DJ boyfriend Keoki heard Repete play at a West Village after-hours club called Tokyo. Impressed by the monotonous severity of the music that came crashing out of the speakers, Alig told Keoki, who also worked as a TWA ticket taker, "He's a much better DJ than you are. He makes you sound like an amateur," and then ordered him over to Repete's booth to copy down the names of the records being spun that night.

Alig proposed that Repete should come and play at the Limelight. He introduced Repete and Caruso to Peter Gatien, who was looking for a new musical format to revive his flagship venue. Gatien suggested the Staten Islanders start throwing parties in the small upstairs chapel area.

Caruso's new Future Shock parties were a huge hit. Steven Lewis, the tuxedo-clad, hyperactive hard-ass who had ruled the velvet ropes at many of the most important New York clubs of the last twenty-five years, was then one of the executive directors of the Limelight. "It blew up right away," recalled Lewis. "It was the only place in Manhattan that played techno music at the time."

In 1992, '60s acid guru Timothy Leary visited the club. Leary was eager to ally himself with the mushrooming rave movement. He'd heard about the Future Shock parties. Caruso gave Leary a hit of the special Ecstasy he reserved for VIPs, and together they tripped, while trying out a virtual-reality machine. Caruso, who always craved the spotlight, felt like he'd finally arrived.

In the early days, Caruso claimed he was building a new youth move-

ment, populated by a "new breed," the antithesis of the ethnic stereo-
type that bedevils young Italian-American males. "Techno kids aren't
Guidos," he kept insisting when I first met him in 1991. "Guidos wear
gold; we wear silver," he told me with a straight face. He maintained
that his crowd listened to progressive music and got along with blacks
and gays. He told me his growing band of followers represented a kind
of working-class avant garde rebelling against their more conservative
older brethren. At the time, I believed him. Caruso always had the gift
of the gab. He was good at gaining your confidence. But what he was
really doing, I found out later, was laying the foundation for a highly
successful criminal organization.

To a certain extent, any party promoter has to deal with criminals in
order to make the party swing. If there are no drugs, the vibe suffers as
a result. But Caruso went far beyond casual illegal associations by using
the Limelight as a base of operations to take over the local Ecstasy market. He deliberately encouraged the encroachment of organized crime
upon the rave scene. To protect the drug commerce at the Limelight, he
gathered around him a small army of Italian-American toughs culled
from dangerous Brooklyn and Staten Island street cliques. His taste for
rough trade soon infected the whole milieu.

"The sudden success of Future Shock transformed Caruso," said
Lewis. "Practically overnight, he morphed from this shy, polite guy into
a wannabe gangster who was always talking about having people beaten
up or killed."

"After the initial popularity of the Future Shock parties, a lot of
gangsters started coming," agreed Repete. "They saw the success we
were having, and they wanted a piece of it. Greed and ambition were
Caruso's undoing. All he needed to do was stay with the scene, and he
would have ended up making more money than he did by robbing people and selling drugs."

The gangsters at the Limelight were easy to spot. They were poseurs,
much like the club kids. They always made a grand entrance. You could
see them flashing rolls of Franklins at the bar, flirting with the waitresses, and strutting around wearing too much jewelry and cologne.
"Show that you're earning money" seemed to be their motto. Spending
up to $3,000 a night was no problem for these young big shots, and

$100 tips were common. By the time the club closed, the bar girls would be complaining that their hands hurt from opening so many heavy bottles of champagne.

One of those gangsters was Brendan "Fats" Schlitz, a gruff, squat, drug dealer whom Caruso knew from the Port Richmond Crew.

"Being from Staten Island, the first time I went to the Limelight I was overwhelmed," said Schlitz. "Mike met me at the rope and took me up to the chapel area, where we drugged and drank bubbly all night. Mike introduced me to a house dealer who took out a bag of cocaine and poured some of it on the face of my Rolex. The thing about the chapel that caught my eye was the painting on the ceiling over the bar of a white hand and a black hand greeting each other. That's what it was about. Color didn't matter. Straight or gay didn't matter. Black, white, or Latino; drag queen or Guido—everybody got along."

The common interest that bound these disparate elements together was, of course, drugs. When he first arrived at the Limelight, Caruso cleared out all the freelance dealers and installed his own. The seed money for his new venture came from a gangland source: He borrowed $10,000 in cash from Vincent Rizzuto, Jr., son of reputed Gambino soldier Vincent "Vinny Oil" Rizzuto, to set up the Ecstasy franchise. Caruso divided the labyrinthine club into separate sections assigned to different brokers. Designated sellers were given up to a couple of hundred tablets each night on credit. At the end of the night, they turned in the currency to Caruso, minus a cut for themselves.

"Business was so good at the Limelight, Caruso paid me back within three weeks, and I then started making him buy E from a friend of mine," said Rizzuto.

If the police visited the club, the dealers were tipped off via walkie-talkie, whereupon they stashed the drugs until the cops left. If a rival was found selling unsanctioned substances, Caruso would demand $300 from the dope peddler to be allowed to stay, and then get security to heave him out on the sidewalk. A regular occurence at Future Shock was when Caruso would descend from the DJ booth to the dance floor, to be mobbed like a rock star as he handed out free pills to frenzied partygoers.

Limelight doorman Kenny Kenny was appalled at this goon invasion but felt powerless to stop it. He had a minimal interest in guns and drugs and thuggish behavior; he got into clubbing for the fun fashions and the cute boys. "It was mob mentality dressed up as techno," he said in his melodic Irish brogue. "I would try to keep them out, but Lord Michael would just overrule me and let them in, even though some of them were carrying guns. You felt like you were being spat on. I'd ask the security guards why are these guys walking in, and they would just shrug. I thought I was there to fight Lord Michael, I really did. I didn't understand why this guy was allowed to wield so much power. That job put me in therapy."

Another time, Caruso threatened to have Executive Director Steven Lewis kidnapped because the gatekeeper wasn't letting in Lord Michael's drug dealer buddies from the neighborhood. "Caruso told me that I'd made the wrong people mad, that someone called Al Dente wanted to whack me," Lewis recalled. "I thought he was kidding. But sure enough, one day I get a phone call: 'Hey, this is Al Dente. If you don't start letting my boys into the club, you're gonna have to deal with me.' I didn't know whether to be afraid or order the pasta special."

But despite his gangster ties, real wise guys saw right through the techno promoter's tough guy façade. "Caruso was no wise guy," remembered Vinnie Rizzuto, Jr. "He was an alternative kid. He didn't fit in with us. Nobody really liked him, but we put up with him because he was such a moneymaker. He didn't affiliate with anybody; he just needed muscle for protection."

How paradoxical that the first full-fledged rave scene in America—its lovey-dovey ideology notwithstanding—took root in areas such as Bensonhurst, Bay Ridge, and Staten Island, territory traditionally controlled by the Mafia. The nucleus of the Brooklyn/Staten Island rave scene was a chummy alliance of mainly Italian-American promoters and DJs—the vast majority of whom *weren't* criminals—who directly modeled their musical gatherings on large-scale raves in the UK. If you wanted to throw an illegal party in a Mafia neighborhood, common sense dictated that you cleared it with the local mobsters first. Many a nervous promoter had to go for a sit-down with some silk-suited meathead as a prerequisite to throwing a bash.

Initially, the neighborhood thugs, with their gold chains and moustaches, heavy-duty cocaine habits and IROC Camaros, laughed at this oddly dressed strain that appeared on the streets, handing out handmade flyers advertising "outlaw parties" in warehouses and abandoned buildings—something Brooklyn was particularly rich in at the time. "Get the fuck out of here," was the initial reaction among the goodfellas, who couldn't have been more amazed if Moonies or Hare Krishnas had moved into the area. They called the rave kids "freaks" and "homos." But their scorn soon changed when the scene's moneymaking potential became apparent.

With the increased popularity of raving in the New York area in the early '90s, thousands of kids were greedy for Ecstasy every weekend. A sizeable black market was created practically overnight. Since first users are typically evangelical about getting others to try the drug, demand increased exponentially. Raves became big business. And the ruffians who initially appeared on the fringes of the scene started to take over. Soon enough, in order to defend the Ecstasy trade at these events, rival promoters were discouraged with guns and baseball bats. As ravers danced blissfully unaware, their partying was underpinned by a growing thug culture of violence and coercion.

DJ and rave promoter Frankie Bones used to count Lord Michael among his friends. A year before Caruso's UK trip, the then twenty-three-year-old Bones underwent a revelatory experience similar to Lord Michael's, when he was flown to Britain to deejay at a lavish mega-rave in front of twenty thousand people. Held in a giant film studio, the party resembled a teeming mini city, with all the things needed to sustain human life there in abundance: food, water, shelter, drugs, companionship, entertainment, and spiritual nourishment. The elaborate event featured a *Blade Runner* room, a mock-up of Stonehenge, a Greek temple, and an Egyptian room. Bones, who was used to playing small clubs in Brooklyn, had never seen anything like it before. Determined to bring what he had experienced back to America, Bones started throwing "Storm" raves, the groundbreaking affairs whose motto "hard-core only for the headstrong" became the rallying cry of Brooklyn techno and planted the seed for the entire U.S. rave scene. Bones's bashes regularly attracted rowdy neighborhood gangs like the Kings Highway Boys, the Avenue U Boys, and the Bay Boys, who came looking for trouble.

Brooklyn in the early '90s was a tough terrain by any standards, a borough of broad avenues, dark side streets, and dangerous crossroads where stickup kids of every race, creed, and color lurked. The roughneck capital was an unlikely location for rave culture to bloom. This was a place and a time where a burner and a bulletproof vest were regarded as essential fashion accessories and where crime was such an everyday part of life it seeped into the way inhabitants described the very geography: Crooklyn, Crime Heights, Do or Die Bed Stuy, Murder Avenue. Talking about peace, love, and unity in this context was a good way to get your ass kicked.

One day, while Bones was getting out of his car in front of his Brooklyn home, four young guys from Bath Avenue accosted him: "Yo, you throw a party last night." Bones was still hungover from the outdoor rave he had staged called Field of Dreams in a Bensonhurst park near Bath Avenue. His skull ached from inhaling too much angel dust. In his woozy state, Bones thought they were partygoers who were going to congratulate him on a job well done. When he replied in the affirmative, a guy came running out of the bushes with a baseball bat, while the others whisked out guns and proceeded to pistol-whip Bones to a bloody mess. Left bleeding and unconscious on the sidewalk, with his skull cracked wide open, Bones's girlfriend managed to drag him inside, where she called for an ambulance. Once at the hospital, Bones needed multiple stitches to close three gaping wounds. Caruso was angry with Bones because his party had depleted Future Shock's numbers that night.

"Within twenty-four hours, I knew it was Lord Michael who had ordered the attack," said Bones. "He was going around the Limelight boasting about it. He wanted to scare me into not throwing parties anymore. Lord Michael wanted to be the Al Capone of raves. He wanted to control the local Ecstasy trade. And for a while, he did."

Caruso and his followers represented a new breed of gangster who started popping up like toxic mushrooms on the Manhattan club scene in the early '90s. They kidnapped, robbed, extorted, and generally terrorized the effeminate club kid dealers and candy ravers who used to control the narcotics trade at trendy clubs. Before the likes of Caruso came along, the indigenous Ecstasy business was an informal affair, more a cottage industry employing naive enthusiasts selling the drug as a service or to make a bit of spare cash on the side. But passive ravers and infantile club kids were no matches for this brawny new breed, who staged a chain of home invasions of rivals that left clubland dazed by the unprecedented levels of violence and gunplay.

Caruso's first major robbery of record occurred in early 1992, not long after the Future Shock nights started to take off. Prior to the heist, Lord Michael approached Michael Alig at the Limelight and said he was going to rob Goldilocks, a ratty-haired club-kid dealer. If Alig helped, Caruso promised, he would collect a nice percentage of the score. "Are you out of your fuckin' mind? Goldilocks is a friend," replied Alig, who was becoming more and more scared of Lord Michael and his goons.

Caruso's fat face creased into a grin. "I was only joking. You believed me. Don't take me so seriously." He punched Alig gently on the shoulder and then went ahead with his plan.

Goldilocks, who usually supplied Ecstasy, wanted to purchase twenty thousand hits from Caruso. When Goldilocks's assistant, Mr. Purple (so-called because of his purple hair and clothes), arrived at the door of Caruso's luxurious Gramercy Park apartment carting $180,000 in a briefcase, two of Caruso's hoodlums emerged from a side door, flashed fake badges, and announced they were undercover drug cops. The pretend narcs jumped on Mr. Purple and threw him back into the apartment. He was ordered to lie down on the floor, where he was handcuffed, as was the conspiring Caruso. They called the hapless druggie a "purple-haired faggot" and threatened him with maximum jail time. They flummoxed him with phony cop talk and told him how lucky he was. They weren't going to bust him, just confiscate the cash. The terrified Purple nearly pissed himself. He bought the theatrics wholesale and retail. When asked later why he conned Mr. Purple,

Caruso shrugged and said, "It was easier than giving him the pills." Caruso's attitude was if you were stupid enough to allow him to take what was yours, then you deserved to get robbed.

The double dealer's chicanery didn't end there. Caruso subsequently paid one of his lieutenants $5,000 to convince Goldilocks that Caruso had had nothing to do with the rip-off. The dumb-as-a-stump Goldilocks fell for the ploy and continued to do drug deals with his lordship. By his own admission, Caruso ended up blowing most of the proceeds on expensive meals, gambling on sports events, trips to Europe, and a collection of sneakers that would have made Imelda Marcos jealous.

Betraying colleagues subsequently became a Lord Michael trademark. The crime wave continued when Caruso planned another robbery, after a fellow Limelight party promoter named Dan Forrester boasted in the office about the amount of money he was making selling Special K on the side. Caruso enlisted the help of Forrester's supposed friend named Allison, a bad girl from a good family. Caruso had a considerable talent for bringing out the worst in people. Together, they planned to rob Forrester at home, using his upcoming birthday as a ruse to get past the doorman in his luxury Chelsea building.

"Surpri-i-i-ze!" shouted the three masked gunmen, among them Caruso, as they burst into Forrester's apartment, one of them carrying a handful of brightly colored balloons, the other a Tech-9 machine pistol. At first Forrester thought Allison was playing a prank on him. Perhaps Halloween had come early. Allison had just phoned and said she was coming over to help him celebrate his birthday. Surprise quickly turned to terror, however, when the physically unimposing Forrester realized that this was no joke. Shoving Allison through the door, the robbers, who had pulled up their black turtlenecks to cover their faces, then set upon their victim and beat him to the ground, where he was tied up with duct tape alongside his double-crossing friend, whom the thieves were pretending to have kidnapped from the street below. Turning up the music, the robbers ransacked the place, stealing a box of Special K and $12,000 in cash—all the chump change they could find. To cover their exit, the bandits left pills and empty cocaine bottles strewn around the room to deter the injured party from calling the police. "I was so scared, I cleaned up and moved out of the apartment and never went back," Forrester told me later.

Caruso even scammed his own personal assistant at the Limelight, Andrew Lechtanski, who, according to the techno promoter, made the mistake of telling him that he stole $60,000 in cash, a large quantity of marijuana, and some autographed baseball bats from a New Jersey sports memorabilia dealer. Supposedly, the unworldly Lechtanski was worried that detectives investigating the case were closing in on him, and he wanted advice. Caruso demanded half the money as a consultation fee, which Lechtanski handed over to his superior. Then Caruso demanded another $10,000 to register the burglary with local gangsters, who might have been offended that a crime was commited on their turf without their sanction. Caruso also asked for an additional $10,000, supposedly to pay off corrupt cops. As Caruso would later testify, he ended up with $50,000 of the $60,000 plus the grass, and all he did was lie. Caruso would define the essence of a "good scam" to a packed courtroom as "one that's believable but can't be checked."

In March 1993, less than a year after the Mr. Purple robbery, one of Caruso's partners in crime was found shot in the head in the loft space at Caruso's pad. When not dealing drugs for Caruso at the Limelight, Damon Burett worked as Lord Michael's housekeeper in return for room and board. He was widely regarded as a sweet guy but emotionally unsteady. Caruso treated his flunky like a slave. As a party trick, he and Peter Gatien would make Burett get down on his knees to kiss their feet and bark like a dog.

When the police arrived, Caruso was holding a .32 pistol. The medical examiner ruled Damon's shooting a suicide, but private eye John Dabrowski—a retired Nassau County homicide cop working for Peter Gatien—came to believe that Caruso used a suicide attempt the previous Sunday to cover the murder. While Caruso denied he killed Burett, Dabrowski claimed that given the extraordinarily high levels of Valium (the equivalent of over a hundred pills) found in the housekeeper's blood, it's doubtful he could have held a gun, let alone put it to his head and squeezed the trigger. And the content of Burett's suicide note raised more troubling questions: "I took pills and lemons [slang for Quaaludes]. It was better than blowing my brains out." Why would somebody describe one method of killing themselves and then do precisely what he said he wasn't going to do?

"When Peter told me that Damon commited suicide, he made this funny face that I took to mean the kid didn't really kill himself," said Michael Alig. "Whether it's true or not, everybody in the office believed that Lord Michael murdered Damon. I remember telling Peter, if Damon did commit suicide, it was partially his fault, the way he and Caruso humiliated the poor kid. They made him bark like a dog on all fours. It was disgusting. The kid was obviously fragile."

When key Caruso associate Paul Torres, who participated in the Forrester robbery, was later arrested in 1997, he told the DEA that he thought Lord Michael killed Damon because he was being investigated for narcotics. Damon's father, Raymond, confirmed that his son was picked up on serious drug charges roughly a year before his death.

"The detective handling the case didn't do a proper investigation," claimed the pink-faced Dabrowski. "Caruso basically bullshitted the police like he did everybody else. It was an argument over drugs: Damon kept coming up short and Michael was pissed." Dabrowski asked the detectives to run tests on the gun. "Get lost," they told him. "Mind your own business. You work for that drug dealer, Peter Gatien."

After Damon died, Caruso's mood turned ugly. The pressure was getting to him. He retreated behind the human shield his associates provided. "He liked to project that 'I'm-a-king' attitude," said one of his former dealers. "But Michael has never been a tough guy. He's never thrown a punch in his life. It's his following that's tough. He always had others do his dirty work for him."

One of the young toughs on whom Caruso relied to protect the drug trade at Future Shock was an apprentice mobster named Chris Paciello, who got his first taste of big-time nightlife hanging out at the Limelight. Paciello was a prolific car thief and an accomplished burglar. Vincent Rizzuto, Jr., introduced the pair, after he brought Caruso over to the apartment that Rizzuto and Paciello shared on Wellington Avenue on Staten Island. After hooking up with Caruso, Paciello quickly became one of the Limelight's resident tough guys. All three would go club-hopping together.

In those days, Paciello was indistinguishable from the massed ranks of the so-called bridge-and-tunnel crowd that fills up Manhattan night-clubs on weekends. He was nobody's idea of a top-of-the-line trendy. He dressed like a stereotypical Guido in jogging pants and muscle shirts, topped off by a Caesar-style haircut. At over six feet tall, under two hundred pounds, with a perfectly chiseled frame, he could have passed for a budding professional boxer. The strong, silent type, he never said much, preferring nonverbal communication with his meaty hams, practically every bone in which he'd broken at one time or another. The one thing that made this former special education student stand out from the crowd was that he was conspicuously handsome. With his cherubic lips, brooding eyes, a perpetually sulky expression, and an olive complexion unlined by intelligence, he could have strutted down the catwalk as a male model. But those in the know understood well enough to steer clear. "The first time I ever heard his name, I was told he was a freelance hit man for the Mafia," said Peter Gatien, intending to exaggerate. Barely into his twenties, Paciello had a scary reputation.

5   BATH AVENUE BOYS

Richmond Valley, Staten Island, New York, February 1993

The end came suddenly for Judith Shemtov on a bit-ing cold winter night, as a wet wind blustered across the Arthur Kill straits and leafless trees groaned portentously in the darkness. The forty-six-year-old blond housewife was relaxing inside her opulent million-dollar home at 95 Meade Loop, tucked away down a hill and in a private enclave—a semicircle of suburban mini palaces, each more predictably pretentious than the last—located in the far reaches of Staten Island. The brazen light of gaudy chandeliers flooded out of large picture windows, giving a radioactive glow to the surrounding topiary.

Glad to be in from the raw chill, the petite Shemtov had made a steaming pot of tea and flopped down on the couch to watch television with her new husband, Sami, who had just returned from a business trip. Upstairs, her daughter was awaiting the arrival of an old boyfriend. The happy homemaker had no idea that her domestic bliss was about to be shattered by four Mafia punks who had pulled up at the end of her manicured driveway. Three men got out of the black, four-door automobile. One of them, thirty-year-old Thomas Reynolds, concealed a .45 handgun under his track suit; the others, Michael Yammine and Jimmy Calandra, carried a .45 and a 9-mm Beretta, respectively. The volatile Reynolds was a dyslexic sociopath with a couple of murders already on his dance card. Even the mob bosses thought he was crazy and had banned him from his own stomping ground in Brooklyn for disrespecting fellow wise guys. In December 1991, the itchy-fingered hoodlum shot and nearly killed a Gambino family associate outside a Brooklyn bar called the Cropsey Lounge. "Guys are getting mad in the neighborhood," he was told. "It's not right."

Calandra, a reckless bank robber, who was also certifiably crazy, punched the doorbell. A video camera was supposed to activate but didn't. The home's elaborate security system had been turned off, because the Shemtovs were expecting company. Hearing the chimes, Judith Shemtov strolled out of the living room and looked at her watch. It was just before 10:00 P.M. Calandra started speaking into the intercom: "Police, please open up. We have to speak to Mr. Shemtov."

"Ah, coming right away," said a puzzled female voice. Shemtov opened the door heedlessly, only to be confronted by three sullen strangers who barged their way in.

What followed was the briefest of exchanges. "Where's the fuckin' safe? Where's the fuckin' money?" they hollered, their weapons still concealed. Her husband kept his money in a safe in the basement, although Shemtov apparently never had the chance to tell her intruders. The plan was to tie up anybody found in the household. But within moments of the forced entry, the home invasion went awry. First, Yammine pulled out his gun, followed by Calandra, but as Reynolds brandished his weapon a split second later, the automatic accidentally went off, and a bullet drilled through Judith Shemtov's face and into her brain, sending her flying up in the air before she crashed mortally wounded to the hard wooden floor.

After hearing shouts and curses, followed by a popping sound, Sami Shemtov dashed into the atrium hallway, where he was stunned to discover his wife lying on the floor, a small hole in her left cheek, as she choked on her own blood. "What's going on? Oh my God, what's going on?" he yelled in disbelief.

Yammine ignored the distraught husband's cries and shouted at his comrades, "I'm getting out of here," and started walking away.

Calandra screamed, "Let's go, we got to go!"

Reynolds, a look of panicky incomprehension spread across his face, was the last to leave. At first, he was too stunned to move.

Bad weather was the last thing on the minds of Reynolds and his coconspirators—or the "Bath Avenue Crew," as they were known—as they sped away empty-handed.

"I'm going to hell for this one. This one, I'm going to hell for," Reynolds muttered over and over.

Reynolds knew they had to torch the getaway ride. He knew they had to toss the murder weapon. But, mostly, the Bath Avenue Crew was scared that if Sami Shemtov had gotten a good close look at their faces, he'd be able to pick them out of a police lineup.

The crew was named after Bath Avenue in Bensonhurst, a thriving neighborhood of neat, modest, one- and two-family homes that inevitably sported freshly painted aluminum awnings. Despite the young toughs hanging on the corner, graffiti was as rare in the neighborhood as American flags and plastic Madonna statues were common. This stable and closely bound working- and lower-middle-class community, where several generations of the same family often live on one block, seemed to have escaped the urban blight of surrounding areas . . . for one very good reason: Bensonhurst was a mob stronghold.

At the center of that community was a street called Bath Avenue, lined with mom-and-pop stores: five-and-dimes, small restaurants, delis, car services, and pizzerias. But another type of family business was transacted on this strip. Behind bland brick façades, in inconspicuous holes-in-the-wall you wouldn't look twice at if you walked past them, old men drank thimbles of coffee at rickety tables, and orders were given to carry out crimes—ranging from loan-sharking to gambling to drug dealing to murder—from which enormous profits were garnished.

One of these Mafia-run social clubs stood at the corner of Bay Sixteenth and Bath Avenue, and was home base to aging Bonanno family crime boss Anthony Spero. The establishment was called the Pigeon, after Spero's penchant for racing birds. Spero's social club served as a clearing house for information in a wide-ranging criminal venture whose tentacles spread all over the New York area and beyond. One of the frequent visitors was silk-suited Bonanno soldier Joseph Benanti. A group of tough street kids who used to hang around outside the club caught Benanti's attention. They were juvenile petty boosters, stealing car radios and breaking into video stores. But Benanti thought they showed potential to commit bigger and better crimes. He organized them into a gang and put them on record. Benanti formalized the Bath Avenue Crew by having its core members mark their ankles with numeric tattoos to signify their camaraderie-in-crime and willingness to commit murder in the pursuit of the group's objectives.

While the Bath Avenue Crew already had numerous murders and robberies under their apprentice belts, the Shemtov killing was different. Up until now, they'd never clipped a civilian—someone who wasn't a drug dealer, a competing mobster, or a snitch. While Bonanno higher-ups had sanctioned the robbery beforehand, the crew still sensed the full force of a gathering storm on the horizon.

At the wheel of the jumpy car that night was Chris Paciello, the fourth person implicated in Judith Shemtov's murder and the mastermind of the botched robbery. Paciello had met the Bath Avenue Crew through his friend Vinnie Rizzuto, Jr.; Rizzuto introduced Paciello to Jimmy Calandra, who in turn introduced him to the rest of the gang. "Chris didn't know anybody," Rizzuto said. "I was the one who introduced him around. Even though he grew up in Brooklyn, he met the Bath Avenue kids because of me."

Bath Avenue Crew stalwart Anthony "Gonzo" Gonzalez remembered when Calandra first brought Paciello over for a meeting. "He wanted our help in pulling off a number of scores," said the tattooed dope dealer. "The minute I met him, I didn't like. He began to tell us all these scores, which sounded good. The part that didn't sound good was that he never wanted to have a hands-on role. He was a pretty boy, not a tough guy. He was out of his league when it came to gunplay, you know what I mean? Sure, he was good with his hands, but what good is having ten fingers, if none of them are gonna pull the trigger?"

Even though he counted him a comrade, Rizzuto, who first met Paciello at the age of thirteen at a video arcade in the Staten Island Mall, was becoming increasingly wary of his friend. "I always had my doubts about him," he said. "He'd put on this show of being a stand-up guy, but in reality he was a snake. He'd rob his best friends—anything for money."

Paciello planned the Shemtov heist after he received a tip about the wealthy Jewish businessman who owned an electrical supply company. Supposedly, he kept a large amount of money in a secret safe at home.

Before the robbery, Paciello, who had recently moved out of his mother's modest Staten Island home a few blocks away, had gathered his Bath Avenue cronies at his $1,200-a-month duplex, where many a raucous party was held and which he shared with Rizzuto. Sitting on a black leather couch, Paciello told the Bath Avenue boys all about the big score: "Listen, this guy is coming back from a trip, and when he's home and down in his basement he's going to have a safe with $300,000. All you got to do is go there, tie up the people in the house, go in the basement, open up the safe, and take the money. I'm going to be the driver, because if they see me, they're going to recognize who I am." Paciello was worried about taking a loose cannon like Tommy Reynolds on a major job. He was scared that Reynolds, dumb and dangerous in equal measures, might do something stupid. "No one needs to get hurt," Paciello emphasized to his unstable pal. A little while later, Paciello received a beep. "That means the guy's home. We gotta go now."

On the way back to Paciello's place following the bungled heist, Paciello and Reynolds got into a furious row in the front seat of the getaway car. Paciello's concern about Reynolds's involvement in the robbery had proven well founded. Paciello screamed at Reynolds, "You crazy fuckin' idiot, what did you do?"

"Don't worry about it, forget about it."

"What do you mean forget about it? They're going to know it's me; I'm the Paulie G [a reference to Bonanno associate Paul Gulino, the most senior member of the Bath Avenue Crew] from this area. Everybody knows me around this neighborhood; they're going to know I had something to do with it."

Panic gave way to paranoia, for a moment, as Reynolds turned on Paciello and pressed a gun to his temple. "What are you trying to tell me?" Reynolds asked menacingly. "If you're thinking of ratting us out, think again." Reynolds, who was living up to his rep in spades, suspected that beneath the tough-guy exterior, Paciello was a two-faced coward, someone who might not hold his water if the right pressure were applied.

The car screeched to a halt, and, with a dramatic flourish, Paciello deliberately put his head down between the seats before looking up at Reynolds and challenging him: "Tommy, if you don't trust me, then kill me right now. You know I ain't no rat."

Paciello was angry with Reynolds because the Shemtov killing was a blot on his otherwise impeccable criminal resume. Only twenty-two years old, he already had status as an up-and-coming moneymaker for the mob. Recently, low-level crimes had paved the way for more serious offenses. He'd graduated from years of stealing cars and staging small-time burglaries to planning and successfully executing a daytime smash-and-grab raid on a Chemical Bank inside the Staten Island Mall, which netted $360,000.

Around the same time, Paciello allegedly participated in the hijacking of a two-million-dollar truckload of marijuana in New Jersey. According to someone with knowledge of the crime, he sold a portion of the pot to one buyer and then later stole it back from him at gunpoint so that he could sell the leaves again.

Paciello—who gained the admiring nickname "the Binger" because, as one gangster buddy put it, "he fiends to rob people"—wasn't a full-time member of the Bath Avenue Crew. He freelanced for numerous overlapping Mafia cliques—the Bonannos, Colombos, Gambinos, you name it. The way he saw it, he could make more money as an independent contractor. He did numerous jobs with another Bonanno family crew, the New Springville Boys, best known for burglarizing night deposit boxes. Brooklyn's Bath Avenue Crew and Staten Island's New Springville Boys often joined forces to commit crimes. Paciello's mental Rolodex was a *Who's Who* of Mafia movers and shakers.

"Paciello is my stage name," he joked with acquaintances. Born of joint Italian and German heritage, he changed his name from Christian

Ludwigsen (his father's surname) to Chris Paciello (his mother's last name) because he wanted to sound more like a wise guy. He hated his father because he reportedly mistreated his mother and also because his part-German heritage meant that Paciello could never become a full-fledged member of the Mafia.

Paciello grew up in Borough Park but spent many of his early years hanging around neighboring Bensonhurst. His two closest friends were Dominic Dionisio and Enrico Locasio, two up-and-coming Colombo crime family bruisers, who years later used their menacing bulk to settle disputes between rival dealers at the Limelight. Locasio's mom was Paciello's elementary schoolteacher. Paciello was known around the area as a skilled and attentive gigolo. He went to Franklin Delano Roosevelt High, where many top mob spawn were educated, and after graduating dated the beautiful daughter of one of John Gotti's chief soldiers, Johnny Rizzo. The raven-haired Roxanne Rizzo was the love of his life, say some acquaintances; far more so than the celebrity babes he would subsequently court.

Paciello also had a reputation as a strong and capable fighter. He was a tough guy's tough guy. Only the certifiably insane would mess with Chris Paciello. Legend had it that when approached by a rival Bensonhurst gangster who tried to strike him with a baseball bat, Paciello stuck out his forearm for protection, and the bat splintered in two. "Is that all you got?" sneered the unperturbed badass, before pummeling his astonished assailant into submission.

Another story illustrating the Binger's pugilistic capabilities comes from Vinnie Rizzuto, Jr. One night at Filmore's, a local hangout for up-and-coming mobsters, a middle-aged hulk was slapping around a kid half his size. Things threatened to spiral out of control, when the intoxicated bully pulled out a .38 revolver and pointed it at the petrified victim. Paciello casually strolled over to the gunman, knocked him to the floor, then took the gun, which he fired into the ceiling of the bar as he fled the scene. Later that night, after police visited the establishment, Paciello found out that the drunk he'd floored was an off-duty, undercover detective, who had failed to identify himself when he unholstered his weapon. Paciello and Rizzuto put the gun in a brown paper bag and, before anonymously calling 911, dropped it into a trash can, so the cops could retrieve the revolver.

Paciello didn't mean for Judith Shemtov to die. The bloodshed was inadvertent. Though he wasn't the one who pulled the trigger, he was deeply troubled by her senseless slaughter. It was within the rules of the game to tear into a stranger's home, brandishing heat and looking for loot. However, snuffing out an innocent middle-aged woman was strictly forbidden. He knew pity was bad for business, but he couldn't help thinking of his own mother, a lowly hairdresser, and the white-hot anger he would feel if she were harmed. He also understood that more powerful gangsters than he were bound to resent the law enforcement scrutiny brought on by the bungled home invasion. When local detectives began looking into the murder and reward posters depicting a vivacious woman in the prime of her life started sprouting up on telephone poles and street lamps all over Staten Island, Paciello decided to exile himself to Miami, the traditional refuge for Gotham hoods when things get too hot on their home turf.

Weak and scared as he was, Michael Caruso became fast friends with Chris Paciello. Both men had grown up with delusions of grandeur in tightly knit Italian-American communities, where wise guys were the local role models. Both used stage monikers: Caruso changed his name to Lord Michael, because he wanted to sound like royalty; Christian Ludwigsen became Chris Paciello, because he wanted to come off like a powerful mafioso. Both also had reputations for treachery, the sort of guys who would smile in your face and then rob you blind once your back was turned. The bond between the men was symbiotic. Caruso was a successful drug dealer and promoter who admired mobsters but was no hard-core heavy himself. Put him under pressure, and he turned to jelly. Paciello, by comparison, had the balls of a brass bull.

Caruso needed Paciello for protection because he was afraid of reprisals from competitors he'd robbed. "There were times when people made physical threats towards me," Caruso later told DEA agents, "and Chris would tell them 'Anyone who comes near him, they're going to have to deal with me.' " Paciello also told Caruso that if he ever had problems while Paciello was out of town, he should call his old buddy Dominick Dionisio, at the time a member of the hit team—headed by Colombo family captain William "Wild Bill" Cutolo—that was roaming the Brooklyn streets in a gangland shooting war between two family factions, a bloody struggle in which at least twelve people were murdered, two of them innocent bystanders.

In turn, hanging out with Caruso at the Limelight gave Chris Paciello a glimpse of a glamorous life beyond the confines of his outer-borough turf and the bad-man role he seemed destined to play since birth. Gatien's club opened his mind and expanded his horizons. He saw how the intoxicating music bound different types of people together: gay and straight, black and white, stand-up guys from the neighborhood, and freaks from another planet. Impressed by all this, his experiences at the decadent dance hall gave Paciello the idea of starting his own New York–style club in Miami.

Vinnie Rizzuto, Jr., was Paciello's original partner in the new venture. Rizzuto borrowed money from his mobbed-up dad, Vinnie Oil, to finance his stake in the proposed establishment. But after Rizzuto had second thoughts and sold his share to the New Springville Boys leader Lee D'Avanzo, Paciello approached Caruso about coming onboard. Paciello and Caruso talked a great deal about opening a club together in Miami Beach. Paciello's older brother, George, had visited the holiday resort and had returned with stories about a prosperous town— "the billion-dollar bar" as locals called it—with a flourishing nightlife scene ready to be strip-mined.

And Paciello wanted to flee New York not just because of the Shemtov murder. According to Vinnie Rizzuto, "Chris also wanted to leave because he was afraid of being kidnapped. He thought people were out to rob him. A lot of people knew he was sitting on a mountain of cash from his various robberies. He told me he had a million dollars hidden at his grandfather's house in New Jersey."

The Bath Avenue Crew's Anthony "Gonzo" Gonzalez confirmed that in the months preceding his departure, the Binger was one worried criminal: "He'd fucked everyone over. He'd robbed the same guys he just did a score with. He'd fucked other guys' girls. Certain people were gunning for him."

In the summer of 1994, Paciello and Caruso developed yet another urgent reason to move their act to Miami when the two of them were involved in a vicious knockdown punch-up with bouncers at the Sound Factory, a dance hall in New York. After having been kicked out of Club USA that evening for fighting, Caruso, Paciello, and three or four of his Bath Avenue cohorts—all of them swaying under the influence of too much alcohol—approached the velvet rope at Sound Factory and demanded admittance. They claimed they wanted to hear Sound Factory's then-resident house DJ Junior Vasquez, because they were thinking of booking him for their new venture in Miami. They asked the bouncer in front to speak to Alex Coffiel, the deceptively mild-mannered head of security.

Coffiel, who took bribes from designated drug dealers he allowed to work at the club, tried to remain polite, but knowing trouble when he saw it, he rebuffed them: "You're not getting in tonight, guys. The place is full already."

Coffiel had heard that Caruso and Paciello were branching out from the Limelight and were making moves on the narcotics trade at rival clubs. They were going into non-Gatien establishments, where Caruso would befriend drug-dealer targets, following which Paciello would pounce, beating them up and shaking them down. Prior to that night, Paciello had even sent a female emissary to ask Coffiel if Paciello and his Bath Avenue boys could sell drugs in the club. Coffiel told her to tell the Binger to forget about it. Coffiel was well aware of Paciello's reputation. "He was notorious for sticking up drug dealers," Coffiel said. "He used to go to Roseland for the Black-and-White parties and rob all the queens. I also heard that he'd pose as someone interested in 'good weight' [a major amount of pot], and when they'd show up, he'd rob them at gunpoint."

Paciello and his men continued to press for entry to the club.

"I told you to get off the fuckin' line," Coffiel told Paciello, pushing him away.

Paciello's expression congealed into a contemptuous mask. He took off his Rolex watch and put it in his trouser pocket, seemingly as a prelude to one of those *Clockwork Orange* moments that punctuated every sentence of his biography. Coffiel and his only backup, Randy, a registered bounty hunter, stood firm like oak trees. Blood was about to spill. But all of a sudden, Paciello appeared to have second thoughts, and he ordered his boys to vacate the spot forthwith.

The confrontation apparently over, Coffiel went down the street to visit a friend at the nearby Tunnel. Twenty minutes later, as he was walking back to his place of employment, he saw the Sound Factory's front entrance in turmoil. Paciello and his cronies had returned and were pelting the door with bottles. A one-sided brawl had erupted. Coffiel ran up and began throwing punches to back up the sole bouncer, who was defending the entrance. Despite being bigger than their opponents, security was outnumbered. Paciello snuck up behind Coffiel and brained him with a metal stanchion that split open his head. Another bouncer managed to hit one of the Italians over the head with a fire extinguisher before he himself had his face smashed in. After his wounds were patched up, an angry Coffiel—not a man to cross lightly—vowed eternal retribution.

As it happened, an eyewitness managed to get the license plate of the car in which Caruso and Paciello fled the scene. Coffiel had a friend in the Department of Motor Vehicles, who traced it to a house in Bensonhurst. He and his buddies from a Brooklyn motorcycle club he belonged to rolled over to Bensonhurst, courtesy of Harley-Davidson, and patrolled up and down Bath Avenue looking for Paciello. Paciello supposedly saw them but hid. The Wednesday after the assault, Coffiel and his crew went mob deep, some thirty strong, to the Limelight, and stormed the club. They carried ax handles and walkie-talkies, with bandanas covering their faces. But Limelight bouncers tipped off Michael Caruso that Coffiel was coming to "slice you up"; he ran out the back door, just in time to avoid a major beat-down.

6 LAND OF THE LOTUS EATERS

South Beach, Florida, November 1994

They come from far and wide—from Havana and Bogotá, New York and London, Chicago and Madrid—to this transient man-made paradise, this tropical Oz, this thousand-acre spit of valuable real estate, where even the famous pink flamingos and palm trees were brought in from somewhere else. These aspiring supermodels and fashion plates, these leathery-faced playboys with large cigars and puffed-up chests, these fast-talking sellers of pretty pastel condominiums all in a row, these pneumatic Barbie dolls in tight dresses on roller blades and go-go boys in Lycra short-shorts, these DJs and party animals, hustlers and hungover hangers-on, these seekers of fame, fortune, and up-to-the-minute identities have all contributed to the rebirth of Miami Beach as a beacon of international glamour—a fantasy municipality pulsating with neon-lit desire, or so the local boosters claim. Gay and straight, black and white, and every race, nationality, and sexuality in between, they come, in particular, to the southern end of the island, a mile-long, mile-wide section known as South Beach, a candy-colored dreamland of recently refurbished art deco hotels, whose streamlined curves and fanciful features have caught the attention of magazine art directors, music video producers, and movie location scouts across the globe.

Image is everything in South Beach, a fascination with stylized façades that extends not just to the architecture. It's a place to go to empty your mind and pump up your pecs, a district where the only books allowed are tourist guides and where few vocations higher than that of the swimsuit model exist. The cult of the body beautiful is ubiquitous. The citizens who block the sidewalks have the sheen of waxwork dummies dipped in bronze. Everyone wears brand-new designer clothes and seems to have just left a yoga session or a workout at the gym. The palm tree–lined avenues are clogged with Porsches, Ferraris, and Mercedes that come fresh from the showroom. A new generation of the rudderless rich—VIPs by virtue of no meaningful distinction except their willingness to spend a thousand dollars for a hundred-dollar bottle of champagne—frequent the trendy lounges and restaurants, where the food is deliberately designed to look better than it actually tastes. If the panoply of languages spoken in the bustling streets recalls the Tower of Babel, the bawdy antics on the busy beach sometimes summon up visions of Sodom and Gomorrah by the sea. Amplified music—from disco to hip-hop to salsa—thunders night and day. Modeling tiny cell phones and big sunglasses, the black-garbed minimalists have banished to the mid- and upper parts of the isle the white pants, winter loafers, and fossilized end-timers—often Jewish retirees from up north—who used to flock here for the early-bird specials, leaving the southern tip free to become a fad-crazed fashion theme park for the young and well-to-do.

Yet, not so long ago, South Beach was rife with crime and drugs. Many of its unique buildings were threatened with extinction by the wrecking ball. But after preservation activists saved the area from destruction, savvy entrepreneurs flocked back to open hip boutiques, restaurants, and nightclubs. Italian fashion designer Gianni Versace helped spearhead this revival when, in 1991, on his way to Cuba, he made a stopover in Miami and fell in love with the neighborhood. He bought a run-down mansion that occupied a square block on Ocean Drive and reportedly spent $40 million turning it into "Casa Casuarini," an ostentatious showcase for the designer's baroque sensibility that quickly became a tourist attraction. At the same time, major celebrities from Madonna to Cher to Sylvester Stallone were all buying posh residences in the area.

But behind the glossy image there is a more sinister dimension to this "pastel boomtown," as Miami Beach has been called. The Beach has long been a destination with its own special allure for the sinful, the wicked, and the sleazy, like the South of France, another sunny place where shady characters go to reinvent themselves. Miami generally has a reputation as an American city in name only, a place where, as Joan Didion pointed out, the rules that govern the rest of the country apply only in diluted form. Experts estimate that fully one-third of all the unreported income in the United States either originates in or is funneled through South Florida. Down here, people joke that being accused of money laundering by the authorities is only slightly more serious than getting a parking ticket.

Miami Beach has a long history of dirty dealings under the palm trees. In a town devoted to the pleasure principle, opportunities have always abounded for the criminally inclined in the areas of construction, drugs, restaurants, or nightclubs. A place particularly rich in Mafia folklore during prohibition, Al Capone—one of the first to recognize the possibilities for organized crime in Miami Beach—relocated from Chicago and opened a string of speakeasies and gambling joints. Las Vegas pioneer Meyer Lansky, who also called the place home, made a fortune here from illegal gambling as well as from owning substantial chunks of real estate, before in later life donating a picture window to the local temple. In the '50s, when the mob took over gambling at the big hotels, the FBI called Miami Beach "the winter crime capital of America." At the famous Fontainebleau Hotel, Frank Sinatra caroused late into the night with his gangland buddies, while crime bosses Sam Giancana and Santos Trafficante supposedly conspired with CIA spooks to whack Castro after he kicked them out of Havana. In the '60s, Miami Beach—a short hop to the Caribbean and a smuggler's paradise since bootlegging—became a major staging point for marijuana distribution in America. In the '70s, pot millionaires became billionaires, as another processed plant, this one more compact and a hundred times more profitable, became all the rage. Cocaine money built many of the glittering beachfront towers that subsequently transformed the landscape.

Today, the resort is a home-away-from-home for Russian organized crime, not to mention a major hub for the international Ecstasy trade.

Ever since Capone, Miami Beach's nightlife scene has played host to hoodlum elements imported from elsewhere.

When Chris Paciello and Michael Caruso landed in Miami Beach in the late summer of 1994, most of the city clubs were rather unpretentious establishments. South Beach was still recovering from a long period of decay. While the scene was lively and infectious, it was obvious to the scheming duo that there was room for growth. The biggest venue on the strip was Glam Slam, the cavernous disco owned by absentee landlord Prince, which consistently failed to attract enough people to turn a profit.

Paciello and Caruso knew that opening a nightclub in South Beach was a crapshoot. Given the seasonal nature of the economy, you only had six months to make the big bucks. Establishments that opened and closed in the same week were not uncommon. But on the plus side, it was an open field for newcomers. And their timing might have been just right. South Beach was on the upswing, and they could feel the momentum in the streets, the energy of a place on the very cusp of becoming one of the planet's most fashionable destinations.

Paciello knew nothing about the nuts and bolts of running a nightclub, except what he'd picked up providing protection for Caruso's drug operation at the Limelight. Caruso was supposed to serve as the new venture's front man. Unlike Paciello, Lord Michael had juice in clubland; he knew how to book the top DJs who would bring in the punters. Still worried about the Shemtov murder, Paciello intended to stay in the shadows. "People know you from the club world," Paciello explained to his partner. "You've been the face everybody knows. You know how to deal with people. I'm a goon, I'm not a high-fashion pretty boy."

With a realtor in tow, they toured half a dozen vacant spaces looking for the ideal spot to turn into a smallish nightclub. Dissatisfied with what they saw, Paciello suggested to Caruso that they should meet with a friend of his from the old neighborhood—Carlos Vaccarezza, once John Gotti's limousine driver. Vaccarezza was selling a bar he controlled called Mickey's Place on Washington Avenue. Paciello persuaded Caruso that it was a great opportunity because Vaccarezza needed to get rid of the place in a hurry and didn't want much money up front, so they could pay the remainder when the club took off.

The next day, Caruso and Paciello walked over to Mickey's to meet the owner. Unlike his stylish former boss, Vaccarezza was a sartorial mess. Graying and paunchy, wearing sandals with black nylon socks, he stuck out like a sore thumb on the style-conscious beach. Vaccarezza knew Paciello from Brooklyn wise guy circles, and he liked the spunky kid who had a reputation as ambitious and mature beyond his years, not at all like the drug-addicted, disrespectful punks that make up the Mafia's lower ranks these days.

Vaccarezza had bolted to Miami after the feds investigated his Manhattan restaurant, Da Noi, claiming it was a currency-washing operation for Gotti. In partnership with actor Mickey Rourke, whom he met at Gotti's 1992 murder and racketeering trial, Vaccarezza journeyed to Rourke's hometown, where they opened up Mickey's Place.

The watering hole was known as a hangout for hoodlums, a perception that the owner did little to dispel. Caruso noticed how Vaccarezza decorated the club to look like a Brooklyn boxing gym and festooned the walls with framed portraits of Gotti in what resembled a religious shrine to the jailed don. Bull-necked toughs hung outside the entrance. "It was a little patch of Brooklyn on South Beach," said one local wag. Rumor had it that Rourke was given a stake in the club by the Gambinos for his public support of Gotti.

Mickey's location was an established site for failed mob businesses. Before Mickey's, the place had been a struggling restaurant named Mario's, whose owner—later convicted of laundering money for the Genovese crime family—was desperate to attract bodies to his establishment. He allowed local promoters to start a night in the eatery's back room called Fat Black Pussycat. The rear alley–entrance party—to which you needed a password to gain admittance—became the hippest, most musically eclectic party on the Beach, everything from swing to '70s funk. The rendezvous was pumping at 4:00 A.M. on a Monday night with the coolest crowd in town. But when Mario's was sold to Vaccarezza, Fat Black Pussycat folded, only to be revived after Paciello and Caruso decided to take over the place.

Paciello paid $140,000 to assume the lease in a deal brokered by Janet Navarro, Micky Rourke's sister-in-law, who subsequently became Paciello's full-time accountant. Where that considerable coinage came from was moot. The government believed that the deal was financed with the proceeds from robberies and drug rip-offs back home. However, when applying for his liquor license, Paciello told the Florida State Liquor Authority that a Staten Island gym owner named Robert Currie fronted him $125,000 to finance the venture. When the *Village Voice* contacted Currie in 1998, the businessman flatly denied loaning Paciello any money.

Caruso had a 10 percent share of the club, which, by his own admission, he financed with proceeds from the drug trade at the Limelight as well as by selling his Harley-Davidson motorcycle. He also borrowed $6,000 from Peter Gatien to help decorate the club. Vinnie Rizzuto, Jr.—the man who provided the seed money for Caruso's Ecstasy operation—also had a stake in the fledgling enterprise but quickly sold it to the New Springville Boys leader Lee D'Avanzo, who himself had second thoughts and backed out, but not before warning Caruso, "I don't want to be involved with Chris; he's shady. I heard he's involved with some heavy mob guys, and he's going to shake you down. You might as well get out of here and not be involved. They're eventually going to take over the place anyway."

Caruso also noticed that Paciello had private closed-door meetings at the club, confidential sit-downs from which he was pointedly excluded, with two frequent visitors from New York, John "Jackie Nose" D'Amico, reputedly a powerful captain in the Gambino crime family, and his soldier Johnny Rizzo, whose daughter Roxanne Paciello used to date. The government would subsequently become convinced that the Gambinos secretly controlled the new venue.

In November 1994, with little fanfare, Chris Paciello and Michael Caruso opened their first ever club at 1203 Washington Avenue, a location overshadowed by the cavernous Glam Slam a few doors down. The debut of the 300-person-capacity establishment registered barely a blip on the social radar screen, its snob appeal being nonexistent. It was called Risk, and as the name suggested, it was a decidedly dicey venture from the get-go, an unprepossessing launchpad for the remarkable transformation of Paciello.

Inside, the atmosphere was as hot and steamy as a conservatory, a point underscored by the club's one unusual design feature—a public shower where patrons cooled off. The disco was filled with secondhand furniture bought from the clubs that go out of business on the strip every season. A partitioned-off area in the corner was devoted to drug taking.

Paciello's gangster roots were obvious from the names on the opening night's guest list. A thirty-strong crew of Versace-clad junior mobsters flew down from New York especially for the occasion, among them Tommy Reynolds, who had shot Judith Shemtov; Dominic Dionisio and Enrico Locasio, the two Colombo family torpedoes that Paciello grew up with; and Vincent Rizzuto, Jr., who would soon be the subject of a nationwide FBI manhunt. All night they clogged up the tiny VIP room, making bottle after bottle of Cristal and Moet disappear down their muscular necks.

"Risk had a real New York attitude," recalled Gilbert Stafford, the grande dame of South Beach doormen, who patrolled Risk's velvet rope during its short six-month existence. "The opening night was very mobster chic. I thought they were just dressed up like mobsters; it wasn't until later I found out they really were gangsters. They were perfect gentlemen, though. They all seemed on their best behavior. But you did get the sense that could change in an instant."

Stafford, one of the original doormen at the legendary early '80s New York club Area, had moved in the early '90s to Miami Beach, where he became something of a local celebrity, famous for bringing a bit of old school wit and wisdom to an attention-deficit scene that had trouble remembering what had happened the previous Saturday. Stafford first noticed Paciello and Caruso in the gym in the basement of the Clevelander, a cross between a hotel and a nightclub on Ocean Drive and a favorite hostel for students on spring break. With wet T-shirt contests by the pool during the day and obnoxiously loud dance music played at the outdoor bar by night, not to mention the constantly rotating cast of drunken revelers, it was an ideal setting that enabled a couple of young crooks like Paciello and Caruso to reside in relative anonymity, hide in plain sight, while they found their bearings and planned their next scam.

"I used to see these young Italian guys at the gym every day who always seemed to be holding a secret meeting," recalled Stafford in his booming theatrical voice. "One day, I looked up, and they were all staring at me for some reason. A couple of days later, one of them came to see me at the Spot, the club I worked for at the time. He said his name was Lord Michael, and he said he had a friend named Chris Paciello who wanted to meet me. He told me, 'We've heard you're the best doorman on the beach, we're opening a new club and we'd like to hire you.' I'd already heard the name Chris Paciello before. The biggest fight that ever happened at the Spot was a fight that began when Paciello, Caruso, and their boys went into the club and starting throwing their weight around. But what Chris didn't know was that the Spot had the toughest and the most notorious security team on the Beach. They weren't going to take shit from a bunch of out-of-town punks. Chris took a beating that night. It was one of the few times he didn't walk away victorious."

The colorful Stafford, a dark-skinned, white-haired gay man, gladly took the job offer. He became fast friends with Paciello, who, unusually for someone from his background, felt perfectly at ease in the company of blacks and gays.

"He was unfailingly gracious to me," said Stafford. "He was incredibly modest. He treated his employees like family. We had dinner parties every couple of weeks, and he would thank the whole staff. He was the kindest employer I'd ever worked for. We would bicker like husband and wife sometimes, but there was a real friendship there."

Risk was a rough-and-tumble spot. Punch-ups were not uncommon. Bottles and fists sometimes flew. Stafford was instructed to clean up the crowd and keep out the knuckleheads. One night, a group of rowdy frat boys—the intoxicated children of privilege—created a commotion at the front door. "There were like these six obnoxious creeps in Lacoste T-shirts that I wouldn't let in. All of them were white jocks, except for this one guy, who was black, who had the mouth on him and would not get off my back, to the extent I couldn't do my job anymore. Believe it or not, he ended up calling me a 'nigger.' Chris heard him and strode over. He always stood up for his employees. It was one shot, and the guy was out cold. If you blinked, you would have missed it. His friends picked him up and carried him away unconscious. It was poetry."

To woo the sizable gay population in South Beach, Paciello and Caruso swiftly initiated a decadent gay night called Risk Your Anus. To court black patrons, they shrewdly resumed Fat Black Pussycat, which was reinvented as a hip-hop night. The weekly event attracted not only A-list night crawlers who relished the amazing DJs that Caruso imported from New York, but the name itself carried on a tradition for South Beach trendsetters. But try as they did to court a more fashionable set of people, most of the club's core clientele consisted of what locals dismissively call "the bridge-and-causeway crowd," the invaders from the Miami mainland, who travelled via causeway across the glassy waters of Biscayne Bay every weekend.

"Business was only ever OK," said Stafford. "Risk struggled to survive. As clubs go, it was eminently forgettable."

As the club floundered, Paciello became increasingly disillusioned with Caruso's promoting abilities. Lord Michael had resumed drugging after a period of abstinence, and as a consequence Paciello didn't want his partner handling money anymore. "I took him in because he claimed to know about the club business, but he really didn't know as much as he led me to believe," Paciello told the *Village Voice*. "He was a name-dropper and eventually thought he was more fabulous than the people I paid him to attract." To help Paciello run the club, his younger brother, Keith, and his older brother, George, a bank robber with a permanent sneer, moved down to Miami. The unreliable Caruso increasingly was frozen out.

Gilbert Stafford vividly remembered the first time he met George at Risk: "I happened to pop my head into the office for some reason or another. George was reaching down and taking a gun out of his ankle holster. 'What's that for?' I asked him innocently. 'Well, we're in a new city, and we don't know anybody,' and I'm like, 'Wow. That's how you go to a new town. Most people I know would just take a guidebook and a credit card.'"

Despite this introduction, Stafford became close to the Paciello clan, especially after Chris's mother, Marguerite, moved down from Staten Island to live with her son. Like many members of the criminal classes, Paciello was excessively pro-family, as if loving your nearest and dearest somehow compensated for unleashing horrible violence upon the rest of the world. "Chris loved his mother," said Stafford. "Marguerite was one of those women who was always full of life; she always had a smile. She doted on her kids."

But Stafford kept his distance from Chris's father, George, Sr., a former bouncer and petty thief, who stole to feed his heroin habit and was a bad dad to boot: "He scared the hell out of me. He was this hulking giant of a guy who obviously had some skeletons in the closest. Chris told me he had a drug problem. Chris said that now he was successful, the only time he ever heard from his father was when he wanted money. The thing I remember most about George, Sr., was that he was scared of cockroaches. If he saw one, he would shriek like a hysterical woman."

But even as he tried to forge a new career as a club owner, Chris Paciello's criminal genes still got the better of him. His fondness for boosting luxury rides remained unabated. Two months after the opening of Risk, the Binger, who by now had deserted the Clevelander for a luxury high-rise building on Collins Avenue, decided to steal his cardiologist neighbor's brand new BMW. Paciello had just wrecked his own BMW, which itself was reported stolen by a New York resident, and the club owner was on the lookout for a replacement. Paciello tinted the windows and replaced the identification number with that of the trashed automobile. This obvious deception was easily spotted by the attendant when Paciello, brazen as could be, drove the car back to the garage and parked it in his own space. The police were summoned, and Paciello was busted on grand theft auto. But the charges were dropped after the stolen BMW mysteriously disappeared from the police compound, only to turn up a few days later, smoldering by the side of the road.

Michael Caruso could not believe how dumb his partner sometimes acted. By this point, he badly wanted their alliance dissolved, but he was too scared of Paciello to broach the topic. Caruso had come to the realization that he wasn't cut out for the gangster lifestyle; this was a guy, after all, who had to return a Glock handgun he'd bought for protection, because he couldn't figure out how to operate the fearsome weapon. Besides, he'd recently received a visit from his girlfriend, Gina, who had arrived with their newborn son. He told friends that he now wanted to turn his life around by swearing off drugs, adultery, gambling, and crime. He was going to return to New York, where he intended to transform himself into a model father. Around this time, a drunken and emotional Caruso cornered one of Risk's waitresses and spilled out his emotions. "He told me he really loved Gina," she said. "He said he desperately wanted to get out of the club business. You could see the anguish in his face."

The final straw for Caruso came when Paciello insisted on hiding out their old friend Vinnie Rizzuto, Jr., at Caruso's small, one-bedroom apartment on Washington Avenue, just a couple of blocks down from Risk. The authorities were looking for the fleeing gangster. Indeed, the FBI had put a bounty on his head, after he ran away from a murder indictment following the gangland slaying of a Colombo family capo's son (Joey Scarpa, scion of secret FBI mole Gregory Scarpa) in a dispute over a drug-related robbery in Brooklyn. Unknowingly, Rizzuto had ripped off the wrong marijuana dealer, one protected by the Gambinos, the same crime family to which Rizzuto supposedly pledged allegiance. Though he enjoyed a measure of protection because of his father, Vinnie Oil, it was still a serious matter. A sit-down was arranged under the auspices of his dad, and the decision was made that Rizzuto had to make amends. He did this by luring his partner in the robbery, Joey Scarpa, to Brooklyn's Sheepshead Bay, where Rizzuto blew Scarpa's brains all over the inside of his automobile.

Rizzuto stayed at Caruso's place for about two weeks. Proving that there's no honor among thieves, before he left for Minneapolis, Rizzuto stole Caruso's wallet, containing his driver's license and social security card, and until his capture, Rizzuto proceeded to assume the party promoter's identity.

By now, Caruso had had enough. He was tired of living in fear of his life. Not telling Paciello that he had no intention of returning, in March

1995 he took a flight to New York and begged Peter Gatien to rehire him as a director at the Limelight. When he left for South Beach, Caruso had lied to Gatien that he had to exile himself to Miami for six months as punishment because he was in trouble with the Mafia over a $40,000 gambling debt. Caruso told Gatien the debt had been paid and that he wanted to come back to work in New York. Gatien rehired him, but at half his previous salary. Caruso informed the clubowner he didn't want to resume selling drugs. Gatien said that was fine; he didn't want him getting involved in drugs anymore. After Caruso moved to Miami, the day-to-day running of his drug network had been passed on to his former lieutenant, Robert Gordon.

But before he could resume his position in Gatien's empire, Caruso had some unfinished business to take care off: He needed to make amends with Sound Factory's head of security, Alex Coffiel. Whereas Paciello had countered the death threats issued by Sound Factory bouncers in the wake of the brawl with his typical "Anytime, anywhere, motherfucker" attitude, Lord Michael had been seriously shaken up by the episode.

With Gatien's help, Caruso attempted a rapprochement with Coffiel. A clandestine meeting between Caruso and Coffiel was set up at a Manhattan coffee shop, after Coffiel promised the promoter "safe passage." Caruso, who was visibly shaking and extremely paranoid, blamed the bad blood on Paciello. He said that he had quit the drug business, and he begged Coffiel not to hurt him for the sake of his family. He offered him thousands of dollars as compensation. Caruso also supplied Coffiel with intimate knowledge about Paciello's routine in Miami, including where he lived and what gym he went to every day. In addition, he gave up the names, addresses, and phone numbers of the other Bath Avenue toughs involved in the assault. "He developed diarrhea of the mouth," Coffiel said afterward.

The bouncer secretly tape-recorded the conversation and then played the tape to Paciello in Miami. A ticking time bomb on the best of occasions, Paciello exploded in rage when he heard about Caruso's disloyalty. His brain bubbled with anger, and he hit the warpath without delay. He hopped the next plane to New York, spending the whole flight imagining the heavyweight harm he was going to administer when he tracked down Caruso. He intended to exact a supersize measure of revenge because Caruso had broken the cardinal rule of the streets: He'd snitched out a comrade. From the airport, Paciello hurried over to the Tunnel, where he bumped into Caruso. "Straight away, I could tell something was wrong," Caruso would say later. Caruso thought that the Binger was mad because he had left Risk for good without telling him. "How come I haven't seen you lately?" asked Paciello. He was unaware that Paciello knew all about the meeting with Coffiel. Caruso apologized, explaining that he had to come back to New York to care for his girlfriend and their newborn son. Paciello seemed to accept this explanation and told him he'd come by and visit soon.

The next day, Paciello went over to Caruso's Staten Island apartment accompanied by a second male, found him home, and then, in a flurry of fists, beat the promoter to a pinkish mush, before sticking a gun in his bloody face and screaming, "You treacherous motherfucker. You set me up. I ought to shoot you right now." According to Caruso, only the intervention of Paciello's companion prevented him from pulling the trigger. Before he left, Paciello told Caruso, "You're lucky that I didn't kill you. From now on I want you to pay me whatever I tell you to." Neighbors called the cops, but the techno promoter was too petrified to finger Paciello as his attacker.

In January 1995, the Miami Beach police swooped down and raided and padlocked Paragon, Twist, Groove Jet, and Glam Slam, all prominent South Beach clubs. The police were acting on information from a professional informer named Sean Kirkham, a fine-featured descendent of Inuit Indians from the Arctic circle, who told them about drug dealing in the local clubs. One club was noticeably absent from the list. Kirkham says that several days after meeting the club owner by the pool at the newly opened Delano Hotel, he took $3,000 from George Paciello at a South Beach Denny's. In exchange he agreed to omit Risk from the report he gave to his handlers.

Kirkham was born inside the Arctic circle on a reservation in Canada's Northwest Territories. Orphaned at an early age, he grew up with foster parents in a middle-class suburb of Toronto. In 1990, after his surrogate parents found out he was gay, the troubled teenager ran away from home with $90 in his pocket. He eventually ended up in New York, where he stayed in homeless shelters and slept on the subways. He eked out a modest existence by hustling in the old Times Square, living off "the generosity of some sympathetic strangers." In December 1993, Kirkham secured a job as a busboy at Club USA, Peter Gatien's sex-themed Times Square dance hall. It was here that Kirkham met Gatien, Michael Alig, and Lord Michael Caruso for the first time. Kirkham immediately disliked Alig, then at the height of his influence. "He was snotty, sarcastic, and disgusting," recalled Kirkham. "He used to throw pee out of the window onto the crowd below waiting to get in." And he wasn't particularly impressed by Gatien, either. "Personally, the man left a sour taste in my mouth," he said.

Kirkham was given a crash course in the criminal element that hung out at Club USA, when he claims one of the bouncers spotted a coked-up drug dealer, an easy mark, who was stumbling around the venue. Kirkham was told, "Come with me for a minute." Kirkham and the steroid-pumped bouncer went downstairs, approached the dealer, announced themselves as security, and told him to empty his pockets. The bouncer took the drugs, while Kirkham kept the money. Kirkham claims he was fired from Club USA after he approached a local politician with the accusation that Gatien was paying off the fire department to ignore fire code violations. The politician, who requested anonymity, confirmed that she spoke to Kirkham. "He came to me with this accusation, but there was no specific evidence, so there was nothing I could do," she related. "He seemed very innocent about the ways of the world." While Gatien insisted that his former employee was mistaken, Kirkham still claimed, "I saw cash being passed from a club employee to a fireman."

After leaving Club USA, Kirkham sought a new life and moved to Miami in 1994. Kirkham worked for the FBI. His first job was trying to infiltrate a famous Russian mob strip club called Porky's near Miami International Airport. Russian mobsters were trying to forge alliances with Colombian drug traffickers in the area. He attempted to befriend the club's owner, reputed top gangster Ludwig Fainberg, known as "Tarzan" because of his long hair and muscular frame. Kirkham failed to get a job at the club, and Fainberg was later arrested trying to sell two Soviet military helicopters and a submarine to the Cali cocaine cartel.

Kirkham's next project was more successful. He set out to penetrate the stylish South Beach party scene. He dug the lifestyle—the drugs, the glamour, the sex, and the ostentatious displays of wealth—even though, strictly speaking, his job was to put a damper on the festivities. His delicate good looks made him stand out among the thickset muscle boys on the circuit. Unfailingly polite, he easily penetrated the trendiest clubs, where he spent many a night getting bombed on champagne, courtesy of the authorities. "Sean used to be at all the fabulous parties," remembered Maxwell Blandford, then manager of Miami hot spot Warsaw. "He had Madonna's home phone number in his address book as well as what looked like an A-to-Z of Florida law enforcement." Kirkham claimed he obtained Madonna's number after he stole a famous film director's address book from his bungalow at a Miami Beach hotel where Kirkham briefly worked as a front-desk clerk. Kirkham says he held hostage the virtual *Who's Who* of the entertainment industry until the director threatened legal action. Kirkham FedExed back the book to the production company but not before copying five hundred numbers and addresses. He later sold the information to Sound Factory promoters, who called up stars like Bianca Jagger and Liam Neeson to invite them to parties.

Kirkham kept his ears open and heard a lot of gossip in the clubs and bars, tales of Madonna, Gianni Versace, and Elton John; stories about who was boning who and who was snorting what. He mingled with celebrities at parties, dancing with Donatella Versace at Salvation, sitting next to Madonna in a VIP room, using the urinal next to a well-endowed Vanilla Ice, and crawling around the dance floor on all fours at Paragon with a temperamental disco diva who was out of her mind on Special K.

Kirkham got to know many of the local club owners and promoters, and took detailed notes about which establishments were the big drug spots. Unbeknownst to his handlers, he worked both sides of the fence.

He took favors from drug dealers to rat out other drug dealers. He befriended Chris Paciello and secretly told him about his status as a federal informer. Paciello thought this a useful tidbit of information. Money passed from one hand to another. Kirkham continued to work as an informer until December 1995, when he returned to New York and put himself back in the heart of Peter Gatien's clubland.

Paciello poured his heart and soul into Risk. But even with the success of the Fat Black Pussycat and Risk Your Anus nights, he just couldn't make it work on the economic front. "Risk wasn't the biggest money-maker," he admitted to his friend, society reporter Jacquelynne D. Powers. "But I took home a nice paycheck. Ultimately, I made a bad business deal, and the notes that I was paying were the profits of the place. But it was a great learning experience."

Then, on April 21, 1995, a month after a disillusioned Michael Caruso returned to New York to care for his girlfriend and newborn son, Risk burnt to the ground in disputed circumstance. At around 9:00 A.M., nearly four hours after the last club-hopper had left the establishment, a Miami Beach patrol cop spotted smoke escaping under the club's back door. Inside, a ravenous fire raged, consuming furniture and decorations. The place was literally gutted by flames. Gilbert Stafford described a distraught Paciello, the morning after the inferno, tears welling up in his eyes, sitting on the curb outside the space that formerly housed Risk, now a blackened shell: "He was not a happy guy. He was clearly in shock. He could hardly speak. The club was totaled. Whoever did it did a damn good job."

Investigators believed that sometime after the establishment had shut, someone shoved a lit cigarette into the cushion of a semicircular couch in the back VIP area. The incident looked suspicious. For one thing, the material that covered the couch was supposed to be flame retardant. But lacking sufficient proof of arson, the fire marshall ruled that the conflagration was an accidental smoke fire.

Back in New York, a puffed-up Caruso was going around boasting he burnt down the club to make himself look like a tough guy. But the feds came to believe that Paciello had his own club torched for the big payoff from the insurance company. "The fire wasn't properly investigated because Chris was bribing the local cops," said informer Sean Kirkham. A federal prosecutor once told me that Paciello hired the head of security from a rival club to put a match to the venue and rewarded him with a new truck, money, and a job. Another theory was that Paciello brought in "outside talent"—members of Caruso's Limelight drug gang—to do the deed. Whatever the exact scenario, nobody believed the fire was unintentional. When later confronted with the accusation that he torched his own club, Paciello shot back via fax: "Utter nonsense. The fire marshall investigated the incident thoroughly and found it was an accident."

When he first showed up on South Beach, the locals considered Chris Paciello a tacky "gym bunny." He was dismissed as a vulgar interloper, a suspicious carpetbagger—one of the many fun in the sun–seeking outsiders who trek down each season to start up nightspots that end up failing fast. "I was a big Guido from New York opening up a club," Paciello once recalled. "Everybody thought I'd be out of business in a week." A socialite friend, who met Paciello back then, recollects mocking the crude speech patterns and the impossibly loud jogging suits that he'd arrived with from New York: "I remember him guzzling champagne straight from the bottle as if it was mineral water." But Paciello stood out from his rough-hewn compatriots. "He was stunningly good-looking," the socialite stated with a wry smile. "That counts for a lot down here. In South Beach, beauty is like having money in the bank. It's collateral."

With Caruso out of the picture, Paciello was determined to forge an alliance with the locals. After all, with the investigation of the Shemtov murder heating up, he couldn't boogie on back to New York. He decided he wanted to open another club. And he already had his eye on a suitable partner for the new venture, a petite, dark-haired beauty named Ingrid Casares. They had met for the first time just before Risk closed, introduced by a mutual friend named Hojie, and Paciello and Casares clicked immediately. Casares was known to have a penchant for collecting young, talented macho males as arm candy. "I thought Chris was a good-looking guy," Casares once recalled. "I was from Miami, but I had been living away from home. I didn't know any of the clubs or the locals." The duo became unlikely kindred spirits. Paciello's physical magnetism and his no-nonsense approach to business appealed to the feckless party girl. Even though she had been raised in Miami in the lap of luxury and dressed in the latest expensive European fashions, Casares cursed like a sailor and despite (or maybe because of) her diminutive frame, affected a tough street attitude. Here, standing in front of her at Risk, was the real deal.

At this time, Casares was perhaps best known for French kissing a naked Madonna in the pop star's controversial book *Sex*. *New York* magazine described her look as "a kind of butch Audrey Hepburn." She lived on her father's mountains of cash and ran with a fast crowd that attended drug-steeped parties late at night. She was a flipped-out flapper devoted to style, the bad seed who shunned the elite Latin world of lavish quinces and communions in favor of a bisexual lifestyle that shocked the conservative Cuban exile community. Her life was a long way from the tiara and ruffled skirt–wearing Cuban-American princess she had been bred to become.

Born in 1964 in Miami's Little Havana, just a couple of years after her parents Nancy and Raul had fled Castro's Cuba, Casares grew up in a wealthy Coral Gables neighborhood. Her father, a supporter of anti-Castro causes and a union buster, owned RC Aluminum, a company that supplied the windows for many of the major high-rise construction projects in the Miami area. Casares attended Our Lady of Lourdes Academy, a strict private school for girls, where she was always getting into trouble for skipping class and dating boys. She suffered from attention deficit disorder, was weak at learning, but strong at sports, especially basketball. She was the class clown who later morphed into the school freak and was lucky to graduate. As a teenager, she became addicted to cocaine.

For seven years after high school, Casares floated around Miami doing menial jobs, such as working in a tanning salon and as a valet parker. Eventually she headed north to obtain a degree in English and public relations from the University of Maryland. In 1991, she moved to Los Angeles and worked as a booker at the Wilhelmina modeling agency. Casares first sprang to public attention in the early '90s, when her name began to appear in boldface in the gossip columns as a member of Madonna's lesbian inner circle, which also included the comedian Sandra Bernhard and the country crooner k.d. lang, both of whom the pixie-cute Casares dated. She was frequently photographed at fashion shows or sporting events with her pal Madonna. She had started going out with Bernhard in 1990 after meeting the comedienne backstage at one of her shows in Miami. Bernhard took Casares to Madonna's birthday party, where Casares struck up a lasting friendship with the pop singer. They shot *Sex* together in Miami Beach. The complicated love triangle was simplified when Madonna supposedly stole Casares from Bernhard.

When Chris Paciello returned to Florida—his anger having subsided since his encounter with Caruso in New York—he regaled Ingrid with plans of opening a new Miami nightclub by using the $250,000 fire insurance settlement from Risk. The place was to be called Liquid—a rather appropriate name given not only the ethical fluidity of life in Miami Beach but also the club's alleged role as a money laundromat for organized crime. Paciello remembered how Carlos Vaccarezza used Mickey Rourke to give Mickey's the sheen of legitimacy. He figured that Casares, even though she wasn't exactly a celebrity, was close enough. She would make a good front person for the operation. "When Chris approached me about Liquid," Casares claimed, "I said 'Yes' immediately. I didn't know anything about nightclubs, but I did know a lot of famous people." Casares didn't own a share in Liquid initially, although she was paid handsomely to be the club's public façade. Only later, after Paciello feared Casares might leave him, did he give her a 25 percent stake in the club.

With Casares onboard, Paciello's social circle started to broaden dramatically. Instead of Jackie the Nose or Frankie the Baker, Paciello started hanging out with Madonna, Gianni Versace, and Calvin Klein. And because of Casares's influence, Paciello gained membership to one of Miami Beach's most exclusive male cliques, a group of wealthy playboy swingers, many of whom were a bit on the shady side themselves.

During the summer and fall of 1995, while Ingrid and Chris were overseeing the construction of Liquid, Paciello used the upscale lounge

Bar None as his finishing school. Bar None was a celebrity hangout where, it was said, there were more beautiful women per square foot than anywhere else on the Beach. A consortium of international jet setters who became Paciello's new best friends owned the deluxe den. Among them were Jason Binn, copublisher of *Ocean Drive* magazine; Ugo Colombo, Miami's answer to Donald Trump; major real estate developer Craig Robins, who was Chris's landlord at both Risk and Liquid; Shareef Malnik, co-owner of the venerable Forge restaurant with his father Alvin, a former associate of Meyer Lansky; and even Sylvester Stallone, who was supposedly a silent partner in the venture. At Bar None, Paciello learned about table manners and ordering the right wine, how to dress appropriately and engage in social intercourse without the use of profanities. He adopted the habit, unusual for his generation, of standing up when a lady entered the room. His pal Shareef Malnik was driving a Range Rover, so Paciello bought one too, instead of stealing the luxury automobile, as he normally would have done. Elaborate dinners at the opulent Forge and late nights at Bar None were de rigueur. Celebrities, including Demi Moore, Whitney Houston, Bobby Brown, Cindy Crawford, Jack Nicholson, Russell Simmons, David Lee Roth, and Donatella Versace, all graced Bar None's VIP room with their presence. Paciello was there, soaking up the glamour and taking copious mental notes.

"Chris really wanted to be a man of the world," said Gilbert Stafford. "He craved sophistication. I remember one time I said to him, 'What did you do today?' and he replied, with a big smile on his face, 'I played polo.'"

Paciello wore his first-ever tuxedo for the Make-A-Wish Foundation Ball at the Hotel InterContinental, the premier philanthropic event of the year. In Miami Beach the November to April winter season was, and still is, an endless whirl of receptions, openings, parties, balls, and benefits. But the Make-A-Wish occasion is always the most elaborate. Drowning in a sea of champagne and fortified by the best available caviar, the upscale and wrinkled were out in force that night: Mickey Arison, who owned Carnival Cruise Lines and the Miami Heat basketball team; Jeffrey Chodorow, who ran the China Grill restaurant group;

Don Shula, the then-coach of the Miami Dolphins, who married into money; Frosene Sonderling, the grand dame of local charity events; Marcy Lefton, another major socialite; and Stephen Sawitz, owner of the Miami institution Joe's Stone Crabs. Broadway star Bernadette Peters was the host for the evening. At the end of the night, as part of an annual tradition, nightlife czarina Regine sang Gloria Gaynor's "I Will Survive." Walking across the red carpets and marble floors, taffeta swirling around him, a tanned and toned Paciello looked amazing in his evening wear, which fit him like a second skin. Even old-school matrons in gliterry gowns had to suppress a gasp at the sight of him, beauty and the beast rolled into one. While a long way from Staten Island, the beneficent malefactor felt right at home frolicking with the swells and the power brokers. The social possibilities of his new life in Miami seemed infinite to Paciello. At the end of the Make-A-Wish ball, Paciello couldn't think of an inscription to write in the guest book, so a socialite friend stepped in. "I loved the lobster, but I'm not a mobster," she wrote tongue in cheek.

Chris and Ingrid's relationship seemed to help Paciello more than Casares. With this A-list acceptance came power, money, success, and bevies of beautiful women. But Casares gained a lot, too. She was taken seriously for the first time in her life. When Casares met Paciello, she was known as a "star-fucker": "I was famous, but I was famous for certain reasons," Casares confessed. She made celebrity friends easily but needed a substantial profession to prove she was more than just a drug-addled sycophant. "I could discover a cure for cancer, and I'd still only be known as Madonna's best friend," she liked to complain. When Gloria Estefan and her husband, Emilio, gave Casares a job as singer Jon Secada's image consultant, this vocational incarnation was widely derided by insiders. Ingrid had gone to high school with Gloria's sister and had known the family for years. Her job was to update Secada's image. But during her tenure, no one could discern any change whatsoever in Secada's bland and conservative persona. Paciello provided Casares with the dose of credibility she so desperately needed, not to mention the thawing effect that he had on her icy persona. "I was a spoiled little rich kid until I met Chris," she admitted.

In September 1995, Paciello also ended Casares's decade-long love affair with cocaine by teaming up with Madonna to check their mutual friend into rehab. Paciello never touched the usual vices that made the party swing in drug-saturated South Beach. But the brittle and determinedly superficial Casares did. A frail-looking creature in a well-tailored suit, she desperately needed a vacation away from the slopes. The dope drama might have had a tragic denouement if Paciello hadn't stepped in. After all, he needed her clean and sober for Liquid's debut. Years later, before a packed courtroom, Ingrid's father, Raul, tearfully told the judge that his daughter was a "walking disaster" until she met Paciello: "Ingrid did a lot of drugs as child. . . . Then she met Chris. Chris is the one responsible for stopping her taking drugs."

Under a lurid purple sky illuminated by arc lights, Liquid debuted on Thanksgiving weekend 1995. The club was located above a Payless shoe store, two blocks from the ocean in a raw, hard-edged, second-floor warehouse. It was one of the biggest, most crowded unveilings in South Beach's nascent clubland history. Ten thousand invitations had gone out. The national media had been notified. Limousines stretched around the block, waiting to disgorge famous face after not-so famous face. The hype was so all consuming that two hours before the club was supposed to open, a mob besieged the front entrance, overflowing across the sidewalk and into the street. The evening started out bright with promise, but, by the end, many patrons waiting outside were assaulted by the crash of broken glass and the shrill, brain-penetrating wail of a store alarm going off across the street. Such was the hysterical crush of bodies surrounding the velvet rope in front of the club that some of the would-be scene-makers actually feared for their lives.

While Paciello's old crowd from Risk was left fuming on the sidelines, desperately waving worthless invitations and straining to catch the attention of the diffident bouncers in dinner jackets, inside the bare-walled establishment, with its exposed pipes and steel wire decor, some of the most famous names from the worlds of film, music, and fashion gyrated to the pulsating grooves of world-renowned house music DJ

Junior Vasquez, who was making his first Miami appearance. There was Madonna, sporting her *Evita* look, whose brother, Christopher Ciccione, was celebrating his birthday in the VIP room; David Geffen and Barry Diller, both dressed like Wall Street accountants on casual Fridays; Calvin Klein, Kate Moss, Naomi Campbell, Gloria Estefan, and Sean Penn. Denied entry to the pantheon of showbiz gods, incensed members of the swelling mob started spitting at the few lucky enough to gain admittance. At the end of the night, as the celebrities started to exit, bouncers had to escort them to their vehicles for fear they would be set upon by the remnants of the livid throng.

"The South Beach equivalent of Truman Capote's Black-and-White Ball," local gossip columnist Tom Austin gushed afterward. "A watershed gathering that blended fame, beauty, talent, and shiny new money."

Liquid was a sign of the times in more ways than one, representing the new regime of money and celebrity starting to take over clubland. The glitterati were co-opting underground dance music. Supermodels were dating DJs, who now were treated like superstars. The counterrevolutionary forces of elitism and posing, VIP rooms and VVIP rooms, were overwhelming the inclusive and idealistic democratic dance floor of the early '90s. Appearance and social standing were now more important than the music. The old golden rule of nightlife was being reasserted: It's not who you let in that counts but who you keep out. The fact that a socially ambitious Staten Island gangster was crucial in engineering this snobbish trend only made it more ironic.

Despite the bad feelings at the front door, the starry opening established the club—and the Paciello-Casares team—as gossip column staples. In the pages of newspapers and magazines, Liquid became known as Madonna's favorite nighttime habitat. "In the early days, Madonna helped carry Liquid a lot," said a grateful Paciello. "She's been very supportive of Ingrid and me."

Liza Minnelli dubbed the establishment "the Studio 54 of the '90s." Like the famous discotheque, Liquid had an extraordinary ability to attract boldface names on a regular basis. Soon, in the outdoor art deco cafes along Ocean Drive, the questions on the lips of any self-respecting club-goer were: "Have you been to Liquid, yet?" and "Who was there last night?"

Liquid's spectacular success also had something to do with good timing. Ian Schrager's ultrachic Delano Hotel—another shrine dedicated to hype, fame, and fashion—had opened the previous year, and Miami was in the midst of celebrity influx, with many big-name stars purchasing holiday homes there. Liquid attracted famous people in droves, which attracted tourists in even bigger droves, who shopped at the stores, ate at the restaurants, and stayed in the hotels—all of which helped fuel Miami Beach's fleeting seasonal economy. Even after the celebrity sheen started to wear off, Liquid continued to pack in the locals with a stellar cast of DJs that overshadowed all the other musical gatherings on the Beach.

By early January 1996, Paciello was still buzzing from the fabulous launch of Liquid. But his propensity for violence was once again getting the better of him. According to the statement that Michael Caruso gave to the DEA after he was arrested in 1997, Paciello decided to fly back to New York, where he allegedly murdered Limelight drug dealer Billy "Ilber" Balanca in a dispute over a narcotics deal gone sour. Balanca, his big-boned body caked in ice, was found stabbed to death in the trunk of a tan four-door Oldsmobile on Johnson Street, a deserted, weed-strewn cul-de-sac, not far from the Balanca family's Staten Island home. When he was questioned about Balanca's murder, Caruso blamed Paciello for the homicide, saying Paciello had Balanca "whacked" in a dispute over fifty pounds of marijuana. According to Caruso, Paciello had vouched for the large pot consignment, which Balanca failed to make good on. Caruso told the DEA agents that Paciello killed Balanca "to protect his name."

In the wake of the murder, which is still officially unsolved, Caruso and his right-hand man, Robert Gordon, were interviewed at Peter Gatien's Tunnel by Staten Island detectives investigating the case.

Paciello was phoned in Miami, but after initially offering to help the detectives with the murder probe, he cut off all contact. At the time, the persistent rumor on the street was that Lord Michael had Balanca eliminated. Caruso adamantly denied that he had anything to do with Balanca's brutal death; in fact, Balanca peddled drugs for Caruso at Gatien's club and participated in at least two robberies with Lord Michael.

When Paciello was later confronted about Caruso's story, he claimed never to have heard of Billy Balanca. "I'm dumbfounded," said an indignant Paciello. "Caruso is either lying or as delusional as an informant as I knew him to be as a promoter. After he's admitted to being a liar, a drug dealer, a thief, and an all-round lowlife, it shocks me that I have to defend myself against his ridiculous allegations."

7

HOMETOWN OUTCAST

New York, 1995

By the time the *Village Voice* published the story about Special K in that summer of 1995, Michael Alig was no longer playing at being sordid and perverse. He and the club kids really had become sordid and perverse. The scene had grown sullen and sour, the crowd a lot rougher and druggier. Alig had always preferred illusion to reality, but his penchant for artificiality and his love of eccentricity had degenerated into a taste for filthy and disgusting highs. His entourage seemed like a desperate throng determined to squeeze the last drop of pleasure from life, even unto death itself. As Alig said, "It's hip to be a mess."

The club kids now clothed themselves according to the principle of loathsomeness. They painted bruises on their arms and hollow shadows under their eyes to cover the real bruises and real hollow shadows. Large metal screws distended their lower lips. They adorned their faces with scabs and plastic flies, as if emulating the look of extras from *Night of the Living Dead*. Lost souls—creatures made up of pure motorized instinct—walked the dance floor. Club culture's utopian project had been turned upside down and inside out, as world-weariness came to rule the scene. What was once joyous now seemed frantic and robotic. Partygoers took a perverse enjoyment in horrible drug trips. Journeys to the emergency room were common, as stomach pumps became the new fashion accessory. Even the music the DJs played sounded unhinged and menacing, a sonic forced-march into madness. Constantly upping the weirdness factor was a full-time job for Alig. This ardent despoiler of youth had to keep outdoing himself, staging sicker and sicker specta-cles, to satisfy his followers.

When Peter Gatien was asked about what was going on at Disco 2000—wasn't he worried that the authorities would crack down?—he responded, "If someone wants to masturbate in one of my clubs, there's nothing much I can do about it," and shrugged. But what about the open drug use? Clearly, here was a world ready to self-destruct in a spectacular manner. Gatien thought for a minute, while he carefully selected his words, and then replied, "I worry all the time that Michael is going to go too far and do something that will put me out of business."

Michael Alig grew up on the outskirts of South Bend, Indiana, in a Mid-western suburb of little interest for those not into beer, heterosexuality, and college football. Before he was born, his colorful German mother, Elke, had already picked out a name for him . . . Lisa. She'd also bought a bunch of pretty pink dresses in anticipation of the happy event. She was astonished when a fair-haired baby boy popped out. Elke had come to live in the States as a teenager after marrying a handsome American GI named John Alig. She'd arrived expecting a brave new Big Mac world but instead found a crushing conformity she soon grew to loathe. Born during World War II, while her father was at the front fighting the Tommies, Elke's early years were spent in Bremerhaven, a town near Hamburg that was regularly illuminated by RAF bombs. After a one-day honeymoon in Cincinnati, where she tasted her first McDonald's meal, the Aligs settled down to a quiet, orderly life in South Bend and had two children, the first son, David, in 1962, followed four years later, on April 29, 1966, by Michael.

"There was something different about Michael," recalled Elke. "He was more of a schmoozer than David. He was very 'Mommy, Mommy, love me, love me.' There was always an underlying sadness to him."

Alig was four when his parents divorced. His father left for Arizona, never to return. "It was like living with a pet rock," Elke explained the breakup. "We just couldn't get along. To this day, Michael still has abandonment issues with his father, which explains why Michael was outrageous later in life. He wanted John to pay attention to him. Michael never felt loved by his father."

Michael's father was a strict, by-the-book sort of guy, someone who worked hard at his job as a computer programmer and even harder to fit in with the prevailing Midwestern morés. Elke was the opposite. She was a bawdy and larger-than-life character, a part-time catalogue model, who enjoyed parading around like a minor Hollywood starlet in hot pants, blond wigs, and go-go boots, hardly the norm at the time in suburban Indiana.

"My mother's influence is fairly obvious," Alig said. "She's flamboyant and emotional and outrageous and exaggerated. While my father was a sharp American pencil, she's a colorful European crayon." At the age of five, Michael realized he was gay: "I thought God had put a girl's brain in my body and I was the only one he had done that to." At age seven at his mom's urging, he started to dress up in women's clothes. School chums noticed that when he went to the bathroom, he would sit down to pee like a girl. When not suffering from a sexual identity crisis, Michael chased deer and romped in the woods behind his home. He watched a lot of television. His favorite shows were *I Love Lucy* and the vampire series *Dark Shadows*. He was obsessed with Lego and would often build elaborate cities and amusement parks to which he would charge friends admittance. "Mama, I'm building you your dream house," he once told Elke. He eventually accumulated thousands of dollars worth of the little plastic bricks.

Michael was what one friend who knew him at the time called "a time-share child." He grew up half the time with Elke, and half the time in the next town over with his nanny, Clarabelle. Clarabelle was a sweet, kind, almost saintlike figure, an older woman who also looked after Michael's brother, David. She and her husband, Earl, had no children of their own so they adopted Michael as their own. "Clarabelle was more of a mother than his real mother," said a source with intimate knowledge of the Aligs' circumstances back then. The family acquaintance continued, "Elke had an apartment with this tacky, gaudy furniture—sort of French provincial knockoff meets Italian Renaissance, mixed with this weird German aesthetic. It was like a museum dedicated to bad taste. She contained Michael in a very small area and had plastic coverings on all the furniture. He had his own room, but there were all kinds of rules about what he could and couldn't do in it. He couldn't have friends over, for instance. Or he had to have his clothes folded in a certain way. His mother kept a very tight lid on him. Basically, Elke didn't want Michael in the house."

Faggot was the first word that Ron Alan—who, in later life, would become Peter Gatien's publicist—ever uttered to Michael Alig, an off-and-on friend for two decades. Alan was twelve at the time, Alig thirteen. The two bumped into each other on a narrow stretch of sidewalk in front of the Topsfield Condominiums, the hillside apartment complex where they both lived. Alan (born Ron Alan Koch) was riding what he thought was a macho Huffy dirt bike, while Alig was peddling along on some girlie, Pee-wee Herman–style conveyance.

Alan had seen the gangly Alig, his arms flapping loose-limbed in the breeze, skipping around the tree-lined complex. Alan came from a rough and ready rural background. His family—all their belongings piled in the back of a pickup truck—had only recently made the move to suburban civilization. In the world he grew up in, "faggot" and "nigger" were used as punctuation points.

After hurling the slur, Alan was extremely surprised when Alig replied by cocking his fist and plowing it into Alan's chest, sending him flying off his most masculine bike and onto a grassy hummock. It was only when lying on the ground that Alan noticed that Alig, despite his puffy pageboy haircut and tight Jordache jeans, was well built for his age, with a husky torso. After their initial encounter, the duo became inseparable bosom pals, as Alan became increasingly fascinated with Alig's sense of style. "After that, I never called him a fag again. If it wasn't for Michael's influence, I would have stayed a redneck," said a grateful Alan.

Alig initiated Alan into the mercenary realm of the future club king's twisted imagination. "We instantly bonded around the notion of being bad," recollected Alan. "He brought me into this weird world of pranks, of playing gags on people around the apartment building and stealing quarters from the laundry room machines. He was conniving even back then." Some of the pranks they got up to were relatively innocent. They'd randomly call people on the phone and tell them they'd won a million dollars in a sweepstakes, just to chortle at their reaction. They'd break into the abandoned Studebaker car factory in South Bend's once bustling downtown area and end up being chased by the cops. They'd shoplift small items from drugstores or go out in the middle of the night and steal flowers from neighbors' gardens. One time, they came across a freshly planted lawn, rolled it up like a carpet, and carried it on their shoulders back to Topsfield. Elke woke up the next morning and found her back garden had brand-new turf, trimmed with boxes of multicolored flowers, as if they had been magically planted by elves overnight.

During his time at Grissom Middle School, Alig was known as "the Candy Man." The headmaster banned sweets as bad for the students' health. Alig saw an opportunity to earn some extra loot. He and Alan would go to the drugstore and buy big boxes of dime candy and then smuggle them into the school. In between classes, he and Alan peddled the contraband out of Alig's locker to sugar-addicted schoolmates at a 400 percent markup, until the headmaster found out and shuttered Alig's concession stand.

"Michael had all kind of scams going," Alan related. "He was like this weird, gay version of Michael J. Fox on *Family Ties*. All he cared about was making money and mischief. The thing about Michael, he had more balls than any straight person I ever met."

But Alig and Alan eventually graduated from minor misdemeanors to more serious offenses like breaking and entering, after Alig stole the master key to the apartment complex. He and Alan would case out the different apartments, figure out who lived where, and track their comings and goings. When they left, the pair would break in—not to steal anything—but to rummage through people's possessions or move around their furniture, so when they came home they would freak out. Michael called it "intellectual burglary."

Over time, that game developed into real burglary, as they started stealing property. "We wouldn't take too much stuff, because we wanted to come back," said Alan. "It was all about the thrill; it was all for the kick." On one occasion, a resident came home while they were still in his apartment. The chain was on the door, so he couldn't get in to his own residence. With the neighbor yelling outside, they had to make a quick exit, and jumped off the first floor balcony. Alig always loved narrow escapes.

A deep Teutonic darkness haunted Michael Alig's teenage years. Mood swings—manic highs followed by crippling lows—paralyzed him for long periods of time. A psychiatrist diagnosed him as bipolar manic-depressive. On the German side of the family, suicide and clinical depression were ancestral heirlooms handed down from one generation to the next. His mother, Elke, had an obsessive-compulsive disorder and also suffered from recurring bouts of sadness. There was a family history of manic schizophrenia. A number of close relatives had committed suicide. (Alig later claimed that when he took Ecstasy in the late '80s, "It made me feel normal for the first time in my life.")

At sixteen, Alig fell in love with a young man in high school named Jeff. Jeff's father found them holding hands on the family sofa and warned his son to stay away from Alig. The next day in school, Jeff acted like Alig was air—he wouldn't speak to him or even acknowledge his presence. "Michael still relives that painful moment to this day," claimed his mother.

Alig's mental health didn't improve when he entered Penn High, a vast redbrick complex with a football stadium in the rear that played host to the Penn Kingsmen, a nationally renowned high school football team. Penn was jock central, one of those suburban gulags for social norming that passes for a secondary-education institution in this country.

Even though his report cards were immaculate, dripping with A's and A pluses, Michael hated Penn with a vengeance. It didn't help matters that his brother was a track star there, while he was the resident poofter. America's teenage heartland did not exactly welcome this gifted but sensitive child to its bosom. The nerdy eccentric with an eye for women's clothing was picked on without mercy throughout his mostly hellish years at Penn. Strapping he-men preyed on the effeminate she-boy. Alig was so ashamed of his sexuality, he didn't report the assaults to his teachers. Many days, Alig would return home in tears, his shirt torn, his nose bloody. Instead of slitting his wrists or shooting up the school cafeteria, Alig retreated into a fashion fantasy world of his own creation, taking along a small social circle of fag-hags, pretty girls, and stylish straight boys, whom he gathered around him as protection from the bullies and queer-bashers that patrolled the hallways—much like he would later do on a more extravagant, better-funded scale at the Limelight.

"That school was the worst, when it came to being gay," complained Elke. "If you looked or were different, you stuck out, and you were immediately labeled. He was surrounded by good-looking women. He smelt nice. He wore European cologne. The jocks were jealous of him. 'How dare this little pansy surround himself with beautiful women?' So they beat him up."

Despite the inner turmoil, Alig could still manage to be a bright, dynamic, and attitudinal fireball. He wrote a gossip column for the high school newspaper in which he demonstrated a precocious interest in fashion, fake celebrity, and media mockery—all themes that would later show up at Disco 2000. According to friends who knew him at the time, Alig was ironic before ironic was fashionable. He devoured *Interview* magazine every month. He was a heat-seeking trend missile ready to explode in a puff of glittery confetti. "He had a Warholian air even back then," said Ron Alan. "He stood out from the crowd."

Alig was always the first in school to debut new styles. He adopted the floppy-fringe/skinny-tie new wave look long before anyone else in South Bend did. Fashion came naturally to him. He loved MTV and listened to Devo and Blondie. He worked part-time in a high-end men's clothing store called New Horizons and made frequent shopping trips on the South Shore train to Chicago to buy the latest fashions. He would take in the seams of his jeans, so they fitted tighter, the way women wore them. For his prom, he had a pretty girl on his arm and wore a brown Pierre Cardin suit with matching shoes, a narrow leather tie with a button-down shirt. It was all a lie to please his mother.

The sartorial transformation that would eventually become the club-kid look began in 1983, when Alig attended a late-night showing of *The Rocky Horror Picture Show* in downtown South Bend. He came back the next week, this time dressed for the occasion, wearing pajamas and an upturned flowerpot on his head, an outfit that presaged the off-the-wall kiddie look he adopted once he got to New York.

After graduating from high school in the top 8 percent of his class in 1984, Alig headed straight to New York City, determined to find his inner freak and live out the capricious lifestyle he'd already constructed in his head. The hometown social outcast saw New York as his refuge from midwestern disapproval. His mother remembered, "Michael couldn't wait to get out of the Midwest because people were so mean about him being gay." He rented an apartment in the Bronx and enrolled in Fordham University, where he briefly studied architecture. Almost immediately, Alig knew he had made a big mistake. Fordham was a Jesuit college with a Catholic faculty. Many of the students were from the heartland. It was like Penn High School all over again. He'd exchanged one conservative environment for another. Alig felt even more wretched when a priest called him into his book-lined study and warned that his chosen lifestyle was endangering his immortal soul. Afterward, shaken by the encounter, Alig tried unsuccessfully to commit suicide by taking too many antidepressants.

Alig did befriend one of the few unusual-looking students on campus. His name was Jacob, and he was Keith Haring's boyfriend. Many a night, Haring—who had been a busboy at the downtown club Danceteria before he became a famous artist—would come over to the dormitory, and Alig would discuss art and nightlife with him. Alig accompanied Jacob (not his real name), whose body was painted head to toe with Haring squiggles, to downtown's then-hippest hot spot, Area. Even though the established trendies looked down their noses at the gauche newcomer from Nowheresville, Alig was hooked. He briefly switched from Fordham to the trendier Fashion Institute of Technology. But his insatiable thirst for glamour was such that he blew off schoolwork with abandon. "At nighttime, there was no way I could write a paper knowing that Andy Warhol and Boy George were partying at Dance-teria," Alig once told *E! Television.*

To Alig, the world only really came alive after dark. He was a firm believer in the notion that the night aroused the body and inspired the head in a way that sunshine never could. He lived for the nighttime, longing for the artificial colors of the dance club. Alig always felt most vibrant when much of the rest of the world was wrapped in sleep and darkness.

After one semester at F.I.T., Michael dropped out to work part-time in an East Village clothes store called Flip. He next finagled a dream job—sweeping the floors at Keith Haring's old haunt, Danceteria, which was on its last legs. He had stormed into club director Rudolph's office and refused to leave until he was given gainful employment. He was eighteen, not even old enough to be in the place. He earned $120 a week and would often bus tables wearing nothing but his white BVD's.

Rudolph was the longhaired provocateur who then ruled the local nightlife scene with a mixture of ice-cold financial calculation (he had a Ph.D. in economics from the Free University in Berlin) and Old World European arrogance (his father was a diplomat). Older trendies sneered at Alig, this annoying creepy-crawly who kept pestering Rudolph five times a day about how much he wanted to throw fabulous parties, even though he'd never staged an event in his life. But the cultured and patrician Rudolph took a shine to the energetic upstart. "Even back then, he had an interesting and creative personality," Rudolph declared. "He was a troublemaker, a rabble-rouser, someone who had the potential to lead others. I liked that about him." Though he admired Alig's enthusiasm, Rudolph thought the concepts he pitched were childish and stupid. "He came up with these zany and retarded ideas like a popcorn party or a lollipop party," Rudolph remembered. "I told him to forget about it." But after much badgering, Rudolph finally relented and let Alig throw his coming-out ball—the Filthy Mouth Contest. People from the audience were invited up on stage to see who could come up with the dirtiest dialogue. "It wasn't the rousing success Michael thought it was, but it wasn't a complete fiasco either," recollected Rudolph.

Alig worked incredibly hard at attracting punters to his bashes.

Rudolph recognized that promoting was in Alig's blood and became the boy's mentor and substitute father figure—a position later occupied by Peter Gatien. Alig spent the day making phone calls in the Danceteria office, while at night he crisscrossed the town, handing out invitations, befriending anybody who looked *interesting* or *different*. Beaming and ridiculous in his gregariousness, he made friends easily. He zeroed in on an underage crowd: fashion-forward and sexually confused kids fresh off the bus from Port Authority, specimens still young enough to be molded to Alig's warped design. Soon enough, Alig had gathered around him a core group of misfits who were christened the "club kids" by *New York* magazine.

"I was the one freak in school," Alig told *Details* magazine. "When I came to New York, I realized there are so many of us and we need to band together in terms of identity awareness. For the first time ever, I felt a sense of belonging to a group."

The original club-kid look first came to fruition at a club called Red Zone on Fifty-fourth Street. Making fun of contemporary commodity fetishism, Alig's clan dressed up like pure pop products. Hats made out of Oreo boxes, dresses made out of Tide detergent containers, shirts made of Saran Wrap, and Fruit Loops earrings were among the bright, pop art–influenced fashions Alig and his cohorts modeled. Said Alig, "It was a reaction to the stale scene at Nell's [the deluxe retro-lounge on Fourteenth Street owned by *The Rocky Horror Picture Show*'s Nell Campbell], with everybody sitting around in Armani suits, sipping cocktails, and pretending to be oh-so-grown-up and sophisticated. It was meant as a satire of celebrity and soulless consumerism. We were walking Andy Warhols."

The second club-kid look—formulated in the basement of the Tunnel when Rudolph ran the place—was the one that became famous: club kids dressed up like babies. They wore diapers and romper suits. They suckled on pacifiers and sported baby bonnets and pigtails. They carried lunch boxes with pictures of Donny Osmond and David Cassidy on them, and smothered their cheeks with enough makeup to bake a cake. They quickly gained a reputation as wild and madcap eccentrics.

One of the original club kids, Kenny Kenny, said, "Whether you're wearing a baby-doll dress or a pinstripe suit, we're all influenced by our childhood. With Michael, it was just more out in the open than with other people."

When they appeared, the club kids seemed emblematic of a general trend in American society, as young people extended their adolescence into their twenties. Their refusal to act like grown-ups—their asexual aversion to the adult world—was at the heart of the club kids' appeal. And their pose turned out to be surprisingly influential. Any raver who has ever chewed on a baby's dummy or carried a teddy bear to a party, or any grown-up woman who has attended a rock show dressed like a ten-year-old prostitute, owes a sartorial debt to Alig's pioneering sense of puerile chic. "Little children have the right idea," Alig reasoned about this utopian world he was tying to create, where play and child-like creativity were celebrated. "Little children are allowed—even encouraged—to lead a life of pleasure."

At the time he arrived in New York, Alig looked relatively normal. But he quickly developed an extreme habit of dress that was heavily influenced by Australian eccentric Leigh "Pakis From Outer Space" Bowery, the physically imposing performance artist, who later became one of painter Lucien Freud's favorite subjects. Some of the fashion ideas Alig stole from Bowery included the polka-dot face, the frilly knickers with the ass hanging out, the pajamas with the ass cut out, the light bulbs taped to the side of the head. "Michael made cheap copies of Leigh's clothes and did bad copies of Leigh's makeup," said Kenny Kenny, who used to work for Bowery. "It's pathetic to rip somebody off that obviously. But Leigh didn't mind. When he came over and saw the club kids for the first time, he thought it was genius."

When not hosting fashion shows in clubs, Alig staged impromptu "outlaw parties" in various public locations. The contradictory idea behind the outlaw party was the notion that the success of the event was judged by how quickly the cops arrived to break up the festivities. A bad outlaw party was one that went on unmolested by authorities.

Beforehand, Alig asked the permission of Vito Bruno, the king of the outlaw parties, who had popularized the concept of word-of-mouth events held in unusual spaces. He needed Vito's blessing to proceed. Bruno—who by then was more of a manager of musical acts than a party promoter—happily passed the torch.

The first party was held on an abandoned railway bridge overlooking the building that would later house the DEA. Unfortunately, the location was ill chosen. The bridge was hidden from public view, and no neighbor could see their antics to call the police. So one of the drag queens set fire to the trash that littered the tracks, and, sure enough, firemen showed up with the cops. For another party, Alig and his merry band of pranksters set up detour signs on the Williamsburg Bridge and handed out cocktails to astonished motorists, triggering a giant traffic jam. An army of cops on horseback and in riot gear busted the event.

To celebrate Disco 2000 mascot Clara the Chicken's birthday, Alig's crew took over the Union Square subway station. Dressed in leopard-print frocks, vinyl hot pants, and feather boas, Alig and hundreds of others boogied on the platform. Rudolph brought Jessica Hahn—the Monica Lewinsky of her day—to the party. She was appalled at what she saw and left in a huff. Eventually, the police surrounded the station, while club kids made their escape by jumping onto the tracks and running into the tunnels, causing trains to stop in all directions.

Once, at a Burger King in Times Square, Alig arrived wearing silver lederhosen with his limp penis hanging out the front, walked up to the counter, and ordered a hundred Whoppers. On cue, Alig's colorful menagerie invaded and trashed the place, drinking vodka from plastic cups, dancing on the tables, ripping toilets from the walls, and pelting each other with burgers, before security guards finally evicted them. Rudolph had made the mistake of giving the manager his credit card, so the club kingpin ended up paying for all the property damage.

But probably the most notorious of Alig's outlaw events took place in the back of a moving eighteen-wheel big rig outfitted with a sound system, a bar, and a disco ball. "Rudolph and Michael Alig dare you to ride the Disco Truck," read the invitation for what would become a nightmarish journey around lower Manhattan. Two hundred partygoers climbed into the back, and, as they soon discovered, the truck had little in the way of suspension. As a consequence, the disco ball fell and smashed. Then the sound system toppled over. There was precious little air, so people started to faint, while others began to cry. Partygoers pounded on the wall of the truck, begging to be let out, but the coked-up driver in the front failed to hear their cries for help.

The club kids' fame was further spread, this time on a national scale, when Alig was featured in *People, Time, Newsweek*, and *The New York Times*. He and his followers made numerous and much-talked-about appearances on daytime talk shows, shocking Middle America with their outrageous antics. Every time he showed up on the *Geraldo Show*, Alig would be inundated with letters from teenagers in the hinterland wanting to move to Manhattan and become one of his devotees. Soon, every medium-sized city in America boasted a club-kid scene based directly on these lifestyle propaganda spots that aired nationally on afternoon TV. Young outsiders from all over the country flocked to New York to become part of the club-kid phenomenon. They often stayed at Hotel 17, a warren of bleak, claustrophobic cell-like rooms, one step above a flophouse.

"The first time I realized how famous the club kids had become was at my birthday party at the Tunnel," Alig's mother Elke told the *Daily News*. "Five limos came to pick us up. A doorman with white gloves held an umbrella for me."

In the beginning, the club kids didn't mean any harm. At first, it was all comparatively innocent: They were just naughty children playing in the street, one big happy family, where the outcasts of Middle America found acceptance and self-esteem. But over time, the stories about Alig's antics started to take on an increasingly desperate and destructive edge. Alig stole a city bus from a garage to stage an event. Alig flooded the basement of the Tunnel for a pool party. Alig put an ad in the local newspaper urging kids to steal their parents' money and underwear, and then send the stolen property to him. Apparently, several of them did. Alig took a twelve-year-old runaway he picked up at Port Authority, dressed him up in drag to look like Brooke Shields, and then sold his tender behind in a West Village hustler bar. Alig strapped another runaway to a metal Catherine wheel at the Limelight and whipped him raw. Things were starting to get unpleasant.

8

THE DEVIL IN MICHAEL ALIG

New York City, March 17, 1996

On a gray Sunday morning, the urban landscape dingy and blurred, Michael Alig's personal drug supplier and sometime roommate, Angel Melendez, had gone to the luxury skyscraper where Alig lived, looking to collect a sum of money he was owed. Patches of dirty ice left over from the unusually harsh winter still encrusted the sidewalk as he tried to navigate the slippery conditions in his platform shoes. Walking through the redbrick courtyard of Riverbank West, past the feeble attempt at a fountain, and into the echoing lobby of the forty-story building, Angel was immediately recognized by the doormen as a frequent guest at Alig's place, and he was allowed upstairs.

A few nights before, Angel—the winged man who sold me Special K for my article in the *Village Voice*—had been sitting in the Limelight's VIP room, when Peter Gatien spotted the eye-catching drug dealer. Gatien was feeling the heat from the ongoing DEA investigation and, without a beat, ordered his bouncers to eject Angel. Angel had a spitfire temper: He'd once punched a photographer for taking his picture without permission at downtown's annual Wigstock drag festival. Angel didn't take crap from anybody. He was not going to move for Gatien. So the bouncers picked up the feisty dealer and carried him out headfirst.

"Fuck you, get your hands off me, motherfuckers," protested Angel, as he was being forcibly evicted.

In the ensuing struggle, security men broke Angel's beloved wings. "It was a real scene," said one eyewitness.

Livid, energized, Angel once again threatened to go speak to "his friend at the *Voice*"—the clear implication being he was going to dish the dirt about the dope trade at the Limelight to me, even though I barely knew the guy. How dare that one-eyed crook and his bitch wife throw him out, after all the customers he'd brought into the club? He had a following—where Angel went, so did his junkie fans. Screw Peter Gatien.

When he arrived at Riverbank West, still smarting from the snub, Angel found Alig and his sidekick Freeze (Robert Riggs) deep in the middle of a drug binge. "I want my fuckin' money or else," Angel started to rage.

Angel wanted to be paid in full, not just for drugs and money stolen but also for the indignities he'd suffered at the hands of Alig. An avenging Angel was a scary sight to behold. Stubborn and hardheaded, unlike many of the other club kids, he was no nerd you could push over with an index finger. He would walk without fear through Harlem at midnight wearing some outrageous outfit, $10,000 in cash stuffed in his pockets. As a former pier queen (part of the rough crowd of flamboyant young gays, often homeless, who hung around the West Village piers before they were demolished), Angel knew the streets, and he knew how to take care of himself. He also knew when he was being exploited.

For some reason, Angel occasionally kept his bank at Alig's pad for safekeeping. This was a huge miscalculation. Alig felt no compunction whatsoever about digging into his friend's cash and chemicals at will. As Alig saw it, this was his due for being so famous. Previously, after Angel found $2,000 missing from his stash, he had thrown a shot glass at Alig's head and warned him never to steal from him again. Now more money was missing and a sizable quantity of drugs as well.

Angel was sick of the whole club-kid scene. He was tired of being Alig's doormat. The time had come to ditch the wings and move on to something else, something better. Five years ago, when he had fallen under Alig's spell, Angel imagined that through their friendship he would be admitted to an enchanted world of glamour and celebrity. He thought that joining the club kids was a stepping-stone to fame and fortune. But the magic was wearing wafer thin. Alig's mischief was eating into his profit margin, and the money was Angel's lifeline out of this fruitless, dead-end existence.

"Angel wanted a better life," his friend Screamin' Rachael recalled. "He really wanted out of the whole club-kid thing. He was sick of selling drugs. He asked me to find him a job at a record company. He wanted to become a house music singer."

In Angel's eyes, Alig was no longer the fabulous figure of legend, but a "get-over queen," a phony messiah, a pathetic junkie parasite who, because he had no part of his own left to sell, took delight in mortgaging the souls of his followers. Since Angel didn't do drugs personally, it was not fun watching these sad specimens wasting their lives away, craving and scheming their way to their next high. Unlike Michael Alig, Angel was a no-nonsense businessman.

Now, a furious Angel wanted money for all the drugs Alig had snorted and injected, for all the people he had brought to the club, and, yes, the money Peter Gatien supposedly owed him for the chemicals Angel had supplied for the clubowner's hotel sex orgies—a sum of some $1,400 according to Alig, an insignificant amount when you consider all the trouble that would ensue from trying to collect this debt.

Alig countered that it was he who was owed money for rent, since Angel frequently bunked at Alig's place. And, anyway, big deal, he owed half of downtown money for drugs. Only the peasants paid for their pleasures, not Michael Alig, king of the club kids. This only made Angel angrier. Alig tried to calm him down. He offered to go the Limelight later and get some money from Gatien, which seemed to mollify Angel, if only for a while, and everybody decided to chill out by taking a so-called "disco nap" (a short sleep) in preparation for the night.

A short time after he fell asleep, Freeze was awakened by the sound of raised voices coming through the wall. "Help me! Get him off of me!" he heard Alig cry. He rushed into the living room, where he found

Angel violently shaking Alig as he furiously berated him, "You better get my money or I'll break your fuckin' neck."

Freeze immediately interjected, "Why are you yelling at Michael? If it wasn't for Michael, Peter wouldn't give you the time of day."

Angel angrily warned Freeze, "Stay out of this!"

Instead of choosing to calm the situation, Freeze further enflamed Angel when he added, "And nobody likes you anyway. You and your outfits are tacky. You're lucky Michael lets you come to the club, the way you dress."

These catty comments incensed Angel, and he turned to Michael. "Are you going to let him talk to me like that?" he spat in his face. Freeze looked at Alig and made a disdainful expression as if to suggest that Angel meant nothing to either of them. Angel now shifted the target of his anger to Freeze and lunged at him. All three men became embroiled in a tangle of thrashing limbs. Alig was pushed backward through a glass curio cabinet. A long shard of glass pierced his shoulder through to the other side. Alig screamed in pain and pleaded with Freeze, "Get the glass out of me." Then Angel fell on top of Alig and locked his teeth into his chest. The club-kid king screamed in even more pain and tried to push Angel off him. All the time, Freeze was tugging at Angel's shoulders, beseeching him to let Michael go. At least in the early stages of the drama, the only blood being shed was Alig's, as forensic reports would later confirm.

By this time, Freeze was convinced his beloved leader's life was in danger. In the chaos of the moment, Angel seemed possessed by a fury Freeze had never seen before. No matter how hard Freeze shrieked at Angel to release Michael, he wouldn't let him go. As it happened, the apartment was in the middle of a renovation. Workmen were putting in new skirting boards. A hammer lay nearby. Freeze picked up the tool, intending to hit Angel in the back of the head with just enough force to make him release his friend. The blow barely broke the skin. Angel's hand flailed behind his back trying to grab the implement, as Alig continued to yell in agony. The second whack was much harder. Angel's legs buckled, but he still wouldn't release his jaw from Alig's chest. For the third blow, adrenaline prevailed over all the other chemicals sloshing around Freeze's system, as he plowed the hammer into Angel's skull with all the strength he could muster. Angel moaned briefly, before falling to the floor and lapsing into unconsciousness.

The blunt-force trauma and subsequent skull fractures didn't cause Angel to die. He was still alive when a battered Alig—scarlet with rage, blood dripping from his torn shirt, his mouth spewing hateful invectives—pounced on the prostrate body, climbed on the victim's chest, and began to strangle Angel with his bare hands, before grabbing a red sweatshirt with which he smothered Angel's mouth and nostrils, while all the time Freeze was pleading, "Michael, don't do that, are you crazy, you'll kill him." After a struggle, Freeze managed to tear Alig away from Angel's body. "I was trying to prevent Angel from biting me anymore," Alig would later claim in his own defense.

A brief instant of relative calm ensued, as pulse rates plummeted for a while. At this point, Freeze and Alig thought Angel was merely unconscious. So they did what they always did when Angel was asleep. They stole small amounts of drugs from each of his vials, so when he woke up he wouldn't notice the shortfall. Drug time passed, and as the latest set of chemicals started to wear off, the realization emerged that something was seriously wrong with Angel. He hadn't moved in hours. Freeze checked his pulse and put a silver spoon to his mouth. No mist appeared. "He's not breathing," cried Freeze. The crazy mix of panic and adrenaline returned. Quickly they undressed Angel down to his white Fruit-of-the-Loom underwear and dragged him into the bathroom, where they put him in a tub of cold water and covered his body with ice cubes, hoping to revive him. They deliberately submerged his head to see if any bubbles would surface. None did.

Freeze rushed next door to retrieve a medical book. When he came back, Freeze was met by a shocking sight: Alig was sitting on the side of the bathtub, pouring chemical cleaner down Angel's throat. "What the fuck are you doing? Are you insane?" hollered Freeze.

An exasperated Alig clarified the dire situation with impeccable junkie logic: "He's been dead for hours. I'm trying to embalm the body. Help me here." Alig instructed Freeze to go to the closet to get some duct tape, and together they wrapped shut Angel's mouth.

Alig's first phone call following the killing was to father figure Peter Gatien. Gatien paid the rent—$2,400 a month—on Alig's apartment, knowing full well that if he gave him the money directly, Alig would squander it on getting high. Gatien's name was on the lease, as it was on Lord Michael's place, where Damon Burett had supposedly committed suicide. Before he moved into Riverbank West, the club owner had warned Alig, "I don't want any dead bodies in the apartment. One more stiff and I'll lose my liquor license." Gatien was nervous. He'd heard stories about junkies fatally OD'ing at Freeze's pad. Gatien had said to Alig, "If someone dies and I go out of business, you're going to have to go door to door to explain to 900 employees why they don't have jobs anymore."

Alessandra answered the phone. Alig blurted out, "There's a dead body in my apartment. How do I get rid of it?" Alex was appalled. She refused point-blank to put Michael through to her husband. "There's nothing we can do for you," Alex said. And then she hung up. The Gatiens had their own set of problems, and the last thing they needed was a bloody trail leading to their front door.

Stumped about what to do next, Alig and Freeze decided to pay a visit to drag queen Olympia's house, where they discussed the possibility of paying somebody to get rid of the body. But who would accept such a grisly task? Unable to come up with an answer, they took more drugs trying to erase the memory of the dead Angel. A day later, when they came back to the apartment, much to nobody's surprise, the corpse was still floating in the bathtub.

Alex Gatien had a special reason to block Michael Alig's access to her husband after Angel's brutal dispatch. She despised the club-kid king, blaming him for her husband's increasingly self-destructive hotel parties—the same dissolute affairs, held in the presidential suites of posh Manhattan hotels, that Angel supplied drugs to, the monies for which he was trying to collect when he went to Alig's apartment that fateful Sunday.

Long before he met Alig, Gatien had been going on marathon crack cocaine benders with harems of $1,000-a-night prostitutes for a decade. But after the club kid began attending the parties, they took on a crazier

edge. As a special favor, Alex had asked Alig to "wind them down."
Instead, Alig wound them up to even newer heights of debauchery.

"It's basically nude hookers playing charades," Alig told me. "Peter
is so stoned most of the time, he can't even get it up."

The mood was creepy at these lavish but squalid affairs. Containers
of Valium, buckets of champagne, and bottles of vodka stood on the
night tables. Tens of thousands of dollars worth of cocaine covered
every available surface. An atmosphere of joyless eroticism and Catholic
guilt permeated the proceedings. Lord Michael—who, like Angel, supplied drugs for the parties—was shocked at what he saw: his boss, nude
except for a sports coat, walking around holding a leash attached to an
equally naked woman, who was wearing a dog collar while crawling
around on all fours.

After a couple of days of watching porno movies, cavorting with the
call girls, playing scrabble in the nude, and freebasing incredible quantities of rock cocaine, Gatien would start to become paranoid. Though
Alig would try to calm him down, the club owner would get into a terrible state. Muffled sounds in the hallway spooked him. He halluci-
nated aliens coming in through the penthouse windows. He hid behind
the curtains and imagined enemies out to do him no good. Eventually,
the party would end when the hotel management kicked Gatien out for
wandering around the hallways naked or when Alessandra turned up
screaming blue murder.

Alig, who himself suffered a heart attack at a hotel party and had had
to be carried out on a stretcher, recalled one tumultuous night: "Alex
burst into the room and told everybody, 'The show's over. Move out,
kids. Peter, get your stuff; we're leaving.' Peter was as high as a kite. His
speech was slurred. 'I've got something to tell you,' he told Alex. 'I'm
marrying Jenny [teenage club kid and fashion model Jennytalia, who was
Gatien's mistress], and I want you out of the house in two weeks.' Jenny
was young enough to be his daughter. In fact, she and Jennifer Gatien
used to play with dolls together in the sandbox as kids. Peter was not
normally a violent man, but under the influence of the cocaine he could
be. He lunged at Alex, picked her up, and slammed her against the wall.
That was the last, and only, time I ever felt sorry for Alex."

Initially, Alessandra put up with the parties as a form of release for her new husband. She would sometimes book the hotel using an assumed name and attend the wild affairs herself, though she never sampled the illicit wares on offer. Instead she sat stone cold sober in an adjoining room, answering the door and signing for the lavish room service carts, laden down with lobsters, oysters, and caviar. Better to allow Peter to cut loose under her watchful eye and in a controlled environment, she reasoned, than running around the streets getting into trouble.

But Alex had become increasingly alarmed at the deleterious effect that this secretive partying was having on her husband. Now, she disapproved of the out-of-control nights and wanted them stopped. Gatien's heedless hedonism had put a strain on their so-called marriage.

"She could see her husband dying in front of her, and she didn't like it," said one of the paid escorts, who regularly attended the events. "She was very hurt by the whole thing, especially when Peter continued with the parties even while she was pregnant. She saw how destructive the whole thing had become."

What to do about the badly decaying body in the bathtub of his apartment was a pressing concern for Michael Alig in the week after he killed Angel. Sitting there, malodorous in his soiled underpants, his body still sore from the angry fight, Alig thought that not being able to take a shower was inconvenient. He hadn't washed his green hair in ages. But Alig, hardly the most hygienic person in the world, didn't really mind. He'd read somewhere that opiates are more intense when the user is dirty—something about the grime preventing the drug's evaporation through the skin. And Alig was in the middle of a mammoth heroin binge. He jabbed needle after needle into his wan and worn-out flesh and, as one piston after another fired, jolts of joy coursed through his veins, making him sigh like a schoolgirl.

Now the dense fumes of putrefying human fungus emanating from the bathroom—barricaded shut with a mattress—were becoming unbearable. He thought he might be overcome by the rotten odor at any time. Freeze had sprinkled several boxes of baking soda over the body, but that had done little to dampen the stink of mortality that lingered in Alig's nostrils, even after snorting a humongous line of Special K. He could still taste the revulsion in the back of his throat competing with the metal tang of the drugs. Damn it, Angel was spoiling his high. And not for the first time, either.

Alig was used to getting away with murder, at least in the metaphorical sense. He had long held the strong personal conviction that the rules governing the rest of society—like paying for your own drugs—did not apply to him. Sucking on a crack pipe, he would walk through the entrance of the swish building he lived in, and the doormen never said a word. He would pee on people's legs or hand them a glass of vomit, and they would congratulate him on his audacity. He thought of himself as a professional envelope pusher. His bizarre, reckless life was his art form. Alig was paid, and paid well, to be outrageous, to see how far and how fast he could drive things. He had so deepened the spiral of decadence that maybe the only thing left to do was actually kill someone.

Like Angel, Alig was no stranger to violence. You wouldn't have thought it to look at him, but despite his limp-wristed demeanor, if sufficiently riled, he could be quite dangerous. Once at a Baltimore club, a homophobic bouncer offended by Alig's appearance wouldn't let up with the insults: "faggot," "freak," and "cocksucker." In response, Alig took a bottle from behind the bar and brained his brawny tormentor.

But the present situation was far different. There weren't enough uppers, downers, and in-between-ers on the planet to blot out the magnitude of this current crime. Alig knew people were bound to say he'd gone too far this time, that taking a life was no minor matter. A threshold had been crossed. He had made the last stride. The truth about the club kids and their thrill seeking—that violence is inherent in carnival—had become grotesquely apparent.

Still, homicide did have its glamorous aspect, he thought. Imagine all the lurid headlines and column inches to come. What he had just done had all the makings of a bestseller and a box office hit. Books, movies, television shows, pop songs—where would pop culture be without death and carnage to titillate the public imagination? The mainstream, while pretending to deplore evil, secretly needs spectacular crimes, he told himself. He decided Angel's death was all society's fault. But deep in the crevices of his burned-out brain, even he realized this was a lame rationalization.

If Alig squeezed his eyes tight enough, though, he could conjure up an image of happier times: he and Angel sitting at the sewing machine like a couple of elderly women, together whipping up a glorious outfit from old curtains and bits of discarded fabric. In the brief moments of lucidity that pierced the narcotic fog, Alig wondered how the twisted creativity and inspired lunacy of the original club-kid scene had tipped over into outright evil. Drugs were the most obvious answer. Chemicals now owned every voracious fiber of his hungry being. In the twelve months before Angel's death, Michael Alig had gone on what a friend described as "a slow-motion suicide mission." His drug intake, for many years prodigious, had increased dramatically. Alig had overdosed on at least three occasions. A doctor told him he would die if he did any more drugs. Alig polluted his body to such an extent that he grew a hump on his back, which only a rigorous regime of antibiotics managed to cure. Engulfed in a blizzard of white dust, Alig was so screwed up most of the time that he was barely able to walk. But that didn't stop his cronies from propping him up—*Weekend at Bernie's*–style—inserting him into a taxi and taking him from club to club, so they could get in for free.

"In the beginning, Michael was very ambitious and very together," commented doorman Kenny Kenny. "He wanted to conquer the world. By the end, he seemed to wallow in that whole murky, 'drug-outsider' thing. Anybody who wasn't into that wasn't cool."

Alig's parties had pioneered new trends in polydrug use. The fuel that powered the extreme activities was a vast alphabet soup of chemicals: Ecstasy, Special K, MDA (not to be confused with MDMA), GHB, 2CB, LSD, cocaine, crystal methamphetamine, Rohypnol ("roofies"), even heroin, not normally regarded as a club drug, all washed down with lashings of alcohol and puffs of nicotine. Add in the anabolic steroids and AIDS medications some of the thrill-hungry night crawlers were also taking, and you had a volatile jumble of unpredictable chemical cross-reactions that turned many of the participants into dancing drugstores and burned-out zombies.

One evening at Disco 2000, I first heard the phrase "a Calvin Klein special," a reference to the popular mixture of cocaine and ketamine. Then there was Chanel No. 9—an expensive medley of high-quality cocaine, pure Ecstasy, and Special K that supposedly produced waves of euphoria that lasted for hours. At Disco 2000, I also found out about the ultimate downer—"a Special K-lude," a mixture of alcohol, GHB, and ketamine that taken in sufficient quantities could quite easily have stopped a healthy heart cold or induced a coma.

Drugs, of course, were hardly the whole picture. Even Alig must have realized that. After all, drugs only curb self-restraint and amplify what is already present. There are plenty of people who ingest huge amounts of illegal substances but would never consider what Alig was about to do.

Meanwhile, Alig had deputized Freeze, his ever-dutiful courtier, to go out to Macy's and purchase a set of kitchen utensils. "The bigger and sharper, the better," he told him. Freeze came back with two large chef knives and a meat cleaver. "There. That's all I'm going to do to help," he said, throwing the sharp implements down on the bed. Alig had informed Freeze that if he gave him ten bags of heroin, he would dismember the body. Freeze handed over the dope, and a sweating Alig snorted a couple of bags for courage, putting the rest aside for later. "I hate you for making me do this," he told Freeze. Numbed against the horror, Alig went into the bathroom and, with bile rising in his throat, hacked off Angel's legs. By now—over a week later—the body was ripe. The meat fell off the bone with surprising ease. Adding insult to grievous injury, as the autopsy report confirms, Alig also cut off Angel's genitals—a bizarre final insult to his fallen comrade.

Each severed leg was then deposited in a separate plastic bag. The bags were then put in a knapsack, which was carried to the nearby Hudson River. That was the easy part. Next they had to dispose of the rest of Angel's body. Covering his butchered torso with a bedsheet, they packed him into a cardboard box that once housed a Zenith color TV, pushed it out into the hallway, and humped it into the elevator. Freeze had enough presence of mind to cut off the box's UPS code beforehand. An unsuspecting doorman provided them with a trolley to take the package downstairs. A passenger in the elevator supposedly commented on the stink. With straight faces, Alig and Freeze told him that it was rotting garbage.

Wheeling the container through the marble lobby, out into the walled courtyard, the two men found a taxi waiting for a fare. The driver helped them put the box in the trunk and tied down the lid. They headed to a spot along the West Side Highway just adjacent to the Tunnel disco, waited for the taxi to drive away, and then dumped the box into the water. The body was in the box, and the box was in the river. End of story, or so they prayed. Freeze breathed a sigh of relief. If Alig kept his fat yap shut, they'd be in the clear. But the pair of rocket scientists failed to punch holes in the makeshift coffin. Angel didn't sink but instead floated away on the tide.

Several days after the killing of Angel Melendez but before he disposed of the corpse, a jittery Alig turned up at the Tunnel nightclub, where he approached Gatien lieutenant Steven Lewis in his upstairs office. The hour was late. No one else was around. Lewis was surprised to see Alig in his office. Once good friends, they'd had a falling out and no longer talked much anymore. Alig was banned from Lewis's workplace for stealing money and for once too often using the corner as a lavatory.

The club kid was a physical wreck. He looked like a reanimated corpse from one of those gory horror movies he so loved. His usual impish grin had been replaced by a somber expression. He constantly chewed on the inside of his mouth and was obviously worried about something.

"Do you know anybody who has a van?" Alig sheepishly asked Lewis.

"What do you need a van for? Why don't you just rent one?"

"I can't rent it. I need someone I can trust to help me carry stuff out of my apartment."

"Are you moving out of Riverbank West?"

"No. I've got a body in my bathtub and I have to get rid of it."

"Come again?"

"I killed Angel. I'm gonna chop him up and get rid of the body."

"You're delusional, Michael. Stop joking around. You don't need a van, you need psychiatric help."

"I'm not kidding, Angel's dead."

Lewis raised his eyebrows and aped a fake smile. The manager had long since failed to find any of Alig's sick pranks fabulous. He had advised Gatien to dump the club kids and go for a more mainstream, less druggy crowd. Alig and his cohorts were a gigantic pain in the ass. Why continue putting money into them, he reasoned. But there was something about the sober tone of Alig's voice that made him think that maybe this time the trickster was telling the truth.

Alig sat down and started counting out a big wad of bills on Lewis's desk. "That's a lot of money Michael, where did you get it?" asked a puzzled Lewis.

"Peter gave it to me," said Alig.

Lewis thought this rather strange. By now, Gatien had stopped giving Alig large sums of cash because he knew the club kid would immediately fritter it away on drugs. Finding Michael oddly more coherent than he'd been in months, Lewis took the opportunity for a heart-to-heart. Michael confessed how screwed up his life had become because of the drugs. He swore he was going to go into rehab. He talked about "getting my head right."

A month before the killing, Alig's mother, Elke, had tearfully begged Peter Gatien over the phone to send her son to a drug treatment center. "My poor little baby, he will die if someone doesn't do something," she pleaded. While in theory Gatien was all in favor of getting his prodigal executive director cleaned up, he didn't want to foot the bill for an expensive stay in a top clinic such as Hazledon. He was feeling the financial pinch from another Limelight closure. In addition, now that Gatien was under investigation by the DEA, Alig was no longer a lucrative lure but a serious liability. He told Elke, who was on government assistance, that she should pay for the treatment. "I'm not his parent," said the club owner.

Following his meeting with Alig, Lewis went to see Gatien. "Peter, you shouldn't give Michael that much money, he'll kill himself."

"What money? I didn't give it to him," replied Gatien.

"Where did he get it from then?" asked Lewis.

Lewis then broached the tricky topic of the murder rumor, but Gatien immediately shut down the discussion: "I don't want to hear anything about it. I don't want to talk about it."

By this point, Lewis wasn't certain that Alig had committed murder. But he half believed the story. If Alig had stolen money from Angel, they could have gotten into a fight. He concluded that though Alig couldn't have killed Angel on his own, with Freeze's assistance perhaps the pair really was capable of such an act. The district attorney's office, which was looking into Gatien's tax situation, had already approached Lewis, and Lewis was thinking of feeding the authorities confidential dirt about Gatien's finances, but this was the final straw. He vowed to quit the organization as soon as possible. "I had come to the realization that Michael probably did it," Lewis said. "I had no love for Angel. He was a lowlife. If I were on the door, I would never let him into the club. But he didn't deserve this."

Even before this latest atrocity, Gatien's empire was in a shambles. "Anybody who had a brain was looking for work elsewhere," claimed Lewis. Paranoia was in the air. Documents—receipts, invoices, budgets—were being grabbed from desks and shredded around the clock. Newly bought electronic wands were used to scan the office phones for law-enforcement bugs. "Any nightclub is ultimately a reflection of the person running it," said Lewis. "The Limelight was sloppy, confusing, chaotic because Gatien was. He created this environment in which horrible things happened."

Ron Alan, Gatien's baby-faced publicist, first heard the news when arriving at the Tunnel later that day. Lewis pulled him into his office. "Ron, I've got to tell you something," said a worried-looking Lewis. "The story out there is that Michael and Freeze murdered Angel and have his body on ice in the bathtub." Even given Lewis's tendency to embellish, this was an appalling revelation. Alan had a second to digest the news that his boyhood pal might be a killer, when Lewis hit him with another shock. "The reason I'm telling you this," he warned, "is that I want you to know there's a major cover-up about to go down. Freeze and Michael are going to Peter for help to try and get rid of the corpse."

Following his conversation with Lewis, Alan, his head still reeling, barged into his boss's office, making sure to shut the door behind him. "Is it true?"

"Is what true?" asked Gatien.

"Is it true?" Alan said again, this time with more emphasis.

Gatien visibly stiffened and then gave out a long sigh. He appeared shocked that Alan had found out so soon about the Alig mess. He stood and started pacing up and down the room. The club owner stopped for a moment, cocked his head back, and looked at Alan.

"I'll tell you what I know," Gatien finally said. Gatien then admitted that Alig had called the house looking for him but Alex, wanting to protect her husband, refused to put him through. Alig supposedly told Alex some fantastic story about killing Angel. He came to the club the next day, but they wouldn't let him in. Finally, he took Alig's call and told him to clear the drugs out of the apartment, hire an attorney, and then contact the police.

"OK, I'm your press agent. What do you expect me to do about this?" Alan said. "I need to know today what you intend to do, so I can make up my mind what I'm going to do. If you expect me to cover up a murder, you can forget about it. What exactly is the company policy when it comes to homicide, anyway?" added the angry publicist.

Gatien stiffened even more. He'd never seen the even-tempered Alan so furious. He was scared he was going to run to the cops. Gatien never completely trusted Alan, anyway. He was too much of a Boy Scout for Gatien's taste.

"What are we going to do?" Alan repeated.

Gatien replied that he didn't see it as his problem. He didn't kill Angel. He barely knew him. He was just another one of Michael Alig's drug dispensers.

"Don't you think we have an obligation to call the cops?" asked Alan.

"Well, anyone can call the police," Gatien retorted.

Alan was beyond flabbergasted at the depth of his boss's denial. Did he not see a clear moral duty here? He kept dodging the tough questions by giving ambiguous answers.

Finally, Gatien came up with a plan: "We're gonna claim it's got nothing to do with us because Michael is no longer working here. Michael's not an employee here; it's not our situation to deal with. End of story."

"But Michael *is* an employee here. Everybody knows that," countered Alan.

"Oh, yeah. When was the last time you saw Michael show up for work? Alex hasn't paid him in weeks. As far as we're concerned, he no longer works for us. That means he's somebody else's problem now." It was true that Alig had been turning up less and less frequently at the office, but this was the first time Alan heard that his former friend had been fired.

Gatien then claimed he had to take some calls: "Ron, I need a minute."

Alan went back to his office. Forty-five minutes later, he got an angry phone call. "What are you saying about me?" Though the caller didn't identify himself, Alan knew it was Alig. "The tone in his voice really put a chill through me," he remembered. "It was like Jason or Freddy Krueger was on the other end of the line."

"So why are you quitting, and what are you quitting about?" Alig demanded. "Peter says you're about to do something stupid." Alan realized that Gatien had told Alig about their meeting.

"Michael, all I want to know is, is it true?"

"Is what true?"

"Is this a joke or is this for real?" Part of Alan still wanted to believe this was some twisted prank. "Don't make me have to say it, you know what I'm talking about—the story about you and Freeze murdering Angel and keeping him in your bathtub."

Alig dropped the intimidation routine and immediately became flustered. He began to cackle nervously. "Oh, that silly rumor," Alig twittered, before calling to his cohort. "Freeze, you're not going to believe what Ron thinks. He thinks we killed Angel. You know better than that, Ron. I can't believe you really think I'm capable of something like that."

Alan had his answer. He had grown up with Alig and knew when he was telling lies. He had witnessed many of Alig's performances, and this was the worst. "It was then that I knew that he did it. Obviously,

Peter had lied to me. He was in close contact with Michael. I believe that Peter said to Michael something along the lines of your best friend is a loose cannon, he's threatening to go to the police, you better shut him up."

That Thursday night, after consulting with Alan, Steven Lewis went to a pay phone on the corner near his Murray Hill apartment. He called Midtown South and asked for homicide. He spoke to a detective and, without giving a name, related the tale as he had heard it. He emphasized that he believed the account to be honest and accurate.

"Michael was out-of-control," recalled Lewis. "The Limelight was a drug cesspool. And Peter kept disappearing on his hotel drug binges. The situation was chaotic. Somebody had to do something."

Then Lewis called a friend who lived in Alig's apartment building and asked him to keep a close eye on any activity in and around Alig's pad. On Sunday, two weeks after the brutal killing, detectives from Manhattan South turned up at Alig's apartment. The place was completely empty. Sometime between Thursday and Saturday, Alig's place had been cleaned from top to bottom. Not a bloodstain could be found. Unbeknownst to the detectives, Alig had moved temporarily to the Chelsea Hotel.

"It was a professional cover-up," said Lewis. "Alig had help from above. Given the state he was in, and given the bloody nature of the crime, it's inconceivable that Alig could have surgically removed all the clues from his own apartment without the help of coconspirators."

In the days after he killed Angel, Alig tried to play it off as a big joke, parading around the clubs in Angel's high-heeled boots. He refurnished his apartment with antique chairs financed by money stolen from Angel's belongings. He had friends over for high tea, even while the body was still in the apartment. He claimed it was all a hoax perpetuated by a jealous drag queen. He also stated that Angel had gone back to Colombia to see his family. But no, seriously, the real story was that Angel had just left and never came back. It was as simple as that, Scout's honor. Angel, he assured anyone who would listen, had just dropped off the face of the earth.

Bizarre rumors multiplied. Alig and Freeze had sacrificed Angel as part of some satanic ritual. They disemboweled Angel and ate his genitals. Another version had them chowing down on his liver. If Angel was dead, then where was the body, challenged Alig, knowing the answer to his own question. A joke did the rounds referring to Freeze's pre-junkie life as a milliner whose creations appeared in high-end stores such as Barney's. "Why did Freeze hit Angel in the head with a hammer? Because the hat wouldn't fucking fit." Then a story swept clubland that Melendez was alive and well in New Jersey and Michael was planning a "Welcome Back, Angel" party for him next month.

The rumor mill was spinning out of control and the evil little publicist in Alig's head was working overtime. He knew that he had to do something about this messy situation and right away. Angel's disappearance was proving more difficult to explain than he had first thought. The other club kids noticed Angel's absence. People were asking uncomfortable questions.

Alig hit upon a new strategy: "We conspired together to tell the truth, but in a way nobody would believe us," he later said. He claimed Angel's hand was in a freezer on Staten Island. "Do you know the difference between me and a murderer? I haven't been caught," he joked with comrades. "I did it! I couldn't stand him anymore. He bored me. I killed him," he told another. By openly admitting to the crime, he couldn't possibly have committed it. Could he?

Downtown was agog, equally split between those who wanted to believe Alig did the dirty deed and those who couldn't believe it because of the shame it made them feel about their own lifestyles. What did it say about a scene that harbored a stone-cold killer as one of its leading lights? When I first heard the story, I didn't trust its veracity, either. "Get the hell out of here. No bleeding way," was my reaction. I was supposed to be covering Peter Gatien's troubles with the feds, and I didn't want to get sidetracked by one of Alig's digressions. The tale was too strange, too completely insane, even for a sick puppy like Michael Alig. Alig's all-consuming desire to shock, and thereby generate media coverage, seemed the most obvious explanation for this fantastic fable. The acid jokester had a long history of staging pranks, and this was his ultimate hoax.

Yet there was an undisputable logic to the notion that Alig's unruly festivities at Disco 2000 had climaxed with an actual human sacrifice of one of the participants. Maybe Angel was an offering to the god of intoxication and carnal appetites. There were even historical precedents. In ancient times, sacrifice was an essential component of pagan parties—sometimes animal, sometimes not. The more I thought about the story the more it started to make sense.

9

LOOKING FOR ANGEL

New York City, April 1996

A month after the murder, Michael Alig decided to leave town. Now homeless, Michael planned to flee New York in a hired van. He would first drive to Chicago to see Screamin' Rachael; from there to South Bend, Indiana, to see his mother, Elke; and then on to Denver, to visit his former boyfriend, Keoki, the DJ. He intended to kick his heroin habit in the clean air of Colorado. "There's nothing left for me here," he told friends.

But before he fled the city, Alig had a last closed-door meeting with Gatien. One Gatien employee claimed he heard Alig screaming, "I did it! You know that I did it! I did it for you! You're responsible, too." Alig was trying to implicate Gatien in the slaying because the club owner owed money to Angel for drugs consumed at the hotel sex orgies. Gatien agreed to help him out by giving him funds to flee. Soon after, an assistant arrived at Alig's door with sixteen hundred-dollar bills. "This is not from Peter Gatien," the assistant said. "This is a personal loan from me to you, and I expect it be paid back."

"This is not from Peter Gatien?" Alig laughed. "Sure, it isn't."

While his moving expenses were covered, Alig still needed money for heroin. He called Alex at the Palladium, and he and another sidekick named Gitsie went over to pick up $160 he was owed for back wages. From there, they went to the nearby East Village, where they were promptly robbed at knifepoint while trying to score the smack. In a panic, Alig called up Alex for more cash. Alig claimed that Alex told him, "I'll give you $300, but this is the last money you'll get from us." Soon after, Alig said, another assistant met him at a nearby Blimpie with three hundred single dollar bills in a brown paper bag.

But after purchasing what he thought was enough heroin to sustain him during his trip, Alig had something else important to do. He and Freeze had heard on the clubland tom-tom that I was digging around the circumstances of Angel's disappearance. I soon received a phone call from one of Alig's cronies requesting that I meet with Freeze.

Freeze was the club kids' resident intellectual. He'd once read a book on Dadaism. He was said to carry a pouch divided into six sections— one each for cocaine, Special K, heroin, Ecstasy, crystal methamphetamine, and the powerful barbiturate Rohypnol. Cold, imperious, distant, with his furrowed brow and sinister goatee, he was also rumored to dabble in the black arts.

I interviewed a disheveled Freeze at the *Village Voice* office. He reeked of body odor, his store-bought tan was fading, and he looked like he hadn't slept in a week. His tongue could barely connect with the English language, and when it did, his lips barely moved. His once piercing stare trailed off into the middle distance. Whether he was coming down off drugs or feeling guilty about Angel was difficult to fathom. Maybe both, I remember thinking. I'd been tipped off in advance by one of Alig's other chums that the interview was basically a setup. Alig wanted Freeze to find out how much I knew about the slaying. Freeze had no intention of revealing the real deal.

Alig had heard that Alessandra Gatien, prompted by rumors that the authorities were investigating her husband's possible role in Angel's demise, was going to hand over to the *Voice* what she called "conclusive proof" that Alig did indeed kill Melendez. She was going to give me an incriminating tape-recording she had made on which Alig had confessed to the murder.

When Alig heard Alex had an incriminating tape, he was incensed. He went to the Tunnel, and when Peter Gatien refused to see him, he left a note accusing the Gatiens of betrayal. He then began peddling another cover story: the "dead body" in the apartment wasn't Angel but another friend who had overdosed but miraculously came back to life after Alig got off the phone with Alex. At the last minute, Alessandra refused to hand over the damning evidence at the insistence of her husband's lawyer, who threatened to drop Gatien as a client if she talked to the *Voice*.

Now Freeze admitted that once, instead of calling the ambulance, he dumped another friend—Scott, a junkie ex-marine, truly a lost soul even by downtown's liberal standards—in Tompkins Square park after he had overdosed on heroin in his apartment. Scott subsequently died of exposure on what was one of the coldest nights of the year. But other than that, Freeze basically stuck to the story that Alig had told him to tell. In an interview that was mainly off-the-record, Freeze stated that on the Sunday in question, he showed up at Alig's place at noon after spending the night partying at the Tunnel. Angel, getting dressed and apparently in a bad mood, woke up Alig to demand money that was owed him for drugs. According to Freeze, though the argument was bitter, it never turned seriously physical. He said that the last time he saw Angel was when Angel left the apartment saying that he intended to get something to eat. Freeze was a lousy liar who stumbled over every third detail. I could tell he was dissembling, but I didn't have nearly enough to go into print.

Just days after meeting with Freeze, I got a major break when Angel's brother, Johnny Melendez, contacted me at home, after club kid writer James St. James had given him my number. Johnny was a conventionally attired salsa DJ who played at Latin clubs in New Jersey, just across the river but in spirit a million miles away from the weird life in which his brother had immersed himself. Johnny didn't want to believe that his brother was a drug dealer. I broke the news to him that his wayward sibling was a conspicuous figure at the Limelight, where he sold Special K and Ecstasy while wearing his trademark feather wings. I told Johnny I'd personally bought ketamine from his brother and written about it in the *Village Voice*. I theorized this might have something to do with his disappearance. "He didn't used to look like that," Johnny confided about his brother. "When he was growing up, he was a very quiet boy, very shy."

Johnny Melendez's sad dignity and determination in the face of almost certain tragedy greatly impressed me, unraveling my cynicism. He had come to town looking for Angel but had been getting the run-around from Alig's friends, who had refused to talk to him or lied straight to his face. Johnny clung to the hope that his brother was still alive, but he'd heard the widely circulated rumors to the contrary.

The last time Johnny had seen his brother was when he dropped him off in the courtyard at Riverbank West, following a rare get-together over a Chinese meal. Though they loved each other, they had differences. Johnny disapproved of Angel's lifestyle and his friends. The two kept in touch via beeper. When he dropped off his brother at Michael's place, Angel refused to let Johnny come up to the apartment. Johnny had never met Alig, but his brother talked about him all the time, first admiringly, then increasingly with a tone of contempt. "He told me that Alig owed him money," said Johnny. When he first learned of Angel's vanishing act, Johnny contacted Detective Michael Reedy at the Tenth Precinct. Reedy said he couldn't open an investigation without more concrete evidence, which was tough to find, since Johnny didn't even have a permanent address or phone number for his brother. Just the beeper number, calls to which now went ominously unanswered. "If he was an important person, the police would have started looking right away," complained Johnny. "They just didn't want to know."

When I phoned Detective Reedy, he told me, "I have no idea what you're talking about" and claimed to have never heard of Angel Melendez. Did Johnny Melendez contact him? "He could have," he said without a trace of concern before hanging up the phone. In the wake of my call, another detective from the Tenth Precinct buzzed Johnny. He was more helpful, but he told Johnny he couldn't launch an official investigation without a body. After filing a missing person's report, Johnny decided to take his story to the press.

The apathy surrounding the Angel Melendez case was appalling. The cops couldn't have cared less. The disappearance and possible dismemberment of a gay, Hispanic, low-level drug dealer with a penchant for outrageous costumes and no fixed address was not at the top of their list of things to investigate.

Local night crawlers were even more callous, posthumously tearing up Angel's club-kid membership card and ejecting him from their pathological community. Alig denounced Angel as "a scum-of-the-earth drug dealer." Alig's sidekick, Gitsie, wrinkled her nose and said, "Angel was tacky. He deserved to die." The club kids talked about Angel as if he were a subhuman creature. Loyalty to Alig still ran deep. It was all right to kill Angel because he was so low and worthless. After all, compared to Michael Alig, the all-powerful potentate of the pose, he was nothing but an empty costume.

"Nobody was particularly shocked," recalled Disco 2000's Larry Tee. "By that point, we'd seen practically everything. People were so addicted to drugs, it hardly mattered. I remember my reaction was: 'My God, I hope it doesn't fuck up the K supply.' "

Many of the club kids looked down their powdered noses at Angel, not just because he made them pay for their drugs but also because he was a Latino. A pronounced streak of racism ran through the club-kid scene, which was made up largely of the pampered offspring of middle-class whites.

"Behind the scenes, the club kids were very racist," said Screamin' Rachael. "They wouldn't let me put the term *house music* on the party invitations because they thought it would attract blacks, even though they played house music at the club. I would want to invite Afrika Bambaata to deejay, but they always said: 'We don't want that crowd.' "

Once, Rachael invited old school hip-hop legend Melle Mel—the voice on Grandmaster Flash and the Furious Five's rap classic "The Message"—to a party at the Tunnel. Alig turned him away at the door. "We don't want any stupid niggers or lowlife spics coming to the club," Rachael claimed Michael Alig said. "Black people aren't cool. When the niggers start showing up, you know your club is over."

In the face of the widespread indifference about the case, the *Village Voice* was Johnny Melendez's last resort. I followed Johnny around downtown while he forlornly stuck up missing posters on lampposts, offering a $4,000 reward for information about Angel's whereabouts. I accompanied him as he trudged from clothing store to clothing store, holding out Angel's photo and asking the same question over and over: "Have you seen my brother?" Johnny went to the city morgue but to no avail. He traveled to Riverbank West, but the doormen refused to let him look at Alig's old apartment. They did tell me though, that two detectives had recently visited. "In a luxury building like that, somebody must have heard something," Johnny insisted. "To take out a dead body from a place like that must be very hard."

Johnny trekked over to Washington Square Park and down to the West Village piers, both locations where Angel used to hang out. Someone who identified himself only as a friend of Angel's from the Limelight warned Johnny to be careful. "Important people are involved in your brother's disappearance," he said mysteriously. "The people who did this should be strung up."

"I went looking for my brother and found myself in another world," Johnny said of the freaky folks he met on his travels. "I didn't know any of my brother's friends, even though we were close. Everything was a big secret with him."

When Johnny visited Jennytalia, one of Alig's closest companions, she looked as though she'd seen a ghost after Johnny walked into Trash and Vaudeville, the East Village boutique where she worked part-time. Johnny bore a strong likeness to Angel, and though she could hardly talk, Jennytalia immediately recognized him as Angel's brother. She looked terrified as her eyes darted in a dozen different directions at once. Johnny could tell she knew something. But all the flustered club kid would say was that Angel's vanishing had something to do with someone connected to the Limelight. She wouldn't be more specific.

Touring around downtown, visiting Angel's old haunts with Johnny, seeing the grief distorting his face and the tears welling up in his shell-shocked eyes, I became convinced something really bad had happened to his brother. Each passing day, it seemed more and more likely that Alig had mainlined his way into murder and insanity. Both of us became convinced we were pursuing a dead man. "That bastard killed my brother, chopped his legs off, and then dumped him in the river," said an angry Johnny.

My initial stance when I started the story was that of a neutral observer. I didn't want to judge or take sides. "Just the facts, sir, just the facts," was my attitude. Experience had taught me that it didn't pay to become too emotionally involved with sources. But over time that changed, especially after I brought the entire Melendez family, who had flown in from Colombia, up to the *Voice* for a fact-checking mission. As Johnny translated, I heard about Angel's hardscrabble early days and how he had been sent to live with relatives in America so he would have a chance for a better life. Angel was no longer a cardboard drug dispenser, one of Michael Alig's stage props, but a living, breathing human being, whom his parents deeply missed. The idea that Angel put his family through this horror show for the sake of one of Alig's sick jokes seemed inconceivable.

Now, hyped up on indignation that a terrible wrong had gone unpunished, I had a change of heart. With all the righteous rage I could muster, I determined to nail Michael Alig to the media cross.

Johnny was more restrained. "Conscience will take care of Michael Alig," he said. "I'm not out for vengeance. If my brother is dead, I just want to find the body so that my parents can give him a decent burial. Nobody deserves to die like that."

I had half a dozen people telling me off-the-record that Michael had confessed the killing to them, including some of his best friends, such as James St. James. But I needed at least one on-the-record confirmation to satisfy the legal department and enable the article to run. Publicity-mad Screamin' Rachael Cain was the obvious candidate. After promising I would give her latest record a plug in the article, Rachael agreed to go on the record: She confirmed that Alig had admitted to her in gruesome detail that he'd killed Angel.

"Michael is so sick at the moment that the whole thing could be contrived," said Rachael. "No matter how many people he confessed to, I find it very hard to believe that Michael deliberately killed somebody. Either way, though, it's an unbelievable horror. If he did it, it must have been the drugs." (Much later, I would find out that Alig hadn't actually confessed to Rachael but to her friend, when Rachael was out of the room.)

To further complicate matters, on May 15, 1996, DEA agents, among them Matt Germanowski, swooped down and arrested Peter Gatien. Just before 6:00 A.M., half a dozen broad-shouldered G-men, all burly business and aggressive body language, burst into his capacious town house on the Upper East Side of Manhattan, ran up the stairs to his bedroom, and slapped on the handcuffs. Dazed by the commotion, his solitary eye still half asleep, a grim-looking Gatien was charged with conspiracy to distribute MDMA. While his daughter, Jennifer, still in her dressing gown, stood bewildered in the background and with wailing sirens and his wife's sobbing supplying the hectic soundtrack, Gatien was whisked away via sleek illuminated motorcade to the agency's bunker-style headquarters on the West Side, only seven blocks from the Limelight. "I kept thinking it was all a big mistake," he said later. "I kept thinking the agents would apologize for the error and release me at any moment."

Gatien was further startled by the extent of the operation that ensnared him. Following the club czar's arrest, a team of agents fanned out across the city to nab twenty-three other suspects, some of them current or past Gatien employees, whom the government claimed were part of "an extensive conspiracy to distribute the designer drug MDMA, commonly known as Ecstasy."

One of those arrested was club director Steven Lewis. The DEA charged that Lewis was employed by Gatien to stand guard at the door and ensure that Ecstasy dealers "would be permitted to enter the clubs unfettered by security." Lewis told the feds that he was glad that he had been arrested and that he knew that all the drug distribution at the nightclubs was wrong and had wanted to go to the police but was scared of reprisals from Gatien. Lewis said that prior to the arrest, the club owner had promised to pay for Lewis's attorney and the only thing Gatien wanted in return was that Lewis should tell authorities that Gatien knew nothing about the narcotics trafficking at the clubs. Lewis went on to say that on "several occasions" he tried to prevent Lord

Michael Caruso's drug dealers from coming into the Limelight but was overruled by his boss. "Let these people in, they're OK," Gatien was supposed to have said. Lewis further claimed that Lord Michael boasted to him, "I give Peter Gatien more money from my drug sales than he makes at the door."

DEA agents also raided the Tunnel searching in vain for the Ecstasy laboratory falsely rumored to be hidden in the basement. In addition, they ransacked Gatien's office, expecting to discover a stash of cocaine. On both counts, they came up short. But they did manage to cart off boxes of documents that had escaped the shredder. Gatien was charged with participating in a multi-million-dollar Ecstasy ring that stretched as far as Amsterdam. At a press conference, the U.S. Attorney Zachary Carter dramatically accused the club king of allowing the Limelight and the Tunnel to become "Ecstasy supermarkets." He claimed Gatien had "installed a management structure at the Limelight and the Tunnel to ensure successful distribution of Ecstasy to nightclub patrons." The sale of Ecstasy "was the centerpiece of the operation of the clubs, not just a lucrative illegal sideline."

"These clubs existed to distribute these substances," Carter told a packed room of reporters. "They were the honey traps."

Gatien and a host of others were charged on two counts: conspiracy to distribute and possession with intent to distribute MDMA, a Schedule 1 controlled substance. Carlos Boccia, special agent in charge of the DEA's New York Field Division, warned, "The public needs to realize that the high visibility of clubs such as these glamorize the use and distribution of these illegal substances. Those who sell these drugs, albeit surrounded by the splendor and glitz of fashionable nightclubs, are no less the scourge than those who hide in the back alleys of the inner city to dispense their poison."

Gatien's bond was set at a million dollars and he was put in jail in Brooklyn's Metroplitan Detention Center, where he spent two weeks before his bail was raised. Despite being worth $8 million on paper, he struggled to scrape together the money by borrowing from friends, his brothers, his parents, and his ex-wife. He claimed that on the first night, another prisoner offered him cocaine. "If they can't keep drugs out of prison, how do they expect me to keep drugs out of my clubs?" he argued afterward. "I didn't think that law enforcement cared that much about Ecstasy."

By the time of his arrest, Gatien was planning to leave the nightclub business altogether. At the urging of his wife, he wanted to get into producing movies. He'd already had some success as the executive producer of *A Bronx Tale*, which costarred former Limelight bouncer Chazz Palminteri. As frightened community boards became more and more powerful and as the Giuliani administration strictly enforced the hundreds of rules, regulations, laws, and ordinances governing nightclubs in New York, operating a large-scale Gotham disco was becoming increasingly difficult. The implicit understanding between the police and the owners that drugs at clubs, if kept hidden, were permissible melted away as Mayor Giuliani's self-righteous "quality-of-life" campaign invaded the dance floor.

Gatien had been dreading this moment for months. He was well aware that the authorities had his establishments under close surveillance. And he knew he was sitting atop a mountain of corruption and bad karma. He was worried that his chief aides—Michael Alig, Michael Caruso, and Steven Lewis—might feed the feds incriminating dirt about his nocturnal empire. Gatien knew about the extent of the drug dealing in his clubs but felt powerless to prevent the escalating presence of pills and powders. He had built his business catering to ravers and club kids, both subcultures heavily dependent on hard drugs. He had hoped that by not directly financing the narcotics flow he could plausibly maintain his innocence.

The federal indictment presented a damning portrait of a corrupt Gatien hierarchy, beginning at the top and working down:

> The defendant Peter Gatien served as president and chief executive of the nightclubs. . . . His duties included overseeing directors and party promoters; paying, or authorizing payments to certain directors and party promoters to purchase, among other things, controlled substances; and approving invitations and pro-

motional materials to nightclub parties that contained explicit, as well as thinly veiled, references to the availability of controlled substances at the parties.

Directors were below the defendant Peter Gatien in the employment hierarchy at the nightclubs and were responsible for scheduling 'theme' events at the nightclubs. As part of their duties, directors co-coordinated themes with party promoters so that the party promoters could arrange to have controlled substances available for sale consistent with the themes. . . . Michael Caruso, Steven Lewis, and Michael Alig were directors at the nightclubs at various times.

Party promoters were below directors in the employment hierarchy at the nightclubs. Party promoters were responsible for recruiting individuals to attend the nightclubs, distributing invitations and promotional materials for nightclub parties, and ensuring that controlled substances were available for sale at the nightclubs. Among the party promoters at various times were Michael Caruso, Paul Torres, Michael Alig, and Joseph Uzzardi, also known as 'Baby Joe'.

Directors and party promoters employed dealers to distribute controlled substances at the nightclubs. The dealers employed by directors and party promoters acted as house dealers. The distribution of controlled substances by house dealers was supported and encouraged by the employees and management of the nightclubs, while the distribution of controlled substances by non-house dealers was not.

The nightclubs employed bouncers, who stood at the front door and throughout the nightclub premises. Although the bouncers from time to time ejected house dealers, nonhouse dealers, and patrons from the nightclubs for narcotics related activities, the bouncers typically permitted house dealers to enter the nightclubs without being searched for controlled substances and did not typically eject house dealers for selling drugs.

The indictment also took aim at Gatien's hotel orgies:

One of the ways that members of the enterprise and their associates received controlled substances free of charge was at lavish parties hosted by the defendant Peter Gatien at various luxury Manhattan hotels. At these parties, Peter Gatien distributed cocaine base, cocaine, flunitrazepam, (aka Rohypnol, aka roofies) and ketamine to members of the enterprise and their associates, who, together with Gatien, would 'binge' on these controlled substances for several days. At the parties, the members of the enterprise and their associates were responsible for attending to Gatien's safety, comfort, and entertainment, and assisting him in his use of controlled substances.

But, there was one name conspicuously absent from the bill of charges—Lord Michael Caruso, the biggest drug dealer of them all. Even though he was named numerous times in the body of the indictment, he wasn't listed as a coconspirator on the cover page, nor was he arrested. After his partnership with Chris Paciello was violently dissolved, Caruso had abruptly left Gatien's employ in February 1996, just before the feds pounced, which led some insiders to speculate that he had had advance knowledge of what was about to come down.

South Bend, Late May 1996

In the meantime, Michael Alig had washed up in Indi-ana, with a U-Haul truck that contained all the worldly possessions he hadn't sold to finance his getaway—one hundred videotapes of *Dark Shadows*, fifty volumes of *I Love Lucy*, twelve collector cases of Matchbox cars, thirty large boxes of Lego, the complete archives of *Project X* magazine, a suitcase full of press clippings, an eight-piece china set, Angel's green card, and a cat called Kitty. Along for the ride were two other heroin-addicted club kids—purple-haired Gitsie and an orange-haired companion. By this point, Alig was so strung out that he had resorted to shooting up between his toes and under his tongue. In addition, he had seriously underestimated the amount of drugs he needed to survive a lengthy road tip. They were only halfway to Colorado, and already they'd run out of dope.

Gitsie called Alig's mother from the Econo-Lodge out by the airport. Elke hadn't seen her son in three years. When she arrived at the hotel, she was shocked at what she discovered. Her son was curled up on a bed in a fetal position, rattling from withdrawal. He hadn't had heroin in forty-eight hours and could hardly open his eyes. He was sweating profusely. "You could see his pores opening and fluid coming out," Elke said.

"Mommy, please don't touch me," Alig pleaded. "I hurt too bad. I need heroin or methadone." Elke called an ambulance and took her ailing son to the local hospital, but the nurses and doctors refused to treat him, other than to give him a prescription for Valium, because of his unorthodox appearance. Alig passed out in the hallway.

"Michael just couldn't deal with the memory of Angel," said Elke. "He went on the needle because he wanted to be numb, so he could forget what he did to Angel."

In early June, three months after Angel Melendez was butchered, Michael Alig, still stoned, returned to New York from his road trip, to be greeted by Angel's picture on the cover of the *Village Voice*. The combination of numerous off-the-record sources and one on-the-record source saying Alig had confessed to the slaying, along with Johnny Melendez's trail of tears in search of his missing brother, made for a story that implied that Alig and Freeze were the actual killers. The *Voice* article catapulted Angel's murder from the realm of rumor into the province of hard news. The story was no longer merely clubland gossip. Numerous media outlets picked up the report. Alig openly joked with journalists about his reputation as a killer. Surely, somebody would take action.

Alig's career had gone sour. The *Voice* cover story did not immediately lead to his arrest on a murder rap, but it did have the effect of turning clubland against him. Alig's haggard mug was turned away at numerous nightspots, not surprisingly, perhaps, since he appeared sporting his latest fashion outrage—GUILTY in black marker scrawled across his face. He was about as welcome as a cold sore on a first date. The glitter abyss summoned.

Once back in New York, Alig was eventually detained by the authorities but not for the murder of Angel Melendez. DEA agents Matt Germanowski and Bob Gagne arrested and charged him with distributing cocaine and Ecstasy at the Limelight. Alig was head of a coterie of pushers at the club, among them Angel, Freeze, Junkie Jonathan, Brooke Humphries, the It Twins, and Goldilocks, many of whom were sources for the *Voice* stories. This was not a conventional drug ring. Profits took a backseat to pleasure. Money was made, but it immediately went up the noses and into the arms of the coconspirators. These were so-called celebrity drug dealers—human lures used to attract more normal customers, who were known dismissively as "filler."

Unlike other dope dealers, they weren't shadowy figures lurking in some alley but ostentatious, over-the-top characters who didn't mind giving interviews to reporters and frequently boasted about their illegal actions. They weren't just there to peddle product; they were part of the show. With the sole exception of Angel, they were usually much more stoned than the punters they sold to. In marked contrast to Lord Michael and his army of drug-dealing goons, Alig's crew was more of a danger to themselves than anybody else. If it was a conspiracy, it was a disorganized one.

Following his arrest, the DEA offered Alig a deal: Provide damaging information about Peter Gatien, and they'd look the other way on the drug charges. It didn't seem to occur to Gagne and Germanowski, who were well aware that Alig was the prime suspect in the dismemberment of Angel Melendez, that they were doing anything wrong in making a bargain with a supposed killer. Alig now saw a way out of his troubles, and he took full advantage. "The DEA agents wanted me to say that Peter took payoffs from drug dealers and that the hotel parties were rewards for drug dealers," said Alig.

Alig informed the agents that at the end of each night, Gatien gave him a bundle of cash, which he distributed to his hosts, many of whom also sold drugs. He told the DEA that drug dealers like Goldilocks and the It Twins were paid $200 a night by Gatien to simply show up and peddle their wares, while the runners who worked for them were paid $100 a night. "Appearance fees," Alig called them. Alig then went on to say that he and Gatien conspired to make drugs an intrinsic lure to get people to come to the club.

Alig also revealed that Lord Michael and his group of drug dealers had become so dangerous that they were trying to strong-arm the club kids and sell product to the entire club, meaning not just the 95 percent of the Limelight they already controlled but also the small VIP area, where Alig and his pals did business. And, in fact, they did eventually convince Angel and Junkie Jonathan to buy their drugs from them.

In the immediate aftermath of the *Voice* story about Alig, Miguel Rodriguez and Walter Alexander, two investigators working for the

Manhattan District Attorney's office, contacted Johnny Melendez. In an investigation separate from the feds, local authorities were also looking into Gatien's operation. The embattled club czar was at war on two fronts. Rodriguez and Alexander weren't homicide investigators; their specialty was bank fraud and catching money launderers. They were probing Gatien's tax situation, and in the process, they'd uncovered the same story about Angel's death reported in the *Voice*.

The DA knew that the DEA was protecting Alig, as he helped the agency build its case against Gatien. Rodriguez hit upon the strategy of using Johnny Melendez to draw out information from Alig. On August 15, Johnny phoned Alig. At this point, Alig didn't know that Johnny had hooked up with the DA's office. Johnny was noticeably nervous. He was talking to someone who, he was convinced, had murdered his brother. He wanted to reach down the phone and strangle Alig. But he knew he had to act cool in order to pump him for knowledge.

Alig told Johnny that Gatien paid drug dealers to hang out at his clubs to keep customers happy. "Angel was good for business," Alig claimed. Johnny asked Alig if Angel had been paid by Peter Gatien to sell drugs at the Limelight. Alig replied, "Um-hmm . . . it's because if your brother had gone to another club, then all his customers would have gone to another club."

"So Gatien had to pay my brother to stay in his club?"

"Yeah, he was paid $200 a night and worked two nights a week at the Tunnel and the Limelight. . . . Peter was afraid to give Angel the money directly, so he gave me the money, and I gave it to Angel."

As the conversation progressed, Alig pretended to aid Johnny and tried to blame Angel's disappearance on the Gatiens. He told Johnny that the Gatiens had the motive to have Angel murdered because Angel had told Gatien's wife, Alex, that he was going to talk to the *Village Voice*.

"I'll do as much as I can without getting myself hurt, you know?" Alig offered.

"How, how, how you gonna get hurt?" wondered Johnny.

"Because I don't wanna fucking go dig down and bother Alex and get her mad at me, you know? Because I'm, I'm digging into something that, as far as she's concerned is none of my business and could possibly get her in trouble, so she's gonna fuck with me, and I don't want that."

"Is she that bad?"

"Yes, she is. Ask anybody what they think of Alex, what kind of person she is, they will tell you. They're terrified of her. She's the real thing. She's an evil person."

"She had my brother disappear, that's what you think, right?"

"That's what I think. Angel knew a lot, you know Angel knew everything. And he was threatening to go to Frank Owen, his friend at the *Voice*. And tell him all this stuff, you know. That's a real threat to Peter and Alex . . ."

"Oh . . . so my brother was . . . damn, that's messed up . . ."

"You know, and your brother is, was, very stubborn. And he, you know, he shouldn't, he really shouldn't have . . . I mean, I would have been afraid, everybody else, everybody was shocked when he said that in front of everybody at the club, because, you know, you don't say that to somebody like Alex. . . . Peter was hiring drug dealers. Nobody knew that. It was a big secret. That's why Peter was afraid he was going to go blabbing it to everybody. Peter could get into a lot of trouble for that. . . ."

"It's been like four months since my brother went missing, and we can't get anywhere. Nobody wants to cooperate; nobody wants to talk. Everybody just wants to say, 'Oh, the rumor, this and this and that,' but nobody says anything. I just want to know if you can help me out, you know. Can you really help me out? I understand that you might know a lot of stuff you don't want to tell me. I need somebody to come forward, man. I need somebody to help me out real bad. Are you sure you don't know what these people did with my brother? I mean, of course, you're not going to say 'Oh, I know where his body's at,' or 'I know where they put the body,' because you're incriminating yourself."

"Right."

"I'm his brother. I'm messed up. You used to live with Angel. We want to get this thing over with, we want to get on with our lives."

"And right, so do I."

"If we have to pay you to tell us—"

Alig became indignant. "You don't have to pay. I'm really insulted you just said that."

"I'm sorry, but you know, you have to understand me. I'm desperate."

Johnny then asked Alig for Angel's green card and clothes, which Alig had in a storage room in Denver. Johnny complained that all the stress had sent his father to the hospital. Alig commiserated. Johnny pleaded again with Alig to tell him where his brother's body was. Alig told Johnny that he was scared to divulge any more details. Alig finished off the conversation: "Two deaths aren't going to make it any better. You know, I don't want to get myself killed."

Alig was convinced that his cooperation in the Gatien case had earned him a get-out-of-jail-free card when it came to the Melendez killing. That's why he felt perfectly at ease spinning the bogus plot line that the Gatiens had killed Angel, because that's what his DEA handlers wanted to believe. Alig must have thought it was a great deal—trade Peter Gatien's scalp for Angel's torso. He told the DEA agents that the DA investigators were harassing their prime informant. They called the DA and told them to back off; this was their case. The DA's office was furious with the DEA for protecting Alig, but there was not much they could do. Alig started to make fun of the DA probe in front of comrades.

The DA detectives Rodriguez and Alexander also contacted house music singer Screamin' Rachael. They tried to scare her into cooperating by saying she was impeding the investigation. They threatened to arrest her if she didn't tell them everything she knew about Angel's disappearance.

Not long after, DEA agents Gagne and Germanowski, who had been tipped off by Michael Alig that the DA was hassling Rachael, turned up at her door. They were more friendly, even though behind her back they were bugging her phone. Eventually, she agreed to help them and conducted two lengthy interviews.

Whisked before a federal grand jury, Rachael was expecting to be a major source to bring a murder charge against Alig. But to her surprise she found herself answering questions mainly about Peter Gatien. "Both the DA detectives and the DEA agents put on a show of how car-ing and concerned they were, but they really didn't give a damn about Angel," said Rachael. "The whole thing was about Peter Gatien. If they could tie Gatien into the Melendez murder so much the better. The underlying thing always was to get Peter at all costs."

The DA detectives told both Johnny Melendez and Screamin' Rachael not to talk to the *Village Voice*, for fear of jeopardizing the investigation, but they continued feeding me information, anyway, strictly off-the-record. Though the detectives doggedly pursued club kids as potential witnesses, the investigation was not going well. They needed firsthand witnesses. Rodriguez and Alexander marched a string of downtown luminaries through their secret office, located above a Soho art gallery. But no matter how much they tried to pressure them into cooperating, they all said the same thing. Sure, they had heard the rumor. Who hadn't? But they had no specific proof implicating Alig or Gatien. The DA's office got so desperate that an attorney told one club kid that if he didn't give up what he knew, he would have his beloved Chanel outfits promptly confiscated. The DA detectives also visited a drag queen's house—where Alig and Freeze had gone immediately following the killing—vainly searching for the knives with which Alig had dismembered Angel. Another drag queen was temporaily detained and carried away in handcuffs after she refused to assist the murder probe.

Rodriguez and Alexander were stymied, unable to make a case without a corpse. Their theory that Peter Gatien was involved in Angel's death was looking like complete nonsense. Short of dredging up New York harbor, what could they do?

On a horrendously humid day that summer of 1996, Michael Caruso came to the *Village Voice* after I'd told him I had something very important to say to him, something that I didn't want to talk about over the phone. Caruso, who had suddenly left Gatien's employ earlier in the year and moved over to work at the rival club Expo in Times Square, arrived wearing khaki shorts that revealed Together Forever gang tattoos snaking up his chunky struts. I was reminded of Steven Lewis's remark about his former colleague: "Every time he gets a new tattoo, he thinks it makes him tougher."

Caruso had quit the Limelight saying he was leaving the rave scene altogether to pursue another musical direction, namely hip-hop. At Expo, he did his best to ingratiate himself with fellow Staten Islanders the Wu-Tang Clan and often played host to them at his new place of employment.

I'd heard stories that Caruso was back to his old tricks. After he left Miami, he swore he was going to quit selling drugs and robbing people. He also resolved to be a faithful companion to his longtime girlfriend, Gina, and a good father to their newborn son. But once ensconced at Expo, the old Lord Michael returned: He resumed drugging, cheating on his girlfriend, and ripping off unsuspecting marks. Some opportunities were just too good to pass up.

"I saw him spike the drinks of a number of girls at Expo to have sex with them," claimed the Port Richmond Crew's Brendon Schlitz, an old buddy. "He would tell them [Wu-Tang Clan rapper] Method Man was in the backroom and ask them did they want to meet him. Michael was always a 'ho."

Schlitz also told me that he and Caruso had recently teamed up to rob a so-called candy raver (a suburban party person who sucks on a pacifier and waves a glow stick) they met one night at Expo. The goofy kid's name was Ian and he wanted to buy a fairly large amount of Ecstasy. He approached Caruso, who told him, "No problem." The next afternoon, they picked Ian up in a car at Fourteenth Street and Second Avenue. Brendon had a badge from the department of corrections. Caruso had a fake police badge, which he carried on a chain around his neck. Caruso and Schlitz told the scared raver they were undercover cops, beat him up, and took $12,000, which he had hidden in his socks. Despite being a goofball, Ian had some heavy friends, who didn't take kindly to what Caruso and Schlitz had just done. Threats of retribution flew, and as a consequence, Caruso hired two of Expo's bouncers to guard him around the clock.

But I hadn't invited Caruso up to the *Voice* to discuss his current employment situation so much as his old one. After escorting Caruso to a side office, I closed the door and told Caruso to sit down and prepare himself for a shock.

"Michael, I've got some bad news. I'm writing this article that's going to reveal that you were the Limelight's top dog for Ecstasy. I want to get your reaction," I said, hoping to surprise him with the direct approach.

"What the fuck is that supposed to mean?" he snorted and gulped at the same time.

"You were the one who organized the drug dealing at the Limelight."

"That's bullshit."

"No it's not. I've got nearly a dozen insiders who fingered you as the Limelight's drug kingpin. They also said that you arranged and participated in armed robberies of rivals. Plus, they alleged that you frequently threatened to have anybody who pissed you off kidnapped or murdered."

"What fuckin' insiders? You don't know what you're talking about."

"I'm not going to reveal any names, but these are people you worked with at the club."

"That's ridiculous. This is absurd. If you print this crap, I'm going to sue you and your faggot newspaper for libel."

Ashen-faced, he then asked me to turn off the tape recorder. He shifted in his seat and started to shake. I thought for a moment he might launch a retaliatory strike.

Then, to my astonishment, the would-be hard-ass burst into tears. He blubbed like a chastised toddler. He begged me to kill the story for the sake of his girlfriend and child. "I'm trying to turn my life around," he sobbed. "I've known you for years, Frank. Please don't do this to me."

For a moment, I glimpsed the naïve Staten Island kid Caruso once was. "Do you think I need a lawyer?" the red-eyed promoter asked as he was walking out the door. I told him he definitely did. Either that or a priest.

In the interim, Caruso's former business partner, Chris Paciello, despite all his dazzling success in Miami and his newfound social aspirations, was still finding trouble. Sophisticated rules of social behavior aside, lurking just beneath the veneer of propriety he cultivated, the old Chris Paciello was ready to pop out at a moment's notice. Intense spasms of violence regularly marked his rise to the top, even during those times when he was pretending to be a gentleman. Miami Beach's golden boy, who now looked so pumped up that he resembled a comic book super-hero, was dangerous when he got mad. An overheard remark, a display of bad etiquette, or an irritating photographer was often enough to send Paciello into a dark fury.

On the night of June 25, 1996, Paciello got into a major brouhaha in Liquid's VIP lounge with Michael Quinn, a former Mr. Universe, because he overheard the professional bodybuilder hurl a racial slur at one of Paciello's friends.

Quinn's wife, a cocktail waitress who knew the club owner socially, borrowed a cap from a professional basketball player Paciello was friendly with. Quinn, a little jealous and somewhat drunk, told his spouse to "give the nigger back his hat." As with the incident at Risk, when he belted a customer for using the same word to insult the club's doorman, Paciello was incensed. These were fighting words. He told Quinn to apologize straight away. "What the fuck are you gonna do, if I don't?" Quinn challenged.

At 275 pounds, with 5 percent body fat, Quinn was a sturdy wall of mean muscle, twice as wide as Paciello. He was not an easy opponent. But according to Quinn, Paciello picked up a beer bottle lying on the bar and smashed it with all the force he could manage into the side of Quinn's face. Quinn struggled to stay upright for a moment, before crashing to the floor like mercury on a cold day. "You calling my friend a nigger," Paciello screamed at a blood-splattered Quinn and pro-ceeded to kick him repeatedly in the head, while onlookers stood frozen in fear. Paciello ended up breaking the bodybuilder's nose, shattering his teeth, and fracturing numerous bones in his face, which Quinn needed reconstructive surgery to fix.

In the aftermath of the attack, Quinn filed a lawsuit against Paciello but claimed he received a phone call from a friend, boxer Vinny Pazienza, who told Quinn to drop the suit for the sake of his future health. "I got a call from an acquaintance in New York," Pazienza told Miami's *New Times*. "He told me to tell Mike to back off because these are bad people and something could happen to him. He said that Mike would never live to spend the money."

Quinn's lawyer, Peter Mineo, also said that a female witness to the assault suddenly disappeared. "She agreed to give us a deposition and we gave notice of the deposition to Paciello's lawyer," Mineo told the *Voice*. "The next thing we know, after she promises to attend, we get a call that she's not coming in and we can't find her. And she doesn't return our phone calls. There was some talk that she had been offered money to keep quiet."

Paciello told the cops that he acted in self-defense after Quinn attacked him. But Mineo scoffed at Paciello's justification. "In a fair fight, my client would have ripped Paciello to shreds," said the lawyer. "The only way this could have happened, where somebody of Paciello's size could have taken down somebody of Mike Quinn's size, would be if it were a sucker punch, which it was, and with the use of a weapon—in this case, a bottle."

Paciello's rumored use of anabolic steroids may provide the key to his Jekyll and Hyde personality—one minute Cary Grant captivating all the ladies, the next a raging bull administering vicious beatings to rivals, patrons, and employees. There was a strong suspicion on South Beach that Paciello's granite physique was carved out of something other than sweat. At the slightest provocation, steroids can make the user lapse into a sadistic, sometimes homicidal state known as "roid rage"—a temporary psychiatric disorder in which the user "snaps" and commits outlandish acts of violence that may be completely out of character.

"Everybody assumed Chris was on steroids," said Gilbert Stafford, who worked the door at both Risk and Liquid. "He certainly looked and acted like he was."

From conversations with Paciello's close friends about the club owner, a pattern inevitably emerged. Stories concerning Paciello's many acts of genuine kindness were followed by tales that illustrated the club king's penchant for dramatic displays of violence. In the early '90s, Michael Capponi was the most celebrated party promoter on the beach; invitations to his bashes at Dune on Washington Avenue were the hot-ticket items of the day among local trendsetters and young socialites. Then heroin took its toll, as it did on many scions of prominent Miami families at the time. Many a rich kid like Capponi, whose father ran a string of upscale nightclubs in France and Belgium, discovered the harsh truth that privilege was no protection from the pangs of chemical necessity.

After two years of wall-to-wall rehabs in Europe, the costs of which ate up his savings, Capponi returned to South Beach, homeless and penniless. Paciello immediately took him in, fitted him out in new designer togs, and gave the recovering addict walking-around money.

While Capponi had been away, Paciello had taken over the Dune space (after the owner died of a heroin overdose) and transformed it into Liquid, in the process becoming the king of the strip and a far bigger deal than even Capponi had been in his heyday.

One night, not long after he had returned home, Capponi and Paciello were dining with a crew of young swells at a local bistro. "I'd been out of rehab a couple of weeks, and I just had to get high," recalled Capponi. "So I told Chris I needed to go to the bathroom, but instead I split and walked over to the club next door, the Bandouche, so I wouldn't get busted. I went into the bathroom and started chasing the dragon. All of a sudden, Chris turned up and kicked the fuckin' door down, flushed the shit, then dragged me out by my collar. He made the effort to get up from a society table and walk a block to the club in order to save my ass. I always considered him the closest of friends after that."

Yet, even as Capponi remembered Paciello's sense of concern, he couldn't help also recalling another side of his friend, albeit with a bit of a laugh.

"I'd just got out of another rehab, and I was in bad shape," he related. "I must have weighed about ninety-five pounds, staggering like a constipated crab down Washington Avenue. These three Cuban homeboys in hoodies and gold chains see me and don't like the way I look. So they bumped me real hard and called me 'a fuckin' pussy.' Chris was walking like ten feet behind me. I just turned round and looked at Chris, and he nodded at me. Chris strolled up and went boom! boom! boom! He throws three punches, and he decks all three of them. They're lying sprawled out on the pavement unconscious. So we just kept on walking, and we were at the end of the block, before they even started to get up."

Capponi evoked another occasion, during a company picnic at a Key Largo tikki bar. Chris had brought the whole staff of Liquid down on a coach for one of the frequent employee outings he liked to organize.

There was a test-your-own-strength machine in the bar, and some 250-pound muscle man kept swinging the hammer and ringing the bell. Impressed with himself, he sauntered over to where the Liquid people were hanging out and tried to pick up a couple of pretty waitresses from the club in front of the owner. The women didn't want to know, but the meathead persisted. Irritated, Paciello finally intervened: "Why don't you mind your own fuckin' business and get the fuck out of here," he told the unlucky Romeo.

"The big guy starts ranting: 'Fuck you, I gonna kill you,'" said Capponi. "Chris goes, 'Oh, yeah,' and gets up, and he's about half his size, but he just swings one punch: 'See ya, bo-o-o-m!' and the guy goes flying back twenty-five feet on his back. The whole place cracked up laughing. The guy was so embarrassed, he didn't even get back up on his feet, he just crawled out on his hands and knees. It was good to have Chris on your side. The people he beat up usually deserved it."

Longtime Paciello doorman Gilbert Stafford also praised Paciello's compassion. During the time Liquid was open, Stafford became critically ill with severe pneumonia. "Because of my ignorance, I thought I was a dead man, but I wasn't going to make a fuss about it, just slip quietly into that good night," says Stafford. "But Chris insisted that I go to the hospital. I survived largely because of Chris. I couldn't work for three or four months while I was recuperating. Chris raised $10,000 for me at a benefit, which enabled me to take the time to regain my health, and my job was waiting for me when I came back."

But just like Capponi, Stafford also witnessed firsthand Paciello's vicious side. An employee, promoter Carl B. Dread (Carlton Barton) mouthed off to Paciello, telling him to "fuck off" after Paciello had instructed him to do something. Saucer eyes glowing with rage, Paciello dropped his employee with one blow. "Carl was carried out by the bouncers," remembers Stafford. "But Chris didn't drag him out in the alleyway and beat and stomp him after he was unconscious, as some in the press have inaccurately reported." The local police did arrest Paciello, but the charges were dropped when Barton got out of the hospital and forgave Paciello. He came back to work at Liquid after the club owner acted contrite and doubled his salary as penance for the brutality.

Asked to account for Paciello's schizophrenic character, Stafford said: "I've thought about that a million times. And the only thing I can come up with is the steroids."

Paciello wasn't always the instigator of violence, though; sometimes he was the victim. It almost became a rite of passage among some of the local hard men to challenge the pumped-up club owner. "He's not so tough. I can take him" was a commonly heard sentiment along the strip. Later in the year, Paciello accompanied calendar girl and television host Sofia Vergara to the South Beach lounge Bar None. Paciello had just been dating swimsuit model Niki Taylor. The two first met at Liquid and had recently been spotted smothering each other with kisses in the pool at the Delano Hotel. Incensed at this, Taylor's estranged husband, the stocky football player Matt Martinez (who was featured in Oliver Stone's *Any Given Sunday*) went to Bar None with a bulky accomplice who was built like a linebacker. When Bar None's bouncer left the tiny VIP area, Martinez seized the moment to attack Paciello, according to society writer Jacquelynn D. Powers, an eyewitness that night. While his henchman held the club owner down, Martinez, who was in the middle of a messy divorce from Taylor, punched Paciello repeatedly. He beat him until he bled. Tables were overturned and champagne bottles were smashed before fellow patrons managed to drag the professional athlete off Paciello. As a result of the ugly brawl, Martinez was banned from Bar None for life.

After the fight, Martinez told the Miami Beach police that Paciello was threatening to have him killed and had brought "twenty men" down from New York to do the job, which was obviously an exaggeration. But Martinez was scared enough to hire a full-time bodyguard.

During the same period, throughout the summer and into the autumn of 1996, Michael Alig and Freeze were doing their best to keep the truth about what they had done from bubbling up to the surface. Media mockery was one of Alig's specialties. *Details* magazine even ran a light-hearted feature about Alig that depicted him seminaked posing atop a jack-in-the-box. The images recalled the infamous photos of Claus Von

Bulow masquerading in sadomasochistic drag after his wife lapsed into a coma.

In the article, Alig, who was high on heroin when he gave the interview, made the damaging admission: "When a new club opens, all the dealers go, and all the people go with them. We made our clubs last a long time, and the way we would do that is when a new club opened, we would pay the drug dealers to stay."

Alig also told *Details*, "Alex would give Peter X amount of dollars a week that he could do whatever he liked with, and she was slowly shrinking it, just giving him smaller and smaller amounts of money each week. So Peter assumed some debt with Angel, like $1,400."

Nevertheless, by the fifth month following the *Voice* article on Alig, even I was beginning to doubt the veracity of my own story. What if Alig hadn't killed Angel? The cops refused to say anything to the *Voice* while the investigation was ongoing, fearing that Alig would skip town again. It looked like the Melendez killing might go officially unsolved.

Then in September 1996, in a so-called "exclusive," the *New York Post* claimed to have discovered Angel's body floating in the Harlem River. A homeless woman fishing for Sunday dinner had instead reeled in a rotting corpse. Right away, I knew that it was utter nonsense; bodies—even club-kid cadavers—don't float upstream. But the false report jogged the memory of a Staten Island police officer. Back on April 12, Detective Ralph Gengo, assigned to the 122nd Precinct, had responded to a call. A body had washed up on Staten Island's Oakwood Beach, a debris-strewn slip of sand on the eastern side of the borough. A group of children had discovered a box containing the badly decomposed torso of a man in his twenties. An autopsy showed the victim had asphyxiated and had been struck in the back of the head. At first, Gengo thought it was another one of the anonymous "floaters" that turn up all the time on Staten Island shores. Misclassified as being of Asian descent, the body had been stored away for a while in the local morgue under the tag John Doe before being taken to the potter's field and buried in a numbered grave. Gengo arranged for the corpse to be exhumed. The condition of the body was so putrefied that the attempt to match the fingerprints with those of Melendez was unsuccessful. But after receiving Angel's dental records from Johnny Melendez, on the day after what would have been Angel's twenty-sixth birthday, the medical examiner's office positively identified the corpse. The dead body was Angel.

The news had yet to reach Michael Alig when he threw his last-ever party at the end of November 1996 at a midtown club called Mirage. A twin vista of tackiness that looked like it hadn't changed since the heyday of disco, the place had two vast floors of chrome and mirror. The event was called "Honey Trap," after U.S. Attorney Zachary Carter's description of the Limelight as a honey trap for young kids looking for drugs.

The party vibrated with superficial glitz and fleeting expectation. Unbeknownst to the club kids, hiding in the corners, undercover narcs kept an eye on the proceedings. Adding to the surreal nature of the event, too, were numerous media jackals who were out in force that evening. In addition to me, there were reporters from *The New York Times* and the London *Times*, not to mention a small army of hungry producers from the daytime talk shows. Drugs flowed everywhere.

Screamin' Rachael flew in from Chicago to perform her new single "Give Me Freedom/Murder in Clubland," which contained the lyrics "The DA's on my phone, got taps on my phone/The one-eyed don is in jail and hopes to make bail."

"That record doesn't say I killed Angel?" chirped Alig when she walked into the club.

Rachael replied, "No, it says 'Michael, where's Angel?'"

"Oh, that's OK," said Alig, relieved for the moment.

With a champagne bottle in one hand and a pile of drink tickets in the other, Alig—surrounded by a thinning coterie of washed-up trendies—seemed without a care in the world. He thought he was protected from culpability in Angel's murder because he was helping the feds build their drug conspiracy case against his former boss, Peter Gatien. Alig told friends that the DEA agents were his "big brothers." He was gambling that the authorities were more interested in bringing down a big-time club owner than in solving the murder of a low-level Colombian hustler.

The Alig gravy train, which in its heyday had supported a large cast of characters—drug dealers, promoters, and people who were paid simply to show up and be ogled by the less fabulous—staggered on to its last stop, its passenger list thinned by scandal and reduced by financial circumstance. Notably absent from the Friday night party were many of the sideshow curiosities that helped Alig's parties become the red-hot center of New York's whirling nightlife. Alig, still acting like he had a future in front of him, was in a small room off the dance floor. Bloated and unshaven, he looked terrible. Unusual for him, he wasn't wearing some crazy outfit, just a striped sailor shirt and a pair of black bell-bottoms.

Lounging on a pink bed, he sniffed a line of white powder. A bizarre touch was the picture of Martin Luther King, Jr., looking down from the wall. I told Alig that Angel's body had been found. Alig, with a distant look in his droopy, bloodshot eyes, turned away. He was either too stoned or too indifferent to reply.

Detectives from Staten Island's 122nd Precinct and the Manhattan District Attorney's office were finally ready to snatch up the suspects they believed had murdered Angel Melendez. The only problem was that they had no idea where Alig was currently staying. They did know that Alig regularly visited his friend and drug dealer Brooke Humphries at the Chelsea Hotel on Twenty-third Street. Undercover cops swooped down on Humphries for selling cocaine at the Chelsea. DA investigator Rodriguez asked the handcuffed Humphries where Michael was. She wouldn't tell them. They asked her to call Alig on his new boyfriend Brian's pager and set up a meeting somewhere, so they could grab him. They offered to drop all the charges if she did. She refused. Then the DA detectives spotted a yellow sticker on Brooke's bulletin board. The piece of paper had the name of Alig and Brian's hotel, their room number, and the phone number of the establishment. Now they were set to take down the king of the club kids.

The next day, Alig was arrested at a shabby motel in Toms River, on the New Jersey shore. When detectives burst into the room, Alig was playing with his Lego set while his boyfriend was in the bathroom flushing drugs down the toilet in the mistaken belief that the DEA, not the DA, was at the front door. Alig denied any knowledge of Angel's whereabouts and demanded to see his lawyer. The detectives told him he was being arrested and allowed him to pack some toiletries before bustling him into a squad car.

Later that day, Freeze was apprehended, and he surprised detectives when, after initially refusing to answer questions, he made a full written and oral confession, implicating both himself and Alig. Freeze's confession dovetailed with the account in the *Village Voice* down to the smallest detail.

After being arraigned at Manhattan Criminal Court, Alig and Freeze were both sent to the infirmary at Rikers Island, a hellhole where fifty fiending junkies slept on top of each other. The methadone that would salve their psychic wounds was four long days away. With no coterie of pushers to serve their every caprice, Alig and Freeze were forced to go cold turkey. Alig had managed to smuggle a single bag of heroin into the jail, but that was nowhere near enough to get them both straight. Freeze tried to sell his shoes for heroin that was available from other inmates, but that cost $40 a bag, twice the street price.

Alig's days were ruled by terror, his nights by horror. His body throbbed with hurt. His ass and his mouth exploded at the same time. He existed for a while in his own piss and shit. He imagined spiders crawling in his hair. His mind was transported to dreadful places. No matter how hard he tried, he couldn't chase the horrible pictures out of his head. Gargoyles bearing Angel's face haunted his fitful sleep. He cried out desperately for his mother.

Despite the confession, the tug of war between federal and state authorities over Alig wasn't finished. DEA agents Bob Gagne and Matt Germanowski visited Rikers with a clean change of clothing for Alig. Alig claimed that they told him if he admitted to the killing he would get three years. If he didn't tell them what really happened, he would go to jail for the rest of his life. They still wanted to use Alig as a witness against Gatien, even after they knew he was a murderer. Alig confessed to the agents that he killed Angel over a drug debt and implicated

Gatien in the subsequent cover-up. He said Gatien knew all about the slaying and gave him money to leave town. But because of the complicated legal web created by two independent investigations, these allegations were never turned over to prosecutors handling Angel's killing. The DA's office said they didn't want the confession because Alig's lawyer was not present when he waived his rights. Plus, they didn't trust the DEA agents. They thought the feds were trying to interfere with their case.

After Alig was released from the infirmary, he was sent to the Rikers Island gay block where, upon admission, four gangbangers savagely beat him because they thought he was on the phone too long. They smashed his head against a wall and beat him to the ground, where they jumped on his stomach, literally squeezing all the crap out of him. Guards also beat him up and called him a "faggot." Inmates stole his food. He had to pay a bunch of gang members for protection. Alig was also raped several times by a member of the heretical Islamic street sect known as the "Five Percent Nation," which literally believes whites are the devil incarnate. For a while, Alig became the rapist's "bitch."

In the aftermath of Alig's arrest, rumors circulated that the district attorney's office, which claimed to be furious with the DEA for protecting Alig, was going to ask the judge for the death penalty. On numerous occasions Alig had jokingly told friends that he planned to kill Angel for his drugs. Murder in the pursuit of a robbery is a capital crime in New York State. And, there had been a fourth person in the apartment that day—Daniel Auster, the prodigal son of celebrated novelist Paul Auster. The story Daniel told the DA differed from Alig and Freeze's confession in one essential aspect.

The eighteen-year-old Daniel, who met Alig at a record-release party for Mancunian mope-rocker Morrisey and followed Alig around like a lost puppy, was staying at Riverbank West after having been kicked out of his parents' home. Alig and Jennytalia frequently went over to the Auster home for dinner. "Daniel's dad was very cool and liberal—a bit too liberal, perhaps," recalled Alig. In the days prior to Angel's death, Daniel was doing drugs with Alig and Freeze in the apartment.

After the slaying, Auster had been whisked out of the city by his father to a secret location. Paul Auster had then contacted a family friend, who happened to be Manhattan District Attorney Robert Morgenthau. Morgenthau had a reputation for treating celebrities with kid gloves. A meeting was arranged at which Daniel told DA investigators that he'd heard Alig and Freeze plotting to stick up Angel for his stash the day before his death. Angel was lured to the apartment, carrying a big bankroll and a large amount of drugs. As he entered the place, Freeze and Angel were waiting for him behind the door. It wasn't "a sissy fight among friends" that spiraled out of control, which was Alig's version of events, but, according to Auster, a preplanned robbery that escalated into murder.

"I heard he bragged about it to schoolmates," said Alig. "And claimed it was all planned and that he helped me and Freeze murder Angel for his drugs."

Ironically, Alig probably saved Daniel's life the very same day he took Angel's. During the early stages of the fracas, Alig noticed his friend slumped in the corner, his face turning blue. Luckily, Alig recognized the signs. Daniel was OD'ing from the heroin and needed a cure administered immediately. Alig broke away from the struggle and rushed toward Angel's bag looking for cocaine.

Angel angrily protested, "You're not using my coke."

Alig shot back, "I'm taking it anyway; just add it to my tab."

Alig rushed to Auster's side and put some cocaine in a straw and blew it up Daniel's nose. Almost immediately, Daniel jerked back to life.

But after threatening Alig with the death penalty, the DA, in what is now a controversial decision, backed down. The junkie Daniel was an unreliable witness. His story was peppered with inconsistencies. In addition, he admitted to stealing $3,000 from Angel's corpse. It would have been the word of one drug mess against another. In the end, the district attorney offered Alig a deal: ten to twenty years on manslaughter. Alig's lawyer told him he'd be crazy not to accept the offer, which Alig promptly did.

New York City, July 1996

That the overstuffed advocate had an oversized opinion of himself was not difficult to discern from the numerous framed press clippings that decorated the walls of his plush offices. Some called this "little big man" a blustering egomaniac, someone who loved the sound of his own voice and who would go to practically any lengths to get his well-heeled clients acquitted. But even his detractors admitted that few lawyers could win over a jury like Ben Brafman, a much sought-after specialist in the art of discrediting the prosecution by using their own evidence against them. Combining a sense of showmanship with one of the sharpest legal minds around, he would stride up and down in front of the jury box, transforming a dry legal argument into a forceful, easily understandable life-and-death narrative, whose dénouement, more times than not, was the setting free of one of his shady but entirely innocent clients. With a terrier's tenacity, he won an astonishing 80 percent of the cases he took on, often in the face of seemingly overwhelming evidence. He was the guy top mobsters, larcenous rabbis, and crooked politicians called at 4:00 A.M., when they got into serious trouble.

In the middle of July 1996, Brafman was sitting behind his desk on the twenty-fifth floor of a midtown skyscraper when he received a frantic phone call from Alex Gatien. Her husband had just been arrested on drug conspiracy charges. She needed someone to go down to the federal courthouse in Brooklyn and bail him out. Brafman—a short, stout dynamo of a man with bushy eyebrows, a puffed-up chest, and a taste for pinstripe suits he wore like armor plating—usually steered clear of narcotics cases. Although Brafman had defended a number of organized crime figures, most notably Sammy "The Bull" Gravano, the bulk of his clients were accused of white-collar crimes. But Brafman, who had barely heard of Ecstasy and had no idea that Special K was anything other than a breakfast cereal, recognized the publicity value of taking on such a case. He loved the media spotlight as much as any club kid.

The defense attorney had once met Gatien at Club USA, where he was introduced by former Koch administration official Susan Wagner, Brafman's cousin through marriage, who worked for Gatien smoothing over tensions between his clubs and the police and community boards.

"I found him to be fascinating," said Brafman. "I knew he was successful in the club world. I'd seen his face on the cover of *New York* magazine. The whole mystique about him with the black eye patch was intriguing. He was someone you read about all the time in the gossip columns. And being a criminal lawyer who defends high-profile people, I read the tabloids to keep current on what's happening, so the name Peter Gatien was very familiar to me."

Brafman began his legal career in the Manhattan DA's office prosecuting the Mafia. But after going into private practice, the former stand-up comic switched his allegiance. He broke into the big leagues in 1985 by representing one of the lesser-known defendants in a famous Mafia case. Gambino crime family boss Paul Castellano and several of his cohorts were on trial for murder and racketeering. Recognizing that the case would boost his public profile, Brafman had slashed his customary fee. After John Gotti arranged for Castellano to be gunned down outside of Spark's Steak House, Brafman was featured in a front-page photo in the *New York Post* paying his respects at the funeral of the slain mob boss. His former colleagues at the DA's office were appalled. Brafman, a deeply religious man and a pillar of his local temple, was now representing mob clients. His reputation among the criminal classes was secured when Brafman's client was acquitted on all counts, while all the other codefendants got jail time.

Once he'd agreed to defend Peter Gatien, one of the first things that struck Brafman about the government's case was that his client was arrested not because of an indictment but a complaint. Instead of presenting evidence in front of a grand jury, the DEA agents had simply given sworn testimony before a judge who, on his own authority, issued the order that Gatien be apprehended. This told Brafman that the arrest wasn't the culmination of the Gatien investigation but an interim tactic used to further the continuing probe. The prosecution strategy was obvious, one that had been successfully used in numerous organized crime cases: arrest as many people as possible connected to the alleged conspiracy and, one by one, get them to rat up the ladder in exchange for leniency.

"The government made the decision to arrest Peter Gatien and assumed the people he was arrested with would all cooperate to save themselves from the draconian sentences routinely imposed in drug cases," said Brafman. "When Peter was arrested, he was arrested with dozens of other people, many of whom he'd never met or spoken to before."

In addition, after consulting with numerous colleagues more expert in drug matters than he, Brafman was also surprised to learn that Ecstasy wasn't even illegal under state law, though the joy powder had been banned since 1983 by federal statute. There was no precedent for the case. Brafman and his assistants scoured the law books but could find no existing example of a club owner being sentenced to a long jail term for allowing Ecstasy dealers on his premises. Legally speaking, this was virgin territory.

"Peter is under attack by the full force of the federal government in a way I've never seen before," said Brafman. "It's almost become a mission to save him, because I believe he is not guilty of the charges against him. Even if he has done something wrong, he doesn't deserve the kind of punishment the government is seeking to impose. This is a case that, under normal circumstances, if handled by the state authorities rather than the federal authorities, would be resolved very quickly and with little penalty for Peter. He is being singled out for prosecution among many other club owners who are being completely ignored by the DEA. It's as if he's been targeted for extinction by the powers-that-be and it's scary."

Interviewing Peter Gatien in the months following his arrest was a problematic proposition, now that he was joined at the hip with Ben Brafman. The lawyer insisted on being present at all interview sessions, where he would try to deflect difficult questions away from his client, sometimes answering them himself. Finishing each other's sentences and using the same phrases and arguments, Gatien and Brafman spoke in one voice, as they laid out their rebuttal to the prosecution.

Plausible deniability was the basis of Gatien's defense. This impresario wasn't around most nights to supervise his employees, so he couldn't be blamed if they committed serious crimes without his knowledge. His organization was big. He had a thousand employees. He couldn't possibly know everything that was going down at his venues. The club owner acted as if he bore no moral responsibility whatsoever for fostering an atmosphere in which illegal and evil things consistently happened.

After he left jail, Gatien maintained his innocence and improbably told the press that he was unaware of any substantial drug dealing at the Limelight or the Tunnel. In the next breath, ignoring the contradiction, he also claimed that he did everything he could to keep out drug dealers. I wanted to ask how Gatien could believably maintain his innocence, when so many of his codefendants had already pled guilty to drug charges. I also wanted to know how he could credibly insist that he was not aware of the extent of drug dealing by employees at his venues, when everybody else in clubland was.

Gatien made a halfhearted attempt to answer, but Brafman kept jumping in: "Given the dimensions of Peter's operation, and given the amount of people he employs, and given the latitude they were given to be creative, not to mention the looseness of the organization in general, this allowed many people to do things without Peter's knowledge on a regular basis. It's an impossible request to expect that Peter Gatien should be held personally responsible for anything anybody in his clubs did, unless you can prove he was aware of it, and allowed it go on, and was a willing participant in it. Telling me after the fact that certain people did something wrong is no evidence of participation in a conspiracy."

By this point I'd had enough and demanded Brafman leave the room, so I could do my job without interference. "I refuse to do an interview under these circumstances," I pouted. "Don't waste my time."

Brafman refused and snorted. "You're lucky I even let you talk to Peter. I've turned down interviews with *60 Minutes* and *The New York Times.*"

Angered by his response, I stormed out of the room. Gatien came into the hallway and persuaded me to resume our heavily circumscribed chat. The club owner had learned his lines so well that it was as if Brafman were speaking anyway.

After tempers cooled, Gatien went on to say that the government was using a double standard to prosecute him. "Short of strip-searching people, it's impossible to keep drugs completely out of clubs," he argued. "When I was arrested, that particular facility I was in, thirteen people, including guards, were apprehended for dealing drugs there. If a high-security prison can't keep drugs out, how am I supposed to? You have to have hard evidence that someone is a drug dealer or drug user in order to ban them from a club. It's a public place."

Gatien admitted to occasional personal drug use during the wild hotel parties. "They've supposedly got me four times over the last five years. If they were to apply that same standard to the media, Wall Street, and the music industry, and say that if we find in your life that on four occasions in the past five years you've gone to a party where you used small amounts of controlled substances for recreational purposes, then there'd be more people in jail than out on the street."

But the most compelling argument for Gatien's innocence was the government wiretaps. The DEA agents had compiled a log consisting of hundreds of hours of secretly recorded conversations between drug dealers, and not one of the tapes featured any talk about the club owner either sanctioning or personally financing narcotics transactions.

"Anyone who's been in the nightclub business for as long as I have," said Gatien, "knows you can't keep a secret for more than thirty seconds. If I was running any sort of drug ring at the Limelight, it would have been all over town. Surely, if I was involved in the distribution of drugs, the DEA would have some conversation that surfaces that says: 'Bring the drugs to Peter tonight' or 'We've got to do a deal with Peter.' I'm supposed to be at the top of the totem poll, but my name is never bought up in connection with any conspiracy. How come?"

The reaction to Gatien's arrest among some in clubland was gleeful. His rivals were openly jubilant, unaware that they themselves would soon become targets of drug probes. But other, more thoughtful types recognized the troubling precedent that was being set.

Ecstasy is the devil drug du jour, the subject of a nationwide moral panic, but for years the authorities turned a blind eye to the drug's recreational use in discos. E wasn't that big a deal. Psychiatrists used it in therapy, for chrissakes. Heroin and, to a certain extent, cocaine were the killer drugs. Ecstasy was like pot, generally harmless. Many clubgoers sincerely believed that the little capsules and tablets were perfectly legal. Gatien told a story about personally handing over an E dealer he caught in his club to the cops, who merely shrugged and said, "What do you expect us to do about it?" Many partygoers had no idea that dispensing happy pills could land you behind bars for up to twenty years.

Gerard was a mild-mannered Ecstasy dealer who used to peddle his wares at a variety of clubs. He started selling as a sort of social service to fellow disco denizens and as a means of making a bit of spare cash on the side. He never made more than a couple of thousand bucks a week from his illegal activities and often made a lot less. He finally quit the business because of the increasing levels of violence associated with selling the love drug.

Gerard (not his real name) was a freelance dealer, not a house dealer, which meant that he jumped from one disco to the next and that his illegal activities were unsanctioned. He had wide experience dealing party favors not just at the Limelight and the Tunnel but also at such non-Gatien clubs as the Roxy and Sound Factory.

"I'm not surprised that Peter Gatien got arrested," he said. "I'm more surprised it took the authorities so long to clamp down. When I used to deal at the Roxy, other drug dealers used to joke that we might as well be replaced with vending machines because we were so obvious and blatant. I used to walk around the club in a silver hat with a big silver money pouch on my waist that would progressively fill up over the evening, to the point where it was bulging."

Still, Gerard thought it a little unfair that a club owner like Gatien got nabbed, since in his experience, the bouncers are the ones who organize the narcotics flow at most of the big-box dance halls. "It usually begins when security spots you dealing and asks you to pay a certain amount each night," he related. "Those that won't pay are eliminated from the club; those that do become the so-called house dealers. I got forced out of the Roxy because I wouldn't pay the bouncers $500 a night. That was practically my whole profit."

After the Roxy, Gerard relocated to another underground dance hall, Sound Factory, the same place where Chris Paciello and Michael Caruso got into a brawl with the head of security, Alex Coffiel. "Sound Factory was a messy situation," he reminisced. "I got busted three times by the bouncers. The first time it happened, I ended up in a closet with two huge bouncers who took all my drugs and gave them to the house dealers to sell. The second time, I walked into the club with about fifty bottles of K in my pocket, and one of the security patted me down and found the K. He dragged me outside and started emptying the bottles one by one into the street, all the time asking me how much money they were worth to me. He had about $1,000 worth of my drugs in his hands, so I gave him $300 and he gave me my K back. The third time was the scariest. They punched me in the stomach, took all my money and drugs, and said they were going to call the police. After that, I quit the business."

While Gerard allowed that the authorities had good reason to crack down, given how out-of-control the scene had become under the influence of polydrug mania, he still considered it a tad unjust that Gatien was being made the scapegoat for the ills that affect New York clubland in general. "I believe that Peter Gatien wanted drugs in his club. He knew if you took all the drugs out of his clubs, no one would go. But the idea of him getting directly involved in the drug dealing, I don't believe that. He would have to be incredibly stupid to do that."

Private eye John Dabrowski had never heard of Peter Gatien when he got a phone call from his boss, Les Levine, telling him they'd just been hired by Ben Brafman to work a big case involving the Canadian businessman.

"Who's Peter Gatien?" asked Dabrowski.

"He owns the Limelight, Tunnel, and Palladium," Levine explained.

"What are they?"

"Don't worry, you're going to make a lot of money."

Dabrowski, a white-haired bulldog of a man with a pink face and an impressive beer gut that expanded prominently over his belt, was a former Long Island homicide detective and not easily shocked by the darker impulses that vein the human condition.

Dabrowski's first impressions of Gatien were of "a quiet guy, mild-mannered, didn't like confrontation much, smoked a lot, and drank a lot of ice tea." The club owner swore on his children's lives that he wasn't a drug dealer. "He kept saying that he didn't even know half the people he was arrested with, that he met most of them for the first time in lockup," said Dabrowski. In the end, the private eye would grill over seven hundred employees, from bouncers to bartenders to drag queens. "Not one of them said that Peter was involved in the drug dealing," he claimed.

While his boss, Les Levine, took all the credit in the press, Dabrowski was what is known in law enforcement lingo as "the carrying detective" on the case. In other words, he was the one who did all the hard labor in the trenches. Dabrowski complained all the time about Levine's constant hogging of the spotlight; he ridiculed the way his boss went on undercover surveillance operations, sitting conspicuously in a brand-new Jaguar, complete with vanity license plates that read "Les P.I." "I do all the goddamn work," he bellyached. "Les gets all the publicity."

Once aboard the counterinvestigation, Dabrowski started to methodically dissect the case against the club owner. One of the first aspects he focused on was the search warrant the DEA agents had used to rifle the club owner's office at the Tunnel. Agent Matt Germanowski had sworn to a judge that a month before the dance hall king was arrested, while sitting in the surveillance room overlooking the Tunnel, he saw Gatien using cocaine in his office, after which he returned the banned substance to his desk drawer. Dabrowski inspected the desk but could find no compartments, hidden or otherwise. He then contacted the North Carolina company that made the desk, and they confirmed that the piece of furniture was originally made without any drawer. "The search warrant for the Tunnel was bogus," alleged Dabrowski. "They were trying to railroad Peter."

Dabrowski then turned his attention to the circumstances surrounding the suspected drug overdose death of teenager Nicholas Mariniello, who expired at his politically plugged-in parents' New Jersey home, supposedly after coming home from a night of tripping on Ecstasy at the Limelight. The alleged drug death of Mariniello was the pretext for local and state probers to launch their investigation into Gatien's troubled operation, which was separate from the federal inquiry. Dabrowski drove over to the Morris County Medical Examiner's Office to obtain a copy of the death certificate. He was surprised to find out that Mariniello didn't die of a drug overdose but instead had hanged himself. No toxicology report was done, so it was impossible to know for sure if MDMA was in Mariniello's blood.

Dabrowski then tried to interview Michael Alig at the Chelsea Hotel. Alig was staying there with his good friend, cocaine dealer Brooke Humphries. The investigator knew all about Alig and how he had dismembered Angel, but what really shocked him about the club kid were the infamous Emergency Room parties he'd heard about. "The fact that he would urinate on people, and they would accept it," he said. "That's disgusting." Dabrowski knocked on the hotel room door, and Brooke answered. "She was one of the ugliest women I'd ever seen," claimed Dembrowski, no bathing beauty himself. "Her face looked like a pincushion, she had so many bits of metal embedded in it. She and Alig were both so stoned that I could see I wasn't going to get anywhere, so I gave them my business card and left."

Next, Dabrowski began digging for dirt on Lord Michael, fully expecting that the former Limelight techno promoter would sooner or later turn state's evidence against Gatien. He zeroed in on the death of Damon Burett, who supposedly shot himself in the head with Caruso's gun at the promoter's fancy downtown apartment. Ruled a suicide by the medical examiner, Burett's death had many suspicious circumstances. Caruso's fingerprints were all over the suicide weapon, and the suicide note described a method of dispatch different from the one Burett actually used. After reviewing forensic and toxicology reports, Dabrowski became convinced that Lord Michael had killed his live-in housekeeper and then concocted the suicide scenario to camouflage the deed. He confronted Lord Michael at the door of Expo, the Times Square club where he had moved after quitting Gatien's employ, but the promoter refused to talk to him: "I've got nothing to say to you, pal." The private investigator also made several trips to Miami Beach and talked to Chris Paciello at Liquid, but Paciello denied even knowing Caruso.

The middle-aged, overweight Dabrowski looked out of a place in a clubland setting. He walked, talked, and looked too much like the cop he used to be. Disco denizens distrusted him. Only when he hooked up with Peter Gatien's daughter Jennifer—the rosy apple of her father's one good orb—did his investigation really take off. Jennifer used to date Caruso, and she was intimate with all the key players in the unfolding drama.

"Jennifer opened up a lot of doors," admitted Dabrowski. "She used to work the door at her father's clubs so she knew all the club kids personally. She was a huge help."

One time, Jennifer, who was still friendly with Caruso, set up a meeting at a Staten Island basketball court to try and gauge his intentions toward her father. Caruso told her to be dressed in only light clothing so he could see if she was wearing a wire. He assured Jennifer that he had no intention of ratting out her dad to save his own skin. "I would never betray Peter," Caruso said. "He's closer to me than my own father." Putting on a show of bravado, he told Jennifer not to worry; he was going to tell the DEA to go screw themselves.

Together, Dabrowski and Jennifer Gatien also visited Alig in prison, after he was arrested on the murder rap. Jennifer begged the club kid to aid her father. "We have to band together and help each other," Jennifer told Alig. "Both our families are being threatened by the same people." After much cajoling, what Alig eventually told Jennifer and Dabrowski would alter the course of the entire prosecution.

The government's case against Peter Gatien started to seriously derail after Sean Bradley, the original informant in the investigation, and the teenager who dressed up undercover agents Gagne and Germanowski as club kids to get them into the Limelight and Tunnel's VIP rooms, made a number of serious accusations of government misconduct.

In April 1996, Bradley went to the same Woodbridge shopping mall where he had been previously busted on counterfeiting charges. A young woman whom Sean had met at a rave wanted to buy twenty hits of Ecstasy and some Special K. Bradley was out of drugs to sell, but luckily his girlfriend Jennifer had the ketamine. As for the Ecstasy, they decided together that they would try and pass off ephedrine tablets as MDMA. Once at the shopping center, Sean spotted the raver girl, but she was with an older guy whom Bradley suspected was undercover heat. Jessica, the drug mule, was standing nearby, pretending to shop. Sean walked up to the pair and said, "The deal is off. I don't have anything." He then hurried away. As Sean and Jessica left the mall, police surrounded them from all directions and detained and searched them. The cops found five bags of K and twenty Ephedrine tablets, which they presumed were Ecstasy. The couple were hand-cuffed and transported to the Woodbridge Police Department, where Bradley revealed to detectives his status as a DEA informant working on an important case.

One of the prosecutors in the Gatien case, Michelle Adelman—dubbed "Unibrow" by the agents because of her connecting eye-brows—rushed over the Hudson River to the Middlesex County jail, where she challenged Bradley: "You know what an embarrassment you are. Our prize informant gets arrested on drug charges," the purple-faced prosecutor supposedly screamed at her charge. "I wrote you a 5K letter [a letter to the judge recommending leniency] in the counterfeit-ing case, and now I'm going to look like an asshole. If you fuck up this case, I will come after you and bury you," Bradley claimed she angrily threatened. Bob Gagne and Matt Germanowski were also there. Bradley pleaded with them to get him and Jennifer out of jail. Angry that their pet rodent had messed up, the DEA duo decided to let Bradley stew in his own juices for a while.

Bradley had become a major embarrassment. He was a screwed-up informer from a screwed-up milieu in an increasingly screwed-up investigation. The feds wished he would disappear from the picture.

In early May, after he got out of jail, Bradley maintained that the agents called him up and asked him to track down John Charles, who supplied Ecstasy to many of the top Manhattan nightclubs. They wanted him to do one last buy. Bradley phoned up Charles and set up a deal, involving two hundred hits of Ecstasy, to take place the following Friday. The deal had to be done quickly. Bradley didn't have the full cash amount on tap to pay for the pills. So he decided to rip off Charles and then later get the DEA to reimburse him for the transaction. Bradley arrived at New York's Penn Station carrying forty single dollar bills in a roll with a twenty on top, so, at first glance, it would look like a couple of thousand bucks. He handed Charles the money and received two hundred pills in return. Bradley took the train back to New Jersey, very pleased with himself that he had suckered a big-time dealer like Charles. Unbeknownst to Bradley, he had in return been fooled: The Ecstasy was entirely phony.

The next afternoon, Bradley was awakened from a marijuana stupor when the agents came calling at his apartment. "What's up?" he asked. Bradley remembers that Germanowski replied, "We just heard on the wire. You ripped off John Charles for two hundred pills. And he put out a contract on you. Where's the Ecstasy?" Bradley handed over the fake tablets. Germanowski said, "Michelle Adelman wants us to arrest you. Are there any other drugs in the house?" The agents took the remaining weed that Bradley was smoking but left the bong.

The following Monday, Bradley was arrested at the DEA's Manhattan headquarters and charged with selling drugs without the agents' permission. Bradley's cooperation agreement with the government was ripped up on the spot. He was headed to jail, and he was furious. He felt that the DEA had double-crossed him. When Bradley tried to contact Gagne and Germanowski from Manhattan's Metropolitan Correctional Center, the men refused to accept his calls.

Not long after Bradley was incarcerated, Ben Brafman got a phone call from Bradley's lawyer, who told him, "I think you should know that one of the main witnesses in the Gatien case is saying that many of the allegations the agents are making against Gatien are not true. There's stuff he's telling me in connection with his undercover work that I think you should know about. He's willing to meet with you."

Brafman visited Bradley in jail, and what the snitch told the defense attorney startled him. For one thing, Bradley claimed the agents had lied about seeing Gatien using a "one-hitter" (a device for delivering a small jolt of cocaine) in his office at the Tunnel. The agents had repeated this story before a judge in their application for a warrant to search Gatien's home and businesses. Bradley maintained he was present that day in the surveillance room located across the street from the Tunnel when Gatien was spotted putting his hand to his nose. The agents joked that it looked like Gatien was doing blow. Bradley claimed that the joke ended up in the official report of investigation as a real drug incident.

Bradley repeated similar accusations of misconduct in a lengthy Dear Judge letter, in which he began by outlining the important role he'd played in the Gatien case: "Now your honor, I don't want to sound cocky, but I was the whole underlying factor of the case. . . . If I did not get them into the clubs, and introduce them to high-profile targets that I did, or not taken them shopping for clothes so they would fit in, or take pictures for them, it would have taken years to infiltrate this criminal enterprise, and shut it down, rather than the mere months that it did."

Bradley then went on to detail what he claimed was wrongdoing by the agents. According to Bradley, both Matt Germanowski and Bob Gagne popped Ecstasy, snorted Special K, and drank excessively while undercover at the Limelight, just like the club kids they were supposed to track. But another snitch I contacted, who also worked with Gagne and Germanowski, refuted the charges: "Bradley is a lying piece of shit. The agents didn't do drugs and get drunk. Bradley did."

Bradley further claimed that even after he began working for the DEA, he continued to use drugs in the clubs with the agents' knowledge. After he failed a drug test, he says that Bob Gagne taught him how to mask his urine—using a combination of protein, vinegar, and vegetable oil. He also accused the agents of giving him and his girlfriend high-grade Ecstasy for personal use. And he said he continued to deal drugs right under the agents' noses.

"Right from the beginning, they were breaking the rules," wrote Bradley. "They made it very clear to me that they wanted Peter Gatien at any cost. They would tell me what to write when I gave them statements. They blatantly added things or made things up." In addition, Bradley said that Gagne had confided to him, "Because criminals lie and cheat, sometimes the government has to do the same thing to get their target."

Bradley also accused Gagne of making frequent sexual remarks about his girlfriend because she was a stripper: "Does she take it in the ass?" and "Has she ever fucked another girl?" "Agent Gagne is one of those stereotypical males," he wrote, "who think they are very macho and have to prove it by bragging about their sexual conquests. Gagne would always describe his sex life to me, which made me feel very uncomfortable."

At the end of his letter Bradley complained, "I trusted them with everything, my life, my emotions, and now I feel as though I was betrayed," sounding like a jilted lover. "They used me as they needed and when they were done, they discarded me as though I were disposable."

The government denied Bradley's accusations, characterizing them as "perjurious," and saying that Bradley had a strong motive to lie to get back at the DEA handlers he felt had betrayed him. "Bradley won't testify to back up his allegations," prosecutor Michelle Adelman countered. "The only affidavit they have alleging government misconduct omits the more serious accusations from the unsigned and undated Dear Judge letter."

Brafman said the reason that Bradley wouldn't testify was the government had threatened to indict him for perjury and obstruction of justice if he did. "They have essentially told Sean Bradley's lawyer that if he were to testify to the things he alleged in his Dear Judge letter," said Brafman, "that they would consider it a crime." Bradley's lawyer insisted his client wouldn't testify without immunity.

"I feel sorry for Sean," said an affable Germanowski, when I later bumped into him in the elevator at the Brooklyn federal courthouse.

"He's not a bad kid. He just didn't know what he was getting himself into."

The next informant to step forward with allegations of government misconduct was Michael Alig. Alig had initially cooperated with the feds after agents had arrested him in June 1996 on drug charges and offered him a deal. Now supposedly clean and sober, he'd had a change of heart about ratting out Gatien, especially after Jennifer Gatien and John Dabrowski visited him in jail, where Alig was awaiting sentencing on manslaughter charges for killing Angel. Jennifer promised that her father would help pay his legal expenses (a figure of $10,000 was bandied about, claimed Alig) and give him a job when he got out. The story Alig told me, and which he repeated in an affidavit, sounded like a scene from a Sidney Lumet movie: The two thick-necked agents, he said, picked him up from Rikers Island, his body quivering in remission. Gagne and Germanowski were supposed to be taking Alig to the Metropolitan Detention Center, a federal facility in Brooklyn. But when they got to the high-security lockup, there was no room at the inn, so Alig and the agents went out on a day-long jaunt.

According to the club kid, the agents wanted to interrogate their disgraced source about Peter Gatien one last time, but so painful were the withdrawal symptoms that he began to moan and retch in the backseat of their car, and after some persuading on Alig's part, the two agents allowed him to use their handy car phone to contact his boyfriend Brian McCauley in New Jersey—a good source for heroin.

Alig then said the agents took him to a location where he met Brian, who handed over several packets of smack. After Brian left, they then drove to Alig's favorite restaurant—Burger King—where the agents munched on Whoppers in the front, while in the back the informant snorted smack through a straw from the fast-food joint. Later that day, Alig was returned by the agents to Rikers Island.

That night, Alig's mother, Elke, received a phone call from her son, who told her that he had called Brian McCauley's house from one of the agent's phones and asked him to come over with some money. Elke called Brian's mother, and she confirmed that Michael had indeed phoned Brian and that Brian said he was leaving to meet up with the DEA agents. The next day Elke flew to New York, and when she met Brian at Newark Airport, Elke claims he told her that he had met with her son and given him money and "enough heroin to last a couple of days." According to Elke, Brian said the DEA agents knew that Alig was doing heroin because Michael talked about it openly on the phone in front of the agents.

Not long after, Alig was picked up again by Germanowski and Gagne for a second "day trip" during which, the club kid claims, he once more obtained heroin that he ingested in the agents' car. Waiting for the drug connection to arrive, Alig soiled himself, so Gagne and Germanowski supposedly took Alig to his friend Gitsie's place, which was in nearby Queens. Alig changed his pants and then two and a half hours later, Brian turned up with several packets of heroin. Brian had taken so long to get there, Alig claimed, that Germanowksi and Gagne were forced to telephone Rikers Island and inform officials that they had custody of Alig and would be late in returning him to the facility because of "heavy traffic." When the first dose turned out to be junk, Brian went away to find something better. This time, the dope hit the spot. The following week, Brian was arrested trying to smuggle heroin in to Alig at Rikers Island, though the charges were later dropped.

Germanowski vehemently denied that Alig ever did drugs in the back of his car. "We were trying to do the human thing by taking him for a meal," he retorted. "Alig was hungry because he kept getting beaten up at Rikers, and the other prisoners were taking away his food."

Alig further maintained that the agents were well aware of his involvement in the Angel Melendez slaying. But they shielded him in return for information about Peter Gatien. "By the time they find the body, it will be so badly decomposed, nobody will be able to do shit," Alig said the agents had guaranteed him. He also claimed that Gagne and Germanowski had assured him on several occasions that even if he were arrested for the killing, he would get a "slap on the wrist" and serve no more than one to three years, especially if they were to inter-vene on his behalf, which they promised to do, as long as he handed them Gatien's scalp. Alig went on to say that Germanowski even made fun of Angel's corpse, walking on his knees outside the grand jury room in a cruel imitation of the dismembered club kid. Germanowski denied the charges and insisted that Alig was asked on numerous occasions whether he had anything to do with the murder of Melendez. "Each and every time he categorically denied it," he countered.

In addition, Alig claimed that the agents fabricated evidence, spoon-feeding him quotes that implicated Gatien. "On numerous occasions, they attributed information to me that was simply not true. They would take part of what I said and add to it in order to make Peter appear to be personally involved in activities that I knew he had nothing to do with," Alig said.

In an affidavit signed and dated 2nd July 1997, Alig wrote: "I do wish to point out that in the course of my many debriefings with the agents, I told them many things about Mr. Gatien that they were obviously not happy to hear. They openly discussed with me their displeasure with information that I provided them that was exculpatory to Mr. Gatien. I can also state, that on more than one occasion, the agents told me that they had a personal reason to vigorously investigate and prosecute Mr. Gatien at 'all costs.'"

"I don't think I've ever encountered two more renegade law enforcement officials than these two," fumed Alig's lawyer Jerry McMahon. "They're abusive, high-handed, out-of-control bullies who've overstepped the line of what a law officer should do. They've threatened witnesses, and they've threatened me. To say they're out to get Peter Gatien at any cost is an understatement."

"These charges are ludicrous," Michelle Adelman shot back. "It's the government's position that the defense is playing to the press. It's a PR ploy designed to deflect attention away from the very serious charges facing Mr. Gatien."

Just when things couldn't get any more down and
dirty, Sean Kirkham resurfaced from his time as a police and FBI
informer in Miami's South Beach, where he had traded information
with Chris Paciello and been part of the scene at Paciello's clubs, Risk
and Liquid. The professional informer and onetime male hustler not
only backed up Alig and Bradley's charges that the government was trying to frame Peter Gatien by embellishing and manufacturing evidence
but also made the startling accusation that he had been brought into the
case after having what Ben Brafman called in court documents "a rather
extraordinary personal relationship" with one of the Gatien prosecution team.

I first saw Kirkham in a Brooklyn courthouse in 1997 after he had
been arrested for trying to sell Gatien what he claimed was taped proof
of government misconduct in the case. He'd briefly skipped the country
but turned himself in and was now being charged with failure to appear
as well as with the initial charge of lying to a federal agent. Though the
stylish designer gear he once sported had been replaced by blue prison
scrubs, accessorized with a pair of handcuffs, the twenty-five-year-old
cut a striking if bewildered figure as he was escorted into the room. At
six feet, four inches tall, with thick charcoal hair and traces of teenage
acne still on his cheeks, he towered over his escorts. It was easy to see

why this lofty, slender, and fine-featured descendent of Inuits—with his high cheekbones and arched, carefully plucked eyebrows that gave him a permanently startled facial expression—was so effortlessly accepted into the fabulous demimonde of New York and Miami nightlife.

Before his arrest, Kirkham was a club-buster in South Beach by trade. Beginning in 1994, Kirkham claimed, he worked with agents and officers from the DEA, the FBI, the Bureau of Alcohol, Tobacco and Firearms, the Hollywood Police Department, the Miami Beach Police Department, and a number of special narcotics task forces. Kirkham said he sometimes netted $5,000 a case plus expenses. In addition, he contended that his clandestine efforts had led directly to the seizure of 10 kilos of cocaine, 5,000 hits of Ecstasy, 2 kilos of pot, and 400 vials of Special K. The information he provided Miami Beach police also resulted in the temporary closing of a number of local clubs.

To supplement his income, he took bribes from club owners and drug dealers. He worked both sides of the fence. "I was feared by the local drug dealers," he said. "They would arrange meetings with me to verify my status as an informant. They would then provide me with information on rival dealers and vice versa. I was befriended by a number of dealers who thought it was in their best interest to keep me out of harm's way." Kirkham claimed to have helped Chris Paciello by omitting Risk from his professional reports.

"The gossip on the Beach was that Sean was an informer," said nightclub manager Maxwell Blandford. Initially, Blandford took the rumors with a grain of salt. But when he noticed Kirkham flashing big bills and put that together with the fact that "Sean definitely knew a lot of cops," Blandford began to suspect he really was in league with law enforcement. He was none too surprised when he "heard through the grapevine that Sean was the one who got the clubs shut down." Some law enforcement sources tried to downplay the importance of Kirkham's undercover activities. "I'm telling you straight up, we never worked together," said one FBI agent, speaking off-the-record. "Kirkham was basically nothing. He claims to have worked with the whole world." The agent's partner would only say, "I can't make any comment on Sean Kirkham. I could lose my job. I can't even confirm that I knew the guy."

But another anonymous FBI contact praised Kirham's undercover prowess. "Ninety percent of what Sean says is right on the money," he said, before warning. "It's the other ten percent you've got to worry about."

Wilfredo Fernandez, a spokesperson for the U.S. attorney's office in Miami, confirmed that Kirkham did indeed help the feds in a major drug bust involving ten kilos of cocaine: "Mr. Kirkham was a confidential informant for us in December 1995 and testified in the case of U.S. v. Mario Santoro et al. about a shipment of cocaine from Miami to New York." In addition, Kirkham provided me with a number of confidential government documents that proved he also "satisfactorily worked as a DEA informant" out of their Ft. Lauderdale district office.

After Liquid's 1995 Thanksgiving opening, which Kirkham described as the most fabulous party he'd ever attended, he moved back to New York. While he'd been away his drag queen roommates had redecorated their apartment, turning their Upper East Side walk-up into a brothel dubbed Hotel 72. They advertised their services in the weekly gay rags and via sex phone lines. They did a thriving commerce among buttoned-down, closeted types in business suits.

Not long after he got back to New York, Kirkham says he saw a picture in the *Daily News* accompanying a piece about Peter Gatien's arrest and recognized someone in the photo. According to Kirkham, he then rang one of the prosecutors in the case at his Brooklyn office. After identifying himself and assuring him he meant him no harm, he offered his services. Kirkham said he had considerable field experience in this dangerous line of work. He detailed his past activities as a club-buster in Miami Beach. He also mentioned he was currently a registered informant for the FBI Organized Crime Unit, working on a case that involved infiltrating mob-run strip clubs.

At first, said Kirkham, the prosecutor was nervous. Their conversation was pitted with long pauses. Kirkham expected the official to hang up at any second. But eventually he told him he would mull the matter over. A few days later, he called Kirkham back. This time, his tone was clipped and businesslike. He asked if Sean had a pen. "Take down this number," he instructed. Kirkham was given two names: Matt Germanowski and Bob Gagne. The prosecutor then told him never to contact him again.

Kirkham met the agents at a coffee shop on the corner of Twelfth Avenue and Fifty-seventh Street, just across from the old DEA building. Kirkham arrived early and ordered breakfast, making sure to keep the tab open, knowing full well that the feds would pick up the bill. He'd been told what the agents looked like in advance, but that turned out to be unnecessary, when Kirkham spotted two giants trying to squeeze their way through the front door. He waved in their direction. They strode over to greet him like soldiers on parade, then sat down with ramrod backs and ordered stale coffee.

The agents' jaws dropped when Kirkham revealed he used to work for Peter Gatien in a menial position at Club USA. Germanowski pulled out a microcassette recorder, and they bombarded him with questions: What was his position at the club? Did he know Peter Gatien and Michael Alig? Why did he leave? What about Gatien's wife, the Dragon Lady, Alex—was she really the daughter of the Benihana restaurant chain's Rocky Aoki? The meeting lasted for four hours. As he was leaving, Germanowski handed Kirkham $50 for his time and told him he would call tomorrow. Kirkham was excited to be back in this adventurous line of work.

The next day, Kirkham took the subway to the DEA headquarters in Chelsea, where he was officially registered and then activated as a "regular use informant." There are several categories of government snitch; a "regular use informant" is one who works strictly for money. Kirkham's job was to provide information and introduce agents to targets. He would be paid for his efforts; how much depended on results. Like Bradley, Kirkham was promised 25 percent of everything confiscated from Gatien, if the club owner was convicted. If the sound system were worth $100,000, Kirkham would get $25,000. Since the DEA planned to seize all three of Gatien's clubs, Kirkham thought his payday had arrived. Six-figure numbers danced in his head. He remembered a story an FBI agent had once told him about a government informant who had access to a private plane and was shuttled all over the world in search of information. He stayed at only the best hotels and led a lavish lifestyle, all courtesy of the U.S. taxpayer.

Kirkham was fingerprinted and photographed. He signed a "cooperating individual agreement," which read in part: "I will not violate criminal laws in furtherance of gathering information or providing services to DEA and any evidence of such a violation will be reported by DEA to the appropriate law enforcement agency." He promised not to pose as a DEA agent. He was handed a fake beeper—actually a miniature recording device—and a 1-800 number to call if any other branch of law enforcement arrested him. Last, he was given a nightly stipend to circulate in the clubs. He pocketed the money. Because door people knew him already, he got in for free.

Kirkham and the agents sat down in a cramped boardroom and came up with a plan of action. They started off by going through the employee records recently seized from the Palladium. Kirkham was asked to identify drug dealers, club kids, and drug users; who they worked for; and how likely they were to turn state's evidence. He was shown a board depicting a pyramid. While the apex of the triangle was strangely blank, immediately below were pictures of Michael Alig and Lord Michael Caruso, and below them, Manager Ray Montgomery and Executive Director Steven Lewis. A host of club kids and drug dealers clogged up the bottom of the pyramid.

Finally, Kirkham was told to find out as much as he could about the whereabouts of the missing club kid Angel Melendez. The city was awash with rumors about Michael Alig's role in his disappearance. Kirkham knew Angel. "He wasn't a bad person. He was just very tight with money," he said. Kirkham was shown a grisly Polaroid and asked if he could ID the corpse that had recently washed up on Staten Island. The blurry picture showed a twenty-something Hispanic male whose head had been caved in by a blunt object. It looked a little like Angel, but Kirkham said it wasn't him.

The agents trained Kirkham. They taught him to pay attention to small details. They would take him out for a meal, then the next day, they would quiz him on what they had to eat, the color of the waitress's hair, what she was wearing, and so forth. They told him that particulars were important if he was ever called to testify.

Kirkham started to hang out at the Tunnel and soon enough befriended Yvette Gil, a bubbly New Jersey party promoter who handed him a business card that was embossed with the disco's logo. Her legitimate job was to schmooze with guests at Gatien's clubs. But Gil, a pretty Puerto Rican woman in her early twenties, made her real money (sometimes thousands of dollars a week) selling drugs at both the Limelight and the Tunnel. Kirkham showed Gil's card to Gagne and Germanowski, who then decided that the time had come for Sean to start making "controlled buys" in the clubs.

In the spring of 1996, Gagne picked up Kirkham and took him to a meeting at the DEA building, where he was handed a computer printout containing the same set of instructions that Sean Bradley had been given for buying drugs at Gatien's clubs. The agents stressed to him that drug purchases were supposed to be made under the supervision of a law enforcement officer. He was ordered to make a mental note whether the drug deal was "quick and quiet" or "open and notorious." He was given marked money to purchase the party favors. The dollars were photocopied on both sides beforehand in a specially secured room, "so if they lost the money, they could track it through the banks." A representative from the NYPD legal department was there, and he told Sean that three buys from three separate dealers was enough to get a club shut down under the "nuisance abatement law."

"I was told I would concentrate first on the Limelight, then on the Tunnel, and finally the Palladium," remembered Kirkham. "It was obvious what their strategy was—to systematically shut down Peter Gatien's sources of revenue."

Next, Kirkham was introduced to his partner, who would accompany him to the Limelight. Kirkham was shocked at what he saw—a colossal behemoth in his mid-thirties with a beer gut. Kirkham took Gagne aside.

"I told Gagne that there was no way I could pass off this WWF wrestler as a gay club kid," said Kirkham. "I needed artistic control. If we were going to do this right, we needed a gay or femmelike officer to play the part." Calls were made, and a few hours later, the DEA supplied one—a cute NYPD rookie who happened to be openly homosexual.

"The first buy was complete trial and error," recalled Kirkham. The Limelight was dead that Thursday. Few clubgoers had ventured out for the night. Kirkham and the undercover cop waited two hours before they made their initial purchase—a gram of cocaine from one of Michael Alig's best friends, Brooke Humphries. Due to the recent raids, dealers were wary of selling their wares to strangers. While Kirkham was known to Humphries, the undercover narc wasn't. So the cop stayed at the bar, while Kirkham completed the transaction in the bathroom, using a drag queen as an intermediary. Later on, Kirkham claimed, they doctored the field reports to read that the NYPD cop had been present when the deal went down. Outside the club, two teams of DEA agents waited in unmarked cars in case anything went wrong.

"Sometimes, I got the deals mixed up," said Kirkham. "Instead of handing over the drugs to the agent, I would hold on to them until the end of the night. The cop didn't mind, since he was using his cash allotment on booze and was slowly getting drunk. I forgot who sold me what. Was it Brooke who sold me the gram of cocaine or the hit of E? Germanowski told me it didn't matter and when I was to write the report later, he'd tell me what to say."

Kirkham worked for Gagne and Germanowski for about six months, during which time the DEA agents pampered him. "I was flattered and taken aback by their courtesy," said Kirkham. A snitch needs to be wooed to ensure his full compliance. Knowing a fashion victim when they saw one, they gave him a weekly clothing allowance. He wore Ghost, Gaultier, and Vivien Westwood to the clubs. They also let him run riot in the DEA wardrobe room, where undercover agents went for clothing and accessories. The agents brought him out for nice meals at restaurants. But they chastised him for spending money in a frivolous fashion, and they tried to get him a job at Bloomingdale's. When he was late for his interview at the department store, Kirkham claimed they drove him at top speed with flashing sirens down a one-way street.

Kirkham said that Gagne was manipulative, while Germanowski was down to earth. Matt played good cop to Bob's bad cop. "They were on a mission. They worked around the clock to get Gatien. They really thought he was pure evil," claimed Kirkham.

Once on the Gatien case, the snitch started to feel uneasy about the way the investigation was being conducted. He said that if no illegal drugs could be found at Gatien's clubs, the agents made him call dealer friends and ask them to meet him at either the Tunnel or Limelight. These transactions were then recorded as Gatien drug sales.

"Our trouble was that, after a month and a half of touring the clubs," Kirkham said, "and establishing the working patterns of these dealers, it became obvious that they didn't work for the individual clubs; they followed certain parties or promoters or DJs in a whole range of different clubs. Depending on the party, the drug dealers would go from Twilo to Tunnel to Limelight to Roxy to Sound Factory."

Take Ann Marie Pepe, for instance. She was a petite, red-haired dealer with a taste for baby-doll dresses who became a target of the probe after she became friendly with Kirkham. On Saturdays, she dealt drugs at Twilo, before heading over to the Tunnel to continue doing business after hours. She also supplied Café Con Leche's Sunday nights at the Times Square disco Expo. "She jumped around from club to club to club," said Kirkham.

Kirkham was astonished at the resources the government was willing to devote to prosecuting the Gatien case. One day, he met Ann Marie Pepe outside a Greenwich Village Barnes & Noble to pick up some Ecstasy. The DEA had the surrounding area staked out. "There must have been twenty agents," Kirkham recollected. "There were people on the street, people on the pay phone, people in cars, people in the bookstore. There were agents all over the place. And all for two hits of E."

By the beginning of August 1996, the DEA agents had decided to wrap up the drug buys and start making arrests. "By this point, they seemed maniacal," stated Kirkham. On August 17, Bob Gagne called Sean early in the morning and told him to come to the Lower East Side immediately. Kirkham watched as Yvette Gil, her eyes blinking in the harsh sunlight, was arrested without incident after she came out of Save the Robots, an East Village after-hours establishment. She was then taken to DEA headquarters, where she admitted selling cocaine and Ecstasy at the Tunnel, where she also worked as a promoter. According to the arrest report, Gil also told the DEA agents that Ray Montgomery, the Tunnel's head of security, had advised her to stand in certain spots to be less visible if the police visited.

By now, Kirkham was worried about his safety: "I was paranoid. I didn't know where the case was leading me. Plus, I wasn't making nearly as much money as I thought I would be."

Kirkham started to secretly tape-record conversations he had with the agents, bugging the buggers, as it were. He claimed he struck pay dirt when Gagne, after a visit to his chiropractor, offered up a startling revelation. Gagne had testified earlier in the week before a grand jury that he saw Gatien using a device called a one-hitter to snort cocaine in his Tunnel office. Kirkham told Gagne he thought it was nearly impossible to see such a thing from their vantage point across the street. According to Kirkham, Bob Gagne allegedly responded, "I didn't."

On another occasion, Kirkham claimed he had met with Matt Germanowski outside the DEA building, where the agent was buying a sandwich from a van. "Matt confided in me that he was going to raid the Tunnel and arrest Ray Montgomery," related the informant. "I knew Ray. I knew he wasn't a drug dealer. I'd worked with him at Club USA. In all the months, I never saw one iota of evidence that Ray was guilty of taking kickbacks or dealing drugs. It was all a ploy to have him squeal on Peter Gatien. I liked Ray. I didn't want an innocent person arrested just to get at a bigger fish."

Kirkham made a rash decision. The next night, he went to Bowery Bar in the East Village and told a Tunnel employee what he'd heard. He gave the employee a message for Montgomery: Don't show up for work on Friday because the Tunnel is going to be raided.

On August 20, 1996, at approximately 3:45 A.M. seven DEA agents (including Gagne and Germanowski) and an NYPD sergeant arrested Montgomery at the Tunnel. While the agents were talking to Montgomery, Gatien approached Germanowski and asked, "What is going on here?" Germanowski identified himself as a DEA agent and stated he had an arrest warrant for Montgomery. Gatien interrupted, "Right, right, I knew you were coming, I've been expecting you." Gatien then asked if he could see the arrest warrant. Gagne handed it over. Gatien wanted to photocopy the document and Germanowski said that was allowed but insisted that the agents accompany Gatien to his office. While en route upstairs, Gatien, unprompted, turned to Gagne and asked him, "Aren't you Gagne?" Gagne said yes. Gatien then asked, "Why would you lie like that?"—a reference to the one-hitter allegation Gagne made in front of the grand jury. "You are the one that swore in the affidavit, and man to man, I want to know why you would swear to something that was not true. Man to man, you should not do that. I do what I do, and you do what you do, and if you are going to go after somebody and get them, you should be man enough to do it without lying."

At this point Gatien supposedly became visibly nervous when he noticed Gagne and Germanowski peering into a side room where they observed, according to the DEA Report of Investigation, "two white males each sitting on the floor counting money which was stuffed into two large black industrial-size garbage bags. Each male had a garbage bag in front of him which was filled to the top, high enough and full enough that the bag could not be drawn to a close. The money was predominantly in ten- and twenty-dollar denominations. Neither of the males acknowledged the officers' presence, and they continued to count the money."

Gatien called his secretary from an adjacent room to photocopy the arrest warrant. As the copy was being made, Gatien looked at Germanowski and said, "You're the other one that has been here before." Germanowski said yes and identified himself. Gatien got the copy and escorted the agents back down to the main entrance. Walking down the stairs, Gatien complained to the agents, "I know what is going on in the other clubs, why in the hell aren't you doing something about them? I know you're only doing your job, but you shouldn't have to ruin somebody's life and turn it upside down like this to do your job. It's starting to become ridiculous."

In the wake of Montgomery's arrest (Montgomery was ultimately found not guilty), Kirkham became convinced he was being constantly followed in the streets. He presumed that somebody employed by the Gatien camp was trailing him. Matt Germanowski had taught Kirkham how to detect and avoid surveillance by using reflective surfaces à la *The French Connection*. Kirkham carried a compact mirror everywhere he went. He would also change taxis mid-ride, or enter a building, then exit, and walk around the block.

Even though Tunnel security had discovered Kirkham's true identity, the agents still insisted he set up drug deals at the venue. Gagne and Germanowski didn't care that his safety had been compromised. Because they themselves had also been unmasked, they needed Kirkham to continue making buys.

Kirkham then made another rash decision. In late August 1996, after working on the Gatien case every day for six months, the sorely pissed-off snitch offered to sell information about what he said was government misbehavior in the case to the indicted club czar himself. He claimed to have audiotape on which Gagne admitted to lying to the grand jury about seeing Gatien use cocaine in his office. The price was $10,000.

Sean arranged to meet the club owner at a Park Avenue hotel in early September 1996. The weather was still suffocatingly hot. Kirkham arrived in a powder blue shirt, pastel blue Versace shorts, and baby blue suede Hush Puppies. First, he met one of Gatien's private eyes, Les Levine, at the corner of Thirty-eighth and Park. Levine was sporting gaudy gold jewelry, bouffant hair, a well-tailored brown suit, and a diamond pinkie ring. Underneath his attire, unbeknownst to Kirkham, he wore a body wire. Levine was difficult to miss. At first glance, Kirkham thought he looked more like a pimp than a private eye. The odd couple shook hands and together walked toward the hotel. Levine escorted Kirkham through the deserted front lobby. Gatien, dressed all in black, was waiting in an empty restaurant off to the side. Anxious small talk ensued.

"Can I get you something to drink?" asked the club owner.

"No thanks," replied Kirkham.

"Sure is hot. How you doing these days?" Gatien scanned the room. He was acting like he was expecting somebody.

"I've been better," answered a wary Kirkham, "and yourself?"

Before the club owner could reply, Les Levine reentered the room accompanied by a well-groomed figure in gray pants, a starched white shirt, and a well-tailored black blazer accented with a red carnation in the buttonhole. "Hi, I'm Pat Cole. I'm Peter Gatien's other private eye," he introduced himself. "For legal reasons, I'll be conducting this meeting on behalf of Peter. That way, if anything you say comes up at trial, he can honestly say he doesn't know anything about it, you understand." He then handed Sean a business card. "I hope you don't have a problem with that?" he asked.

"No," Kirkham shrugged his shoulders, after inspecting the card. It sounded somewhat plausible.

"Then Les, you take Peter back to the office." Gatien got up from the table, shook Kirkham's hand, and walked out with Levine. Cole ordered a club soda and then got down to business.

"Peter said you have information concerning government misconduct," he began. "How did you obtain this? Is it stolen? Because if it is, this meeting will conclude right here. Peter has enough problems and doesn't need stolen documents to add to his troubles."

"I understand," said Kirkham "No, this information isn't stolen. It's tape recordings I made between the agents and myself."

Cole asked how Kirkham came across this information. Kirkham had rehearsed the story he was going to tell days in advance. He was taught by his DEA handlers to mix truth with fiction, so he told Cole he got the info about the Tunnel raid from a government official he was having an affair with, when in fact, as Kirkham told me, he really got it from Germanowski. Cole asked whether the official was male or female. Kirkham refused to answer.

"So what do you want from Peter?" he asked.

"I don't know," Kirkham replied.

"Can you prove these tapes exist?"

"I can prove it right now." Kirkham reached into his Prada backpack and pulled out a cassette tape with a player and placed them on the table. He pressed the "on" button. Cole listened to an innocuous conversation between Germanowki and Kirkham about the door policy at the Limelight.

"Can I keep this?"

"Sure, it's a copy."

Cole reached into his breast pocket and pulled out three crisp hundred-dollar bills. "This is for your time, and if the other tapes pan out, we can pay you a lot more." He slipped the money surreptitiously into Kirkham's hand and asked when he could call him.

"I'm trying to leave New York by the end of the week."

"Where are you going?"

"First, to Miami, and then I'm going to use my Canadian passport to go to Havana. I have a friend there I'm going to stay with."

Cole wrote down his home number on a napkin. "Give me a call, day or night." Cole thanked Kirkham for his time, and the meeting came to an end.

After the meeting, Kirkham flew back to Miami Beach and booked in at the Clay, a peeling deco hotel out of which Al Capone used to run his gambling operation. The shabby lodgings were located not far from Chris Paciello's Liquid. Kirkham liked the place, not only because it was cheap and close to the clubs but also because it had multiple exits providing numerous getaway opportunities. Kirkham had done a favor for the hotel owner in the past by getting several drug dealers evicted. As a consequence, the staff guarded Kirkham's privacy jealously. Anybody who called looking for Sean Kirkham was told he wasn't a guest.

Kirkham proceeded to set up shop. He purchased a new pager, activated a 1-800 number, rented two mailboxes and a post office box. With less than a grand left to his name, he went to work for the Miami DEA doing a handful of buys and busts. He quickly became involved in a case involving forty pounds of marijuana, for which he earned a fast $2,500. Periodically, Kirkham would phone Gatien's private eye Pat Cole in New York, teasing him with snippets of information. Cole wanted to come down to Miami to pick up the tapes. Kirkham scolded him that if he did, he would be on the next plane to Cuba.

One day, Kirkham got a call from Bob Gagne. He was coming down to South Beach for the weekend for a bit of rest and recreation as well as for a visit with his girlfriend, a personal trainer at a local gym. They met for dinner at News Cafe on Ocean Drive, after which Gagne suggested they go club-hopping. Sean said, "Let's go to Liquid."

At the club's velvet rope, Gagne flashed his DEA identification at the doormen and was immediately admitted. Kirkham spotted Paciello in the VIP room and introduced the club owner to Gagne. Paciello smiled and palmed them some drink tickets. A little later, out of earshot of Gagne, a fuming Paciello confronted Kirkham: "I want you out now. How dare you bring a fuckin' DEA agent into my club?" Before he left for the night, Gagne instructed Kirkham that he needed to come to New York next week to sign a few papers and pick up the remainder of his monies for his work on the Gatien case.

On a Monday morning two weeks later, Kirkham turned up promptly at the DEA's Chelsea HQ, dressed to impress in a canary yellow Claude Montana shirt and a Kenzo orange and lime-green vest. In his backpack, a tape recorder was silently running. Kirkham was trying to collect additional information about government misconduct to give to Gatien's representatives.

Sitting in the lobby, waiting for the DEA agents to arrive, the snitch daydreamed about how he was going to spend the $3,000 he was owed. He felt he'd worked hard for the money to the extent of putting his own life in danger. Now he could buy that Prada suit he coveted and upgrade his laptop. Lost in thoughts of commodity fetishism, he barely noticed when Matt Germanowki and Jay Flaherty, the third agent working the Gatien case, slipped through the electronic revolving door and greeted Sean, as casually as they could muster, "Hey, how ya doing, man?" They shook hands, and Kirkham was escorted to a small side room. One of the agents switched the sign on the door from "unoccupied" to "meeting in progress—do not disturb."

Despite their easygoing demeanor, Kirkham sensed something was up.

"How was your weekend?" asked Germanowki, as he tried to perch his bulky frame on the too-small metal chair.

"Not bad considering."

"What's the vibe like inside the clubs these days? Are people still talking?"

"I didn't hear anything, but then again I was paying more attention to the music than my surroundings."

"You know," said Flaherty, leaning forward in his seat, abruptly changing the direction of the conversation. "We have a problem with the case."

"Oh, really," Kirkham said, attempting to sound unflustered.

"Yeah, someone is leaking confidential information."

Germanowski jumped in. "Have you spoken to anybody you shouldn't have about the case? What about your roommates?" The agent eyeballed Kirkham intently, trying to gauge whether he was telling the truth.

Kirkham tried to steady his voice. "I was talking to a security guard at the Palladium," he lied. "I think my cover was definitely blown. I think Gatien's people knew what I was doing."

"Why? What makes you think that?" asked Germanowski.

"I think that I've been followed. The other night I recognized a person on Seventy-second Street sitting in a car outside my apartment."

Germanowski and Flaherty both looked at each other.

"Was that the only time you talked to anybody in regards to this investigation?"

"Yes," Kirkham lied again.

Flaherty looked at his watch. He said he was going to see what was taking Bob Gagne so long with the paperwork. Matt also left, saying he was going to the washroom. Alone, with the distinct sense that the flimsy plaster walls were closing in on him, Kirkham had time to weigh his options. He felt trapped by his own double-dealing. What was a bad boy to do? He though about making a run for freedom, but knew he would never make it past the electronic doors. So he waited, all the time boiling under his Claude Montana collar, despite the noisy air conditioner pumping frigid air.

Ten minutes later, Gagne, Germanowski, Flaherty, and a woman dressed in a conservative knitted suit accompanied by a man with a stern expression entered the room. "Mr. Kirkham, my name is Michelle Adelman, and I'm with the U.S. attorney's office in Brooklyn. This is Ken Hosey, special agent with the FBI."

Kirkham groaned inwardly. Any conversation that started with him being addressed by his last name was not good, he thought. Hosey took Kirkham's backpack from the table and searched the bag. He found a tape recorder running, and threw it on the desk in front of Adelman.

Then another man walked into the room. "Do you know who this is?" Hosey asked, pointing to the new arrival.

"Sure, that's Pat Cole, Peter Gatien's private investigator," Kirkham said warily, without looking in his direction.

"Actually, my name is Pat Colgin, and I work for the FBI." Colgin paused to let that tidbit of information sink in.

Kirkham's heart dropped. His double-dealing had been unmasked. He tried to remain calm, but clearly his plan had backfired. Shit, thought Kirkham, Brafman must have thought that his offer was a setup and contacted the FBI. The meeting at the hotel must have been a government sting.

Adelman finally spoke up: "Sean, you're in big trouble." The prosecutor pulled out a black notebook, wet her fingers, and flipped the pages until she found what she was looking for, before continuing. "You approached a Gatien security officer and negotiated a deal to sell information in relation to the case. You lied to these two agents, and you lied to the FBI. That's three counts of obstructing justice and a minimum of five years."

"Actually, Michelle that's two counts, since the underlying offense was ongoing," Kirkham replied, feeling cocky for a moment. "And if these charges are so serious, you would have had me arrested in Miami. And anyway, I'm familiar with the sentencing guidelines, and there's no way I'll do five years. So what do you want from me?"

Kirkham was gambling that Adelman wanted to strike a deal. Again there was silence in the room as the two studied each other, trying to figure out who would blink first. Adelman spoke.

"Tell me what I want to hear."

"That there was no misconduct."

"Yes, and the tapes."

"You mean this one," said Sean, reaching into his bag and pulling out a microcassette. He slid the tiny tape across a Formica table pockmarked with cigarette burns. Adleman grabbed the tape and put it in her pocket.

Adelman relaxed and sat back in her chair. "Let's talk."

She asked the DEA agents to leave. Germanowski gave Kirkham an icy stare. Gagne had a smirk on his face. Flaherty just looked disgusted.

As soon as the door closed, Adelman quizzed Kirkham about the tapes. Adelman wanted to know what was on the tapes and where she could find them. Kirkham said they were back at his apartment. She asked how many tapes were there. He said six in all, featuring conversations between him and the agents recorded on blank DEA evidence tapes. Adelman offered a deal: He was free to leave, he would be driven home where he would surrender the tapes. The following morning, she would listen to the recordings and decide what to do.

Adelman then laid out the situation for Kirkham: "This is the deal. You're being charged with one count of obstruction of justice. I'll recommend home confinement. You won't be arrested at this point. In exchange, you're to return to Miami, and you won't discuss this case with anyone until I tell you to. Lastly, you'll agree not to have any more contact with the DEA agents. You're no longer working on the case."

"Am I free to go?" asked Kirkham.

"I guess so. I'll see you tomorrow morning," said Adelman.

The next day an FBI agent picked up Kirkham from Hotel 72 and transported him to the U.S. attorney's office in Brooklyn. Kirkham wore a black Issey Miyake dress shirt, with matching Prada pants held up by a black Gucci crocodile belt. He was dressed for his own funeral. Adelman wore gray. He sat on a hard bench outside her office, while she listened to the tapes. Half an hour later, she called him into her office. "Well, you have been very busy, I see."

Adelman informed Kirkham that the U.S. attorney's office would hang on to his computer and his address book for the time being; meanwhile, Kirkham was to return to Miami and then disappear. He was to tell no one of these events. He was to steer clear of the DEA agents, Gatien's legal team, or anyone else connected to the case. Last, and most important, he was told not to speak to anyone in the media.

After his meeting with Adelman in Brooklyn, Kirkham was whisked over to the FBI building in Manhattan, where he was photographed, fingerprinted, and formally charged. Later in the afternoon, he headed back to Brooklyn federal court. Judge Sterling Johnson was in charge of the proceedings, and Kirkham's was the last case of the day. The accused pled guilty and signed a plea-bargain agreement that said he "falsely stated and represented to a Special FBI agent . . . that he had information and tape recordings reflecting improper conduct by agents of the Drug Enforcement Administration and a prosecutor responsible for the prosecution of Peter Gatien, when in fact . . . he did not have any such information or recordings." Kirkham's bond was set at $50,000. He signed some paperwork and was let go. His bond package stipulated that he return to Miami and report once a week to pretrial services.

"In a period of thirty minutes, I was arraigned, pled guilty to lying to a federal agent, given bond, and let go, all under the watchful eye of Eric Friedberg, the lead prosecutor in the Gatien case, who was sitting at the back of the courtroom with a smile on his face," recalled Kirkham.

The next day, an article came out in *The New York Times*, in which the U.S. attorney's office claimed that Kirkham had played just a peripheral role in the Gatien case, "only for intelligence information and in an unsuccessful attempt to broker a purchase of the drug Ecstasy." Kirkham was furious that his part in the Gatien case was being downplayed. But he bided his time.

Once back in Miami Beach, Kirkham kept his nose clean and his head down. He worked as a desk clerk at the Albion Hotel. He showed up regularly at pretrial services for court-mandated drug testing. On one occasion, though, Kirkham did violate his plea agreement by working briefly for the Miami Beach Police Department on a case involving a couple of pounds of marijuana.

At the end of the summer of 1997, Kirkham was supposed to return to New York for sentencing. Instead, he decided to disappear. He flew first to Los Angeles and then worked his way up the Pacific coast to San Francisco, then Portland and finally Seattle. In the middle of the night, he crossed over the border into Canada. In Vancouver, he met with a barrister whom he paid $500 for legal advice. The barrister told Sean that as long as he stayed in Canada, he had nothing to worry about. He reassured him that it was unlikely that the Canadian government would agree to extradite him on such a minor charge. Kirkham then called Gatien's lawyer Ben Brafman, who sent the two private eyes, Les Levine and John Dabrowski, to see him. Kirkham agreed to turn himself in and help the club owner by repeating his allegations about his personal relationship with a member of the Gatien prosecution team. The private eyes bought him an airline ticket. On October 20, he boarded a flight to New York. When his flight made a stopover in Los Angeles, he was arrested by federal marshals.

"I've worked with dozens of federal agents but I'd never experienced anything like the Gatien case," Kirkham said from behind bars. "Prosecutors never had to lie in other cases I was involved in because the evidence was always there. I think Mr. Gatien is guilty of knowing drugs were being consumed and sold at his clubs. But I don't think he is guilty of supplying drugs, organizing the distribution of them, or hiring dealers to personally work for him, as the government claims. I'm not the most righteous person in the world, but I know the difference between right and wrong."

Admittedly, Kirkham's credibility, like that of Sean Bradley and Michael Alig, was somewhat tainted, to say the least. He was a prostitute, a snitch, and a shakedown artist. He was hardly the most upstanding of sources. But when three confidential informants, separately and without collusion, all made such similar allegations, one more than wondered what sort of case the government was attempting to mount against Gatien.

Adding to Peter Gatien's woes, on March 13, 1997, District Attorney Robert Morgenthau charged Gatien and his wife Alex with grand larceny for allegedly cheating the city and the state out of more than $1.3 million in taxes. At a news conference, Morgenthau accused the Gatiens (only one of whose three clubs, the Tunnel, was then operating) of consistently underreporting the receipts of their largely cash business. The district attorney also said the club management developed an elaborate scheme of off-the-books accounting to hide the actual proceeds from tax officials.

"Cash was collected as the cover charge and cash was also generated at the bars," Morgenthau accused. "The indictment charges a classic case of skimming from these tax receipts in a concerted effort, executed over a five-year period, to enrich these defendants."

Barely a week after the state tax indictment, a superceding federal bill of charges was announced against Gatien. Already accused of turning his clubs into drug distribution centers by the government, the new indictment added RICO racketeering charges, which are normally reserved for full-fledged mobsters, murderous terrorists, or violent drug kingpins. The RICO (Racketeering Influenced Corrupt Organizations) charges doubled the punishment Gatien potentially faced, to forty years in prison and $2 million in fines. Even those who thought Gatien was guilty of something—like conspiracy to betray the spirit of a whole scene—were appalled that the club owner was being portrayed, in the words of one local tabloid columnist as "the John Gotti of discos."

"The government is turning this into a racketeering case, because once you get charged under RICO, the rules of evidence are relaxed," Ben Brafman angrily complained. "The rules go out the window. You can admit hearsay, you can admit basically anything. What I see developing here is a frightening abuse of government power."

13 LIMELIGHT SOUTH

Staten Island, February 1997

Nobody in clubland, least of all his lordship, was par-
ticularly surprised when in the early months of 1997, Michael Caruso
was finally arrested by DEA agents Gagne and Germanowski at his
Staten Island apartment and charged with conspiracy to distribute
Ecstasy and cocaine during his tenure as an executive director at the
Limelight. What was startling, however, was how quickly he was back
out on the street and in the clubs. Before his arrest, Caruso had already
decided, contrary to what he told Gatien's daughter Jennifer, that if the
feds came calling he'd rat out the club owner to save his own hide. As
soon as he was apprehended, he offered to give the agents any and all
information he had about the drug distribution at the Limelight, a network that he himself had in large part created. He quickly pled guilty to
the drug charges and signed a cooperation agreement with the government—which, if everything went well, he hoped could turn into a get-
out-of-jail-free card. He wasn't promised a particular sentence, but he
was told he could end up with as little as probation for crimes that otherwise should have put him behind bars for twenty years. And so began
months of debriefing sessions as prosecutors and agents poured over
every word that spewed out of Caruso's mouth in preparation for his
expected testimony at the upcoming trial of his former boss.

Caruso told investigators that Gatien had "total knowledge of everything going on." "I never had any problem with Peter when it came to dealing drugs at the club," Caruso claimed. "I always got what I wanted." He said that when Gatien first noticed drug activity at Caruso's Future Shock parties, he approached the promoter and asked, "Who are these people selling drugs in my club?"

Caruso said he assured Gatien they were "people I know."

"Keep it that way," Caruso maintained Gatien told him. "Only your people, right. You got a good thing going here, don't spoil it."

Caruso also revealed that the club owner knew about the Goldilocks/Mr. Purple robbery and laughed about it with him. Caruso said he even asked Gatien to hold $80,000 from the rip-off, which Gatien did, giving the money to Alessandra, who stored it in the safe at the Palladium. Caruso claimed he retrieved the money later, telling Alex he needed it because "My supplier is coming in from London. I have to buy Ecstasy for the club."

Alex supposedly warned him, "That's a lot of money, be careful."

But even after signing his cooperation agreement with the government, Caruso was still managing to get into trouble. For a long time, he'd had a bad gambling habit. He bet heavily on the Dallas Cowboys and the New York Knicks, often as much as $1,000 a day, three or four times a week. He would frequently get into debt with mob-connected bookmakers. "Lord Michael claimed he had a system, but it never seemed to work," said the Port Richmond Crew's Brendon Schlitz, who sometimes met Caruso at Expo to pick up money for bookie Jay Parisi, not the sort of guy who would wait to collect.

In the middle of 1997, several months after he became a government snitch, Caruso didn't have the cash to pay Parisi. So he put in a late-night beep to Brendon Schlitz. Both of them had previously robbed $12,000 from a drug dealer.

"He said he had another target and I should come and meet him at a schoolyard in the Southgate section of Staten Island," remembered Schlitz. "When I got there Mike seemed very nervous: 'I keep hearing a lot of bad things about you,' he told me. He patted my chest to see if I was wearing a wire."

Then out of the corner of his eye, Schlitz saw a shadowy figure about hundred yards away running toward him from across the tarmac. Straight away, he realized something was wrong. For some reason, Parisi—known as "Duke" because he liked to duke it out—was coming to get him. Schlitz ran back to his car and fled, with Parisi in hot pursuit. Parisi caught up with Schlitz a few blocks away, and dragged him out of his car and into the back of a van, where he beat Schlitz unconscious. When he awoke, Schlitz was told by Parisi that Caruso claimed he paid a gambling debt of $1,800 to Schlitz, who had failed to pass it on to the bookie. Schlitz had been set up by his friend.

Three other gangster buddies that Caruso betrayed were Robert Gordon, Frankie "The Baker" Romano, and Paul Torres. Unbeknownst to them, he had fingered the trio to the government as the key lieutenants who helped him run the Limelight's violent drug ring. Following the law enforcement crackdown on the Limelight, Gordon, Torres, and Romano had relocated to Miami Beach, where they were hired by Chris Paciello to work at Liquid, which they quickly dubbed "Limelight South." Torres was a doorman, Romano a bouncer, and Gordon a manager. Even though Paciello and Caruso were no longer on speaking terms, the rest of Caruso's former gang kept close ties with Paciello. Fearful of their new boss's wrath, the crew didn't resume selling drugs. But they did continue to commit armed robberies of rival dope peddlers, often acting on information they'd heard around the club.

In early 1997, the trio got a tip. A major drug dealer had $50,000 stashed in his beachfront apartment. They went to his place posing as delivery men. When the drug dealer opened the door, the armed intruders forced him back into his apartment and, after a struggle, tied him up with duct tape. While they were in the process of ransacking the apartment looking for drugs and money, the dealer freed himself and ran onto the balcony screaming, "I'm being robbed. Somebody call the police." Spooked, the bumbling bandits attempted to leave but were prevented from doing so by the combination lock on the front door. After getting their victim to let them out, they fled empty-handed.

When Paciello was confronted with the fact that Gordon, Torres, and Romano were committing serious felonies while in his employ, he shot back, "Anyone working for me, who I even suspect has any involvement in any criminal activity would be fired immediately."

On June 5, 1997, Matt Germanowski, assisted by the Miami branch of the DEA, arrested Frankie "The Baker" Romano without incident at his South Beach apartment, not for the attempted robbery of the local drug dealer but for his role in the Ecstasy distribution ring at the Limelight. In his postarrest statement, Romano admitted to Germanowski that he had a serious drug problem, which got worse after he started attending the Limelight. He said he knew drugs were being sold there but didn't know who was doing the selling. Then he changed his mind and fingered his former colleague Lord Michael as the man in charge of the narcotics flow. He said Limelight management knew about what was going on because "you couldn't walk through the club without seeing drugs being used or sold." He lied when he said he didn't know Robert Gordon, then said he did but claimed Gordon wasn't a drug dealer, which of course he was. When the feds started to get more specific, questioning Romano about rooms rented at Manhattan's Millennium Hotel for the purpose of cashing out drug proceeds earned at the Limelight, he clammed up, refusing to answer any more questions until he spoke to a lawyer.

Not long after, Jennifer Gatien bumped into Romano's pal Gordon at Liquid. By this time, Gordon, a former male model who carried a gun strapped to his ankle, had struck a deal with the government to testify against Gatien. Jennifer, who was in Miami digging up dirt on Caruso and Paciello to help with her father's forthcoming trial, accused Gordon of selling out her dad. "I don't feel good about what I'm doing," Gordon apologized, before warning her. "Lord Michael is a major liar, and he's going to hurt your father. Give your dad my best; I know he didn't know what we were doing."

Meanwhile, Gordon and Romano's employer, Chris Paciello, was hatching plans to turn Liquid into a franchise. Over the summer of 1997, he and his partner, Ingrid Casares, wanted to copy Liquid's rampant success in Miami by opening a New York version. Casares called her friends real-estate mogul Donald Trump and Sony music head Tommy Mottola for advice, and then hired Trump's law firm to help her secure the necessary liquor license for the proposed establishment. But club owners couldn't just buy a license as they could in Miami Beach; you had to apply and be deemed respectable and responsible by the State Liquor Authority. Even a whiff of criminality was enough to get your application rejected. Casares also hired socialite-cum-publicist Lizzie Grubman, daughter of powerful music industry attorney Allen Grubman, who also happened to be Madonna's lawyer. Surrounded by lawyers and publicists, and better connected than AT&T, she thought she would have no problem winning over the city, the state, and community boards—all necessary steps to open a nightcub in Giuliani-era New York.

In the meantime, Paciello was working his side of the room. According to the government, Paciello visited the Brooklyn social club of Colombo family captain William "Wild Bill" Cutolo, seeking his help for the planned nightclub. Paciello allegedly attended the meeting with a childhood friend, six-foot, six-inch Colombo family enforcer Dominic "Big Dom" Dionisio. This particular branch of the Mafia was going to supply Liquid New York's bouncers and building contractors.

Casares and Paciello spent a year looking for a site to house the club. After several false starts, they finally settled on a 20,000-square-foot space on West Twenty-second Street that once housed a Latin music club called Les Poulets, just around the corner from Paciello's old haunt, the Limelight, in a neighborhood already overrun with bars and clubs. Celebrity chums stepped forward and offered to go before the community board to sing Chris and Ingrid's praises. Trump called Casares "a visionary" and "a major asset to the city." Months of delicate negotiations with the landlord, his lawyers, and city officials ensued.

Downtown Manhattan had changed noticeably since Paciello had moved to Miami in 1994. This wasn't like the old days. The forces of law, order, and a good night's sleep had tamed the around-the-clock party town. In the wake of the arrest of Peter Gatien and the grisly killing of Angel Melendez, a black cloud hung over the bleak nocturnal landscape. Unlike Miami Beach, where nightclubs were welcomed as tourist magnets, city hall was openly hostile to any new discos opening, especially in overcrowded Manhattan.

Paciello's representatives assured community groups that Liquid New York would be the antithesis of the down-market Limelight, the source of much neighborhood antagonism. The club was going to be the sort of place that Madonna and Leonardo Di Caprio would visit. Paciello tried to stay in the shadows, knowing full well that if his Mafia ties became public, Liquid New York would never happen. Casares's name was on the liquor license application. "This is entirely Ingrid's baby," her publicist Lizzie Grubman improbably claimed. "Chris has nothing to do with it."

But after the *Voice* revealed Paciello's mob connections, and the *New York Post* columnist Jack Newfield followed up with a series of columns praising the grass-roots effort to deny Paciello and Casares a liquor license, the deal was taken off the table. Even after Paciello offered the landlord a six-figure signing bonus, the owner refused to let him assume the lease. The deputy mayor vowed that he would oppose a Liquid anywhere else in the city.

"I can't believe those fuckers said no to me," Casares complained. "We were the victims of bad press."

For his part, Paciello told *New York* magazine, "It doesn't make me a gangster because I hung out on the corner with people when I was growing up. They're childhood friends and they will remain so."

That July, on a night that followed another frustrating day negotiating with bureaucrats, Paciello turned up with Julia Sukhanova, a former Miss USSR, at a West Village hot spot called Life. Steven Lewis, then the manager of the club, warmly greeted Paciello and his escort and then asked to speak to Paciello alone.

Lewis first met Paciello in the early '90s outside the Palladium, before Gatien bought the venue. Lewis was working at the front door, when he noticed "a clean-cut guy, with cropped hair, wearing a muscle shirt" leading a bunch of young thugs who were trying to instigate fights with ordinary partygoers on the line to get into the club. Lord Michael had sent them over from the Limelight to sabotage the rival event. Lewis, flanked by two beefy bouncers, approached Paciello and said, "This is not the way a man should behave." To Lewis's surprise,

Paciello replied, "You know what, you're right," and gathered up his goons and left. "You could see it in his face that he knew he was wrong," said Lewis. "Right away, you got the impression he had a little more class than the Guidos he hung out with."

Over a bottle of champagne in Life's VIP room, Lewis and Paciello sat down to discuss the prospects for the New York Liquid. Lewis was amazed at Paciello's meteoric rise—from Staten Island street thug to the toast of Miami Beach in the space of a couple of years. But Lewis put Paciello's spiraling success down to the lucrative alliance he'd forged with the socially prominent Ingrid Casares—that, and the fact that any competitor who crossed him was destined for a brutal beat-down. Indeed, now that the Liquid New York project seemed destined not to happen, Lewis was thinking about approaching Casares to help him reopen the old Studio 54 space in midtown Manhattan. But he was understandably worried about how the volatile Paciello would react. During their conversation, Paciello became irritated when Lewis suggested that Paciello's criminal track record and the puritanical regime installed in City Hall, not to mention all the negative press attention, meant there was little or no chance he would get a liquor license. Paciello eyeballed Lewis with one of his trademark intimidating stares before storming off toward the dance floor.

Within minutes, a fight erupted near the bar. Paciello and his posse jumped a pesky Russian shutterbug, Georgi Kandelaki, who was bothering Sukanova for a photo op. They savaged him with their fists and stabbed him three times in his puny chest. "I don't know if it was what I said to him that set him off, but the photographer he beat up was carried out on a stretcher," remembered Lewis. NYPD cops arrested Paciello for attempted murder. Paciello was carted off in handcuffs to the local precinct house, where he reportedly boasted to detectives, "You make $50,000 a year; I make $50,000 a week. And I sleep with women you can only dream about." The cops would have loved to take the tough guy braggart down a peg or two. But the charges were dropped when security tapes from the club revealed that it was one of Paciello's friends who committed the stabbing—with a fork. And Kandelaki, after he found out who his assailants were, refused to press charges.

———

Later that year, two days before New Year's Eve, Chris Paciello was caught on a government phone tap with Colombo family bruiser Dominick Dionisio conspiring to beat up Steven Lewis. After community groups had rebuffed Paciello and Casares yet again in their attempt to open Liquid in New York, Lewis did indeed contact Casares about helping him relaunch the old Studio 54, as he had planned. He wanted to set up a meeting with Casares in Miami, but minus Paciello. Lewis told Casares that Paciello, given his shady past, could be part of the project only as a top-secret partner. And Lewis insisted on another condition—that Paciello never visit the club. When Paciello, who was notoriously possessive of the women in his life, found out that Lewis had gone behind his back, he phoned Big Dom, his old pal from Bensonhurst, who used to settle drug disputes at the Limelight and was later arrested on stock fraud and money-laundering charges. Paciello was worried that Lewis was trying to "poison her head." Dom called him back from New York about the Casares situation.

"Hello, Chris, what's wrong?" asked the leg-breaker. From the message he'd left, Big Dom figured that Paciello was perturbed.

"This Steven Lewis, right," began the club owner.

"Yeah."

"He calls up today . . ."

"Yeah."

"And he keeps trying to get in touch with Ingrid. So Ingrid calls him back finally . . ."

"Yeah."

"And, he's like, yeah, ya know, he's coming down here and he wants to meet up with Ingrid . . ."

"Yeah."

"It's about doing something down here next season. He wants to open a club down here with his partner [Roy Stillman, the owner of Life], and she's like I'm not gonna meet you without Chris, and he's like, no, I don't want to meet with Chris; Chris has a temper, and my boss, a guy who puts a lot of money in my pocket, doesn't really care for Chris. And anyway, you're the one that's fabulous, and I wanna meet with you Friday, and I don't care if Chris knows, you can tell him fifteen minutes after. He kept trying to pump her up, like he's gonna give her a lot of money. I was thinkin' if I should call up Steven right now, and say Steven, do yourself a favor, stay away from her, don't even bother talkin' with her, or . . ."

"Mmmm . . ."

"Have you stop by the club [Life] to talk to him."

"I'll go by the club and talk to him."

"But, ya know, he's, they're gonna try and pump her up, and fuckin' start offering all kinds of money, and no matter what, even if she's loyal and don't leave me or whatever . . ."

"She'll do that."

"Her head just gets fuckin' like, right away, she wants everything."

"Yeah, but you know what the problem is, if I go talk to him, he's scared shit of me, but he might say somethin' [to the feds]. He's talkin' about [informing on] the guy with the patch on the eye, right?"

"What?"

"The guy with the patch on his eye is his boss, right?"

"No, that's Peter Gatien."

"That's who he works for, don't he still work there?"

"No, he works at Life."

"Who owns Life now?"

"Some Jewish guy owns it, this guy Stillman."

"I don't know how ya wanna handle it, ya know what I'm sayin'. I mean, I'll go talk to him, but then what happens if they say something to her [Ingrid], ya know what I'm tryin' to say like?"

"I don't care if they say something to her. I'm gonna tell her now. But they'll be like, we'll give ya fifty percent of the club, leave Chris, come along with us, and then, she's gonna be like, well, ya know, I'm getting offered all this stuff, 'cause I'm already in this argument with her right now."

Paciello feared that Casares might accept Lewis's proposition: "I gotta start taking care of her, or else she's fuckin' gonna leave me. . . . Lewis is a great manipulator, he'll talk her ear off, she'll start believing him, she's fuckin' stupid. . . ."

"Fuckin' people, that's how people get, and that's the sad part, you know," Dionisio commiserated. "I'll go the club tomorrow night. I'll grab him, I don't care, I'll tell him, Steve, what are you doing with this Ingrid, stay away from her."

"Then say, 'Do yourself a favor, Steven. You better not make that meeting,' some shit like that."

"Me, I'm gonna tell him, 'Steve, me and you are friends, ya know somethin', don't call Ingrid no more. Steve, stay away from Ingrid, don't ever bother comin' to Florida.' That's all I'll tell him. I'll tell him tomorrow night. The worst that could happen, he tells me get outta his club, I knock him out, then walk out. . . ."

Paciello laughed. "Yeah, let's do it. Fuck him. . . ."

Dionisio agreed, "Might as well poison the meat, before it even gets done."

"Exactly."

"You got a number for Steven Lewis?"

Paciello gave Big Dom some digits from his Rolodex.

Three days later, on January 1, 1998, Paciello called Dom.

"Dominick, how ya feelin'? Ya got a hangover?"

"No, I was just out late. I'm just tired . . . I went by Life, right."

"Yeah."

"I went to do the thing, I asked for Steve Lewis, they said he's inside."

"Alright."

"I went inside. And he wouldn't come and talk to me, this guy. Ya know that?"

"He wouldn't?"

"He won't come talk to me. I was in there for like fifteen, twenty min-utes, Chris . . ."

"Yeah."

"I left; he wouldn't come talk to me."

"What do ya mean, he was hidin' in the office?"

"He's scared, he wouldn't come out, this fuckin' jerk-off. They're all stool pigeons these guys. The guy's deathly scared of me, fucking weirdo," said Dionisio.

Paciello replied, "So that cocksucker won't come out, huh? I'll take care of it down here."

To which Dionisio remarked, "Even after you grab him . . . I'm gonna terrorize him a little, too . . . because I called and left him a fuckin' message, the fuckin' jerk-off." (Lewis confirms he was approached by a group of tough guys who warned him to steer clear of Casares, who turned down the offer anyway.)

The conversation ended with Paciello describing an incident at Liquid the night before, when the police were called after Paciello roughed up the night's record-spinner. "I didn't hit the fuckin' kid; he was little, he was drugged off his mind. I grabbed him by the neck, and I just, y'know, 'Get the fuck out' and I flung him, and he slammed to the floor, and just lay there for like ten minutes."

The incident Paciello was referring to involved Keoki, Michael Alig's old boyfriend, who, now that his former lover was in prison for killing Angel, was busy forging himself a career as a sought-after DJ. Ironically, Keoki and Alig were the ones who had first introduced Paciello's former business partner, Lord Michael, to Peter Gatien. When Keoki, then a full-fledged heroin addict, arrived at Liquid that night, he was already stoned. During the course of his set, the DJ nodded off over the turntables, causing the night to come to a grinding halt. Paciello, who hated smack because of what it had done to his father, was infuriated. He stormed over to Keoki, yanked him out of the booth, and took him into the back alley, where he slapped him around while screaming, "Get the hell out of here, you fuckin' junkie, and never come back again."

Keoki pleaded to be allowed back into the club to retrieve his record collection. "You want your fuckin' records? I'll get your fuckin' records," Paciello replied, before going inside, only to reemerge not long after carrying an armful of the DJ's treasured vinyl, which he proceeded to throw onto the ground and smash into pieces.

In the meantime, Michael Alig's day of reckoning had finally arrived. On October 1, 1997, Alig and his partner-in-crime, Freeze, were sentenced at the N.Y. State Supreme Court in Manhattan, after admitting to one count of manslaughter apiece. The courtroom was wooden and creaky, like an old library. The judge was gray-haired and austere. The only emotions Alig could register were fear and bewilderment. He felt numb, as if he'd just been called into the principal's office. The full reality of his situation was blurred by the numerous antidepressants—Trazadone, Klonopin, and Depakote—that he was doped up on at the time.

Through the haze, he'd heard Judge Wetzel thundering at someone before him, who was just convicted on a murder rap. "You see that tree?" Wetzel pointed to a sapling in a planter. "You see that tree? It'll be dead before you ever see the light of day again." Alig had heard that he said that to all those he convicted on life sentences, but he was still scared.

Neither Freeze's nor Alig's family was there. But half a dozen friends from the Limelight did show up to support the disgraced duo. Angel's family also missed the date. "Thank God," thought Alig. He didn't know how he would have been able to face them. The thought of looking into Johnny Melendez's face terrified both convicts.

A solemn and humble Freeze got up to address the court, his hands visibly shaking as he read from yellow sheets of paper.

"That I was a party to the death of another human being wounds me in the depths of my heart and soul," Freeze began. "I can never undo that. I endeavor to understand the aspects of myself that led me down such a gross and destructive path, but I have yet to come to any definite conclusions. What I am certain is that all of us involved, myself, Michael Alig, Daniel Auster, and Angel Melendez are victims of the same hideous evil, whose name is drugs.

"Drugs are, of course, the problem, but they cannot be the excuse. There is no excuse. I know that. However, there are reasons why so many young people end up drug-addicted, drug-dealing club kids, and various outcasts of society. And I for one am commited to finding out those reasons in myself.

"If I can do that, maybe I can help steer others away from this kind of life I led. I stand here a guilty man about to be sentenced. I have very little idea of what lies ahead for me, but I embark upon this phase of my life with the belief that the system can work and with the conviction that I can make it work for me.

"I see these years as a time to reflect on my many mistakes and to learn to be a participating if not valuable member of society again. I had many dreams and goals, some of which I came close to accomplishing, but never in my worst nightmare did I see myself standing here today.

"These final words are for Angel himself. There are many ways I could choose to remember you, but I look through all the bad to that night when you and I were gluing feathers on your cardboard angel wings, you were laughing, and you couldn't wait to wear them out that night. Wherever you are, I hope that you are flying in peace on the real wings that you deserve. I thank the court for its indulgence."

The speech was corny boilerplate, but it proved effective. The judge complemented Freeze. "Remorse is always the first step towards rehabilitation where you have a situation as grievous as we have here," he said. But the judge did point out that during the interim period between the crime and the arrest, there was no evidence of any remorse. "Your articulation of your drug habit having been the monster that compelled you and involved you in this crime perhaps will be helpful to somebody else. I impose the promised sentence of ten to twenty years incarceration."

Next the judge turned to Alig: "Michael Alig, do you want to stand up?" Alig complied. Alig's lawyer jumped in and requested a postponement of the sentencing, pending a psychiatric evaluation of his client. After much back and forth, the judge denied the application and turned to the accused.

"Mr. Alig, do you wish to be heard, sir?"

"Yes. I came here today not prepared to accept my sentence, so I didn't come with a speech because I was told we were going to postpone for another week, two weeks, or something like that, I don't know. All I know is that I've been told lots of different things by lots of different people in exchange for me doing other things, and none of it has come true. I feel like I have just been railroaded. I have been used by the feds. When they were through with me, they sent me over here. I feel like I have been lied to here to get me to accept this plea. And I feel terrible that I don't have anything prepared to say."

"What I find curious, Mr. Alig, and I would be disingenuous if I didn't contrast your approach to this and Mr. Riggs."

"I am not prepared."

"You have been told that you have been railroaded, you have been used, you have been lied to. You are the victim."

"In a way."

"In a way, you are the victim?"

"Yes."

"I don't think you are the victim. I think that Angel Melendez is the victim."

"He is also the victim."

"And he is the victim of your selfish, uncontrolled ego that has yet to be harnessed, that is yet to face reality. For you, the show is over. The party is over. Mr. Alig, you are sentenced to ten to twenty years."

14   THE TRIAL OF PETER GATIEN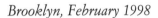

Brooklyn, February 1998

In the early months of 1998, the two-and-a-half-year investigation into drug dealing at Peter Gatien's clubs climaxed with a well-publicized trial at Brooklyn's federal courthouse. Why was the trial held in Brooklyn? After all, Gatien's discos—the alleged crime scenes—were all in Manhattan. Recognizing how thin the case was, Manhattan federal prosecutors wouldn't touch the controversial prosecution. But their ambitious Brooklyn counterparts—who had a reputation for being more interested in big wins and splashy headlines than just outcomes—stepped forward, arguing that it was their turf, since the Ecstasy consumed at the Canadian's hot spots came in via JFK airport, which is in next-door Queens.

In the stuffy, windowless courtroom, the racketeering trial dragged on for more than four weeks, but the expected fireworks failed to materialize. It wasn't as great a freak show as many in the media had fervently hoped. The trial was supposed to provide a window into a world of drugs, sex, and narcissistic indulgence that should have stunned the jury by its decadence. But for most of the time, the middle-aged, working- and lower-middle-class jury members—a truck driver, a retired factory foreman, a collector of money from vending machines, in short, people for whom Special K was still a breakfast cereal—only looked stunned by the boredom of the proceedings.

There were no startling revelations. There was no knockout forensic evidence. The government's case lacked proof and a plausible plotline. Beginning with the opening arguments, the government admitted they had no concrete confirmation that Gatien directly financed the drug dealing at his clubs.

Days and days of painfully tedious evidence pertaining to the club's floor plan—and to the supposed secret drug messages contained in party invitations and promotional material—wore down the collective attention span. By the end of the trial, the jury knew more about the physical layout of the club than the original architect. As the prosecution droned on, I kept thinking, "Where's the beef?" Where's the substance, the smoking gun, the missing part of the puzzle that will put Peter Gatien in prison for the rest of his life? The odd thing was, it should have been an open and shut case for the government. Of the forty people (party promoters, drug dealers, bouncers, etc.) eventually indicted, thirty had already pled guilty before the trial and cut a deal with the government to cooperate against the entrepreneur. Plus, Gatien's defense—that he was so screwed up on cocaine most of the time that he didn't know what was going on at his clubs—seemed less than compelling, even if it was true.

The Gatien trial was more significant for who didn't testify than for who did. The government's case was hobbled before it even got to the courtroom. There was no Michael Alig, Sean Kirkham, or Sean Bradley—the trio of confidential informants who provided the feds with damaging material about the drug dealing at Gatien's clubs in the early stages of the investigation but later turned on their handlers, alleging serious wrongdoing. Also conspicuously absent from the witness list were Matt Germanowski and Bob Gagne, the two DEA agents who infiltrated the Limelight drug scene in drag but who were scratched from the list at the last minute. Prosecutors were aware that Gatien's attorney Ben Brafman was intending to grill the vigorous duo about Michael Alig's allegation that they had allowed him to use heroin in the backseat of their car.

Throughout the trial the government used a visual representation of its case: a big board depicting Gatien atop a family tree of more than fifty known drug dealers with names like Mr. Purple, Goldilocks, Flying Brian, Eugene the Rabbit, the It Twins, Baby Joe, Sir Paulie, and Junkie Jonathan. The monikers alone suggested a mind-bending milieu, where reality was blurred and identities multiplied under a haze of drug cocktails. No wonder the jury, one member of which kept nodding off, had so much trouble distinguishing between truth and drug-induced fantasy.

The judge, Frederic Block, presided over the proceedings with a kind face and an easy wit. The affable Block sparked laughter in the court-room when, following testimony about how to make an Ecstasy punch (mix vodka and orange juice with crushed Ecstasy), a juror began to cough and was given a cup of water, after which the judge quipped, "I'm sure you'll find it's only water." Block believed there was a wealth of evidence implicating the accused ("I think Peter Gatien knew darn well what was happening," he would say later) but took care not to sig-nal that to the jury. He thought the prosecution was stupid not to call Michael Alig to the stand. Even with the manslaughter conviction. Alig, like no other, could have provided intimate and compelling testimony about the depth of corruption at the Gatien-run Limelight.

The club tycoon, who had replaced his trademark black eye patch in favor of tinted glasses, a deliberate ploy to make him look less sinister, sat behind the wooden defense table. Gatien's lips were pressed thin, and his grim expression matched his somber suit, as he heard witness after witness describe the furious drug action at his clubs. The stepmother-and-daughter team of Alex and Jennifer Gatien were a con-stant presence at the trial, squeezed into the front bench, raising their eyebrows and making faces every time they thought the prosecutors stretched the truth. The proceedings degenerated into farce when the prosecution complained to the judge that Gatien's family was trying to sway the jury with their body language.

Bob Gagne and Matt Germanowski sat a few feet away at the prose-cution table, their respective demeanors as expressionless as granite. By contrast, Assistant U.S. Attorney Eric Friedberg looked decidedly ner-vous, as he glumly shuffled through a sheaf of papers, his eyes darting around the room, his beaky countenance a composition in furtive worry. In his ten years as a prosecutor, he'd never had a case blow up in his face like this one. Friedberg, an expert in prosecuting narcotics cases, had come onboard midway through the investigation, after the case had fallen into disarray, to bolster the two young and relatively inexperienced prosecutors, Michelle Adelman and Lisa Fleishman, who were initially in charge. Adelman and Fleishman had believed if they turned enough of his coconspirators, Gatien would be forced to cut a deal and accept a guilty plea. The Brooklyn U.S. Attorney's office never thought Gatien would actually elect to go to trial.

Friedberg had a reputation as a straight shooter: "experienced, smart, and honest" was how one defense lawyer described him. That's why it was so distressing for him to find himself in such a state of affairs, scared that if Gatien's lawyer Ben Brafman called the informant Sean Kirkham to the stand, Kirkham would repeat the story about their alleged personal relationship, and Friedberg would have to recuse himself from the trial. Even though Friedberg denied the existence of any relationship, it was potentially an embarrassing situation for him. What would he tell his wife?

Friedberg was furious with Brafman. He'd heard that the defense lawyer was a bare-knuckles legal brawler of formidable talent who would go to extraordinary lengths to get his sometimes shady clients acquitted. But he never thought he'd stoop this low.

For his part, Brafman was displeased at the news that Friedberg had taken over the prosecution. "To be honest, I was not happy when I heard Friedberg had come on the case. Eric Friedberg is a much, much better lawyer than either Fleisher or Adelman," he claimed.

In his own mind, Brafman's mission was clear. His battle plan was to brand the government's case a "selective prosecution." His job was to show that Peter Gatien ran such a huge operation, he couldn't be held personally responsible for isolated pockets of drug dealing. The argument he would come to make again and again was that the club world was being unfairly held to a higher standard than that applied to other industries or professions. "To maintain that clubs have to be completely drug-free is an impossible standard, one that they don't apply to Madison Square Garden, or at Shea Stadium, or at any high school or any prison, come to that," Brafman said beforehand. "You don't see the warden of Rikers Island, or George Steinbrenner being arrested if one of his players uses drugs or the police commissioner being arrested if some cop sells drugs. Consistently, from the beginning, the government has viewed Peter as a trophy. If he were not a well-known person, I don't believe Peter would have been indicted. They're trying to make an example of him, even if in order to do so they have to break the rules and fabricate evidence. The government has essentially thrown the rule book out of the window and made the decision to get Peter Gatien at any cost."

During opening statements, Michelle Adelman addressed the jury sharply in a harsh voice. "Drugs were a marketing tool at Peter Gatien's clubs," she argued. She talked about party invitations that "referenced the availability of drugs" and said the jury would hear from a writing expert that would prove Gatien "signed off on drug budgets" in a disguised handwriting style. She further declared, "Gatien rewarded employees with cocaine at hotel parties with champagne and high-class prostitutes." After mentioning a couple of corrupt cops that Gatien allegedly had on his payroll, she claimed that Gatien not only invited drug dealers into his club but even gave them an office to divide up the proceeds. She called Gatien's belated attempt to rid his clubs of drug dealers "a joke," though she did allow that dealers were sometimes ejected, but only if they failed to be discreet.

Adelman—whose constant nervous eye blinking throughout the proceedings made it look like she was trying to signal the jury in Morse code: C-O-N-V-I-C-T P-E-T-E-R G-A-T-I-E-N—did admit that some of the government witnesses were serious criminals, especially Michael Caruso, the government's star snitch, who was ratting out his former boss in return for a drastically reduced sentence. But, in the coming days, the prosecutor claimed, she would establish beyond doubt that the club owner "was every bit as much a drug dealer as Lord Michael."

After Adelman finished, Brafman told the judge he'd need two hours to deliver his opening statement, so the court adjourned for lunch, except for the defense lawyer, who spent the break pacing up and down the courtroom, practicing his lines, winding himself up, and waving a pointer at the government's big board of drug dealers. When everybody came back, Brafman, by now a pit bull on a chain straining to be unleashed, launched his opening salvo.

"This man is Peter Gatien," boomed Brafman, as he pointed toward his momentarily startled client. "He is not a drug dealer. He is a creative nightclub genius." Brafman also labeled Michael Alig "a genius," but one "who went nuts." By contrast, he called Lord Michael "a nothing who became a big shot" and labeled his crew "a bunch of urban terrorists who were routinely violent, who impersonated police officers, who threatened people with guns, and who engaged in armed robberies and extortion schemes."

Brafman said, "More police officers have been arrested for drugs than patrons at Peter Gatien's clubs." He made an issue of the fact that one name was missing from the government's witness list—Sean Kirkham, potentially a most embarrassing source of information on what really went on during the government's investigation. He accused the government of injecting the hotel orgies into the case simply to shame his client. He said that Gatien actively tried to rid his venues of drug dealers but shouldn't be expected to run totally drug-free clubs, because drugs were everywhere in New York—from Wall Street to Rikers Island.

"The theory of the government's case is woven with lies," thundered Brafman. "This trial is going to show that life in this city is like life in Peter Gatien's clubs."

During her opening statement, Michelle Adelman had offered a dramatic warning to the jury: "You might be shocked and disgusted by the appearance of some of these club kids, especially Brooke Humphries." Adelman was referring to the body and facial piercings and the dyed hair of the big-boned dope peddler Humphries. She was expected to testify that Alig told her Gatien co-coordinated the drug dealing at the clubs. Putting her on the stand was the government's way of slipping Alig's testimony through the back door, even though Alig—whose conviction for killing Angel Melendez, in the government's opinion, made him useless as a prosecution witness—had already disavowed his own accusations as untrue.

In response, Brafman accused Adelman of being a youth culture bigot. Indignation hardly did his performance justice. "Half the kids in America have body piercings, and they are our sons and daughters, and they are not disgusting," he blustered. "They're different. Brooke

Humphries is not 'disgusting,' because she wears body piercings. When Mayor Giuliani puts on a dress, it's fun; when a transvestite puts on a dress at one of Peter Gatien's clubs, it's disgusting.

"*Disgusting* is a terrible word to use in the United States today," he concluded, trying to wrap himself in the flag. "Not everybody looks and sounds like Michelle Adelman." Frowning and frumpy, the sartorially challenged prosecutor—dressed in a dark conservative suit and black pumps—shifted awkwardly in her chair.

Humphries did indeed end up making a strong impression during the course of the trial, but not in the way that Adelman predicted. Two days before she was due to take the stand, the club kid was charged with making a false statement to federal officials: She had told them she had not resumed selling drugs in violation of her cooperation agreement with the government, when, in fact, she had. (She had been arrested the previous year and accused of being a house dealer at the Limelight, where she allegedly sold hundreds of vials of cocaine. In return for leniency, she had agreed to testify against Gatien.)

As it turned out, Brafman was the one who shopped Humphries to the authorities, after Jennifer Gatien visited Michael Alig in prison. Jennifer was pretending to befriend Alig so he would help her father, and Alig had let slip that Humphries had mentioned in a letter that she was still dealing, all under the inattentive eye of the government. Humphries would come to New York, stay in a nice hotel on the taxpayer's dime, then use the opportunity to purchase drugs, which she would send back via FedEx to her hometown of Dallas. Brafman buzzed the feds. A package was intercepted, and Humphries was arrested. "If we could find out she was still committing serious criminal offences, how come the government officials, who were supposed to be watching her, didn't know?" Brafman challenged.

Humphries wasn't the only Alig sidekick not to take the stand. Limelight regular Cynthia Haatja, a.k.a. Gitsie, was also slated to be a prosecution witness. Gorgeous-looking but also fragile and foolish, she'd once said, "As part of the club-kid world, you don't even realize that drugs are illegal." The skinny blond bubblehead, a topless dancer, was notorious for chatting up guys at the Limelight, taking to them to a hotel room supposedly for sex, then giving them a big line of powder, which she told them was cocaine, when in fact it was Special K. She would wait for the victim to fall into a K-hole and then roll the mark for his money and possessions. According to Michael Alig, he and Gitsie dreamed up a scheme to entrap one of the DEA agents, Bob Gagne, so as to coerce him into helping Alig get a reduced sentence. Gitsie conspired to seduce Gagne and draw him into her bed, where she would feed him drugs, while all the time a hidden video camera recorded the events. She then intended to blackmail the agent. "See how much I love you Michael? I'm willing to sleep with this pig to help you," she told Alig, when she visited him in prison. If Gagne didn't help, said Alig, she intended to testify at the Gatien trial that the agent had tried to get into her pants.

But Gitsie overdosed on heroin and was found dead in her Queens apartment just a few days before she was due to take the stand. Dark rumors circulated in clubland that the DEA had Gitsie eliminated to prevent her from testifying. As it turned out, the truth was more prosaic, though no less sad. The smack that killed her was sent via FedEx from her friend Brooke Humphries in Texas, who was supposed to be under government supervision at the time.

Back at the trial, one by one, the jury was introduced to a rogues' gallery of government witnesses, former patrons and employees of Gatien's clubs who recounted their own transgressions: drug dealing, extortion scams, sundry assaults and robberies, and voracious drug taking. And one by one, Brafman tap-danced all over their heads. Pacing in front of the jury box, sticking out his jowls where his jaw should have been, he attacked what he dismissed as the "coached and rehearsed testimony" of government witnesses, punching holes in their credibility time and again.

The few club kids who did make it to the stand at the Gatien trial were all sedated and sanitized, remade and remodeled for public consumption, the faint traces of hair color the only giveaway revealing their recent racy past. The government's case was not helped by the appearance of Jenny Dembrow, a.k.a. Jennytalia, the former bald-headed bad girl who used to host Disco 2000 nights and attended the lavish parties that Alig and Gatien threw at posh Manhattan hotels. Other witnesses testified that the wild affairs featured champagne, caviar, prostitutes, and mid-sized mountains of cocaine. Gatien spent up to $20,000 a pop on these parties. The government had the credit card receipts as proof.

Dembrow, who had grown her hair out and was nearly unrecognizable in a gray suit and white blouse as Alig's androgynous, raccoon-eyed sidekick of yore, was supposed to bolster the government's hypothesis that the hotel parties were really company picnics at which Gatien's coconspirators in the alleged drug ring were rewarded for their illegal efforts. Dembrow testified to exactly the opposite. "These parties had nothing to do with what was going on at the club," she insisted, angering prosecutors.

The newly demure Dembrow—the same woman who used to delight in telling me about the extraterrestrials she'd met on her frequent K excursions—was nervous and confused, at one point bursting into tears when asked to recall the hotel parties. She appeared dazed and constantly bit her lip. When she testified, she spoke in a whisper and had to be asked by the judge on numerous occasions to raise the volume of her voice.

She recalled some of the more innocent aspects of the parties, such as Alig building a play fort out of hotel sheets and furniture. But she developed amnesia about the shadier details. "I don't remember. I was on drugs at the time," said Dembrow, in the trial's most memorable line.

On re-cross-examination, a furious Adelman tried to discredit her own witness. She asked Dembrow, who used to be Gatien's lover, "Isn't it true that you're scared to testify against Peter Gatien?" Dembrow said no, she wasn't. By the time she stepped down from the stand, Jennytalia looked drained.

Following Dembrow, Ann Marie Pepe testified. She also appeared nervous. Brafman went easy on her, knowing that beating up on a scared little girl wouldn't win him many brownie points with the jury. Pepe admitted she was a house dealer at the Tunnel, where she said her small crew of female sellers worked out of the club's Silver Bedroom. She said she also sold drugs at a rival club, Sound Factory, and continued to do so even after the space turned into Twilo. Pepe's appearance had changed dramatically since the days when she turned up at the

Tunnel in baby-doll dresses and a Mickey Mouse backpack, in which she stored her drug supply. She looked like an accountant, which was what the witness claimed she was studying to become, now that she was no longer a drug dealer.

Pepe said that Alex Coffiel, who she claimed was a Latin King gang member, headed the security team at Sound Factory and controlled her all-girl crew. Chris Paciello and Michael Caruso had gotten into a knockdown brawl outside Sound Factory, before the latter two fled to Miami. Pepe claimed that "Alex told me he killed somebody" to frighten her when she said she wanted to stop dealing drugs. Pepe became upset when she thought she saw someone who was a Latin King in the spectator gallery. The DEA agents cleared the courtroom and interrogated the suspected gang member in the corridor. It was ultimately established that he was not a gangbanger but a regular clubgoer who used to frequent the old Sound Factory, which is probably why Pepe recognized him. (Afterward, Coffiel called Pepe a "liar" and vehemently denied he was a member or associate of the Latin Kings. "I don't wear a crown on my chest; you can check if you don't believe me.")

Everybody filed back into the courtroom, and Brafman plowed ahead. Why did she continue to work for Coffiel, even after she found out that he was a Latin King? "I'm a girl," Pepe replied. "I was scared. I knew what he was capable of."

Pepe overcame her initial anxiety to give compelling testimony about the extent of drug dealing in New York's clubland. But from the prosecution's point of view, most of the damaging evidence implicated Gatien's competitors, not the accused. Pepe testified that she had a sanctioned arrangement at Sound Factory, whereby Pepe and her crew paid $2,000 to the management every Saturday night to be allowed to deal drugs at the dance hall. (The fee was only $500 for the less-busy Friday nights, when underground music god Junior Vasquez wasn't deejaying.)

Under pressure from Brafman, Pepe admitted that no such formal deal existed at Gatien's club the Tunnel, where she said she simply bribed individual bouncers with small amounts of drugs to gain admittance. "I didn't look at the Tunnel bouncers like security," she chirped. "They were my friends."

Next, Baby Joe Uzzardi, the stylish club kid and Gatien party promoter, who ran yet another crew of drug dealers at the Tunnel, and unwittingly welcomed undercover DEA agents into the disco's inner sanctum, entered the witness box. His black hair was slicked back and harshly parted, his shoes were freshly shined, and he wore a blue double-breasted suit that gave off a serious junior executive vibe.

Prosecutor Friedberg began by getting Uzzardi, now a government witness, to describe a typical Ecstasy trip, which he did vividly: "All your fears and prejudices were swept away. You wanted to know every-body. It filled you full of love."

When he first began to work at the Tunnel, Uzzardi was a colorful, intelligent college student who told everybody he abhorred drugs. Gatien was grooming Uzzardi, who by clubland standards seemed like the model of rectitude, as a replacement for Michael Alig, who was by then a dysfunctional mess. "Good riddance to Michael Alig," Uzzardi told comrades. "We're the next generation. His thing is dead." But over the summer of 1995, Uzzardi went nuts after ingesting massive amounts of LSD and Ecstasy. He would talk about how he could taste colors. He started urging Gatien's employees to read Philip K. Dick novels. He kept babbling on about how acid expanded the mind, and he advo-cated that everybody should try Ecstasy at least once. All of a sudden, he had turned into Timothy Leary.

In what could have been some of the most damaging testimony of the trial for Gatien, Uzzardi, now supposedly drug free, claimed that in the same summer of 1995, he had a conversation with the club owner about selling illegal substances at the Tunnel. "I told Gatien it would be bet-ter to organize the drug dealing, because it was out-of-control." Uzzardi claimed on the witness stand that Gatien replied, "I don't want to hear about drugs," before disappearing into his office. Uzzardi further main-tained that Gatien made serious efforts to break up the numerous drug rings that infested his clubs but only after the Limelight had been raided by cops in September 1995. Uzzardi also said the Tunnel's exec-utive director, Steven Lewis, had once commented to him, "Good music and good drugs is what makes a good party," a cue the college kid took to mean he should ensure Tunnel patrons were supplied with a constant flow of high-quality product.

"Ray [Montgomery, Gatien's head of security] and Steve [Lewis, the Tunnel's executive director] told me that I had to keep drug dealers out of sight, because if they could see them, so could undercover cops," Uzzardi testified to the jury.

As it happened, undercover agents had already targeted Uzzardi. One of his own drug dealers, Sean Bradley, ratted him out to the DEA agents Gagne and Germanowski, who arrested Uzzardi after they had spent hours listening to wiretaps of his NYU dormitory phone, on which he boasted openly about major drug deals. On the stand, Uzzardi recalled how Bradley had introduced him to the two undercover operatives who wanted to buy drugs as his "friends from New Jersey."

Fifteen minutes into his testimony, Ben Brafman knew he had to take down Uzzardi to win the case. Uzzardi was no street criminal like Michael Caruso. He was clean-cut. He was soft-spoken and well-mannered. He went to a good school. He was obviously smart, perhaps too smart for his own good. Brafman thought that maybe he could use that intelligence, which smacked of arrogance, against him.

Under withering interrogation by Brafman, Uzzardi had trouble remembering dates of major drug transactions that involved hundreds of hits of Ecstasy, the number of pills sold, the names of the people who participated in the deals, or even whether they actually took place. But he had crystal-clear recollections of minor purchases involving a handful of pills he sold or gave to various Gatien employees. Brafman was trying to underscore the impression that the vast majority of Uzzardi's drug business was conducted out of his NYU dormitory, not at Gatien's clubs.

Brafman also quizzed Uzzardi—who after the trial changed his name to Joseph Quartana and opened a trendy boutique on New York's Ludlow Street—about the DEA wiretaps. On one, Uzzardi advised Sean Bradley to wear a disguise to get past security after Steven Lewis had banned Bradley from the club for dealing drugs. Uzzardi claimed on the stand that Bradley had been eighty-sixed for not being discreet enough: "He was a sloppy drug dealer, and they didn't want that." Uzzardi also admitted that another of his drug dealers was thrown out of the club, after he sold a vial of Special K in front of Alex Gatien.

In a different wiretap, Uzzardi, while talking about the lack of good party favors at the club following the crackdown, observed, "The trippy drug element is gone from the Tunnel. We need to bring that element back." Uzzardi improbably claimed in court, "I was referring to lighting effects on the dance floor." When Brafman asked him if he thought it was acceptable to lie on the stand as long as he didn't get caught, Uzzardi arrogantly replied, "Why not?" The jury rolled their eyes. Uzzardi had hung himself with his own smart mouth. The witness's credibility effectively destroyed, Brafman had no further questions. The lawyer walked back to the defense table, a big smile on his face. The trial was going better than he possibly could have hoped.

Michael Alig was supposed to be the star prosecution witness, but the murder rap rendered him useless. Instead, the government had little choice but to rely on Lord Michael Caruso, now better known to former acquaintances whom he had ratted out as "Sir Shithead," who had been telling what few friends he had left that he wasn't going to do any real time because of his cooperation in the Gatien case. He was the centerpiece of the trial. Gagne and Germanowki accompanied him to the stand for his own safety. Shifting awkwardly in his ill-fitting blue suit, with the collar gaping at the neck, Caruso tried to avoid looking at his former employer. Alex shot a withering stare at her husband's main accuser.

The ex–techno promoter was the government's chief rat by default, because of his allegation that Gatien had budgeted money for Caruso to buy Ecstasy for drug punches given out to Limelight patrons. Caruso testified that he'd made twenty to thirty punches during his tenure at the club. He also said that he put out party invitations advertising the availability of Ecstasy there. On one invite, Caruso was photographed with a hit of Ecstasy on the tip of his tongue. Remarkably, even the prosecution referred to its own witness as a "significant criminal."

Brafman began by impressing upon Caruso the penalties for lying to the court, thus planting the idea that this was not a person to trust. He also asked about his cooperation agreement, making sure the jury understood that Caruso was getting something in exchange for his testimony. Next, Brafman made Caruso lay out the details of his life story. Caruso lost his way in a labyrinth of lies. Brafman scoffed when Caruso claimed he made only $500,000 in total from dealing Ecstasy. With a quick glance at the vinegary look on the jurors' faces, one could easily tell that these men and women had Caruso correctly pegged as a treacherous scumbag.

Gatien's alleged transgressions paled in comparison to the five-year crime wave from 1991 to 1996 to which members of Caruso's team openly admitted. Caruso told the court he oversaw a violent crew of drug dealers at the Limelight and participated in a string of robberies of rival dealers. Brafman called Caruso and his men "a bunch of urban terrorists" who had committed enough criminal deeds to be put behind bars for life.

Brafman nearly turned the Gatien proceedings into a double murder trial, when he forcefully pressed Caruso about the violent and suspicious deaths of two members of his drug gang, Damon Burret and Billy Balanca. The key to the Caruso cross-examination, as Brafman saw it, was to confront Caruso with overwhelming evidence that he had killed Damon. He'd read the police file on the supposed suicide, and he thought it was a joke. The way he saw the forensic scenario, there was enough physical evidence to prove that Burret did not die by his own hand. In clubland, rumors had long circulated that Caruso disposed of Burret because he kept coming up short on drug deals. As Brafman thundered, Caruso looked stunned by the ferocious interrogation. On the stand, Caruso admitted that he had heard the same story but denied that Damon's death was anything more than what the medical examiner had ruled it: a suicide. Brafman pushed harder: "Did you kill Damon Burret?"

"I loved Damon, why would I kill him?" retorted Caruso, his voice rising. The jury's eyes widened. They sat forward in their seats. For a change, the audience was transfixed. All eyes were on Brafman and Caruso.

"You loved Damon?" scoffed Brafman. "You made him kiss your feet in Peter Gatien's office. You treated him like a slave."

"That was Peter's fault. He told me to do it."

"Did the government ask you if you killed Damon Burret?"

"The agents did ask me if I killed Damon," confirmed Caruso.

Brafman then turned his back on the witness and asked the next question to the jury: "Why would they ask you that, if it was a suicide?"

"I never murdered anybody. I loved Damon," Caruso repeated.

Caruso's expression started to crumble. Tears began to run down his pudgy cheeks. His shoulders shook. He looked to the prosecutors for help. Brafman paused for dramatic effect, while Caruso's sobs filled the courtroom. The theatrics continued when Brafman offered Caruso a white handkerchief and a glass of water. He waited for the witness to compose himself, then continued to bombard Caruso with uncomfortable questions.

Brafman smelled blood in the water and strode across the courtroom, moving in for the kill. He interrogated Caruso further about the murder of Billy Balanca, who had sold drugs and participated in robberies with Lord Michael and was subsequently found stabbed to death in the trunk of a car on Staten Island. Brafman took Caruso back to an interview he had given to the DEA agents at the time of his arrest. Once again, Caruso confessed that he had heard the rumors that he was responsible.

Brafman asked Caruso whether in an attempt to deflect culpability, he had blamed his erstwhile friend and business partner, Chris Paciello, as the real killer. Gasps spilled from the spectator section. The color drained from Caruso's face. He emphatically denied it. He was still terrified of Paciello.

"I never said that."

"You never said that Chris Paciello whacked Billy Balanca over fifty pounds of marijuana?"

"No."

Brafman handed him the notes the agents had taken down during the meeting. Caruso read them.

"OK, I said it, but it was just a rumor, one of several rumors I discussed with the agents."

"You mean like the rumor you killed Damon Burret."

Once again, Caruso burst into tears. The crybaby routine was starting to wear thin. Eric Friedberg objected furiously that Brafman was leading the witness. "What does this have to do with Peter Gatien?" he complained to the judge. By the end of his testimony, Caruso was slumped in his chair, looking like someone who had just been bashed in the head with a brick.

The trial moved unexpectedly to a climax. After the government rested its case on a Thursday, over the following weekend Brafman made a decision—one of the most difficult of his professional career. The dogged advocate had beat up on the government witnesses and was confident that they had failed to prove that Gatien was a drug kingpin, therefore he decided to rest his case without calling a single defense witness. The way he figured the situation, he had no need. No impartial jury would send someone to jail for twenty years on this paltry proof. Anyway, you could tell the jury was tired. The proceeding had taken up a big chunk of their time, and to what end?

In closing arguments, Assistant U.S. Attorney Eric Friedberg, who was not a powerful orator, branded the Limelight "a drug supermarket" where "massive amounts" of Ecstasy as well as cocaine, Special K, and the depressant Rohypnol were used as "promotional tools to lure patrons to the club." The government didn't accuse Gatien of personally selling drugs or taking a cut from drug dealers who operated in his clubs. Instead, they argued that he allowed drug dealers into his venues to increase their popularity and profitability.

"Peter Gatien knowingly paid for drug giveaways and E punches," Friedberg maintained, droning on in his usual monotone. "We do not have to show that Mr. Gatien handed out drugs personally. We do not have to show he knew everything that went on. Peter Gatien opened his house to these dealers and let them deal so he could make money off the patrons these drugs attracted. He gave them a home. . . . Look at his American Express bills. He's supporting a very lavish lifestyle."

Brafman began his summation by taping green crosses over the faces of drug dealers who didn't testify on the government's big board. "Why, if they gave a cooperation agreement to a murderer like Michael

Caruso, did they not call Junkie Jonathan or the It Twins?" he asked. "Because if they had, it would have contradicted the government's theory of the case."

Brafman slammed Friedberg and his colleagues for "trying to pull a fast one on the jury." He accused the government of using "venal and corrupt" witnesses to frame Gatien. He argued that the club owner was a target of overzealous prosecutors who were trying to make their name on the back of his client's celebrity. He emphasized that the only physical proof the government had was the party invitations. None of the hundreds of hours of wiretaps contained any evidence whatsoever linking Gatien directly to the drug dealing at his clubs.

"If Peter Gatien is a major drug dealer, as charged, where are the conversations that say 'bring the money to Peter' or 'Peter wants this amount of drugs'?" asked Brafman. "They don't exist."

Addressing the issue of the invitations, and the government's insistence that any use of the letters E or K within said invites referred to illegal drugs and therefore constituted a crime, Brafman mocked, "There were 6,800 invitations in all. Gatien approved maybe thirty percent of them. *The X-Files* is one of the most popular shows on television. According to the government's logic, it must be about pills."

"You can not convict Peter Gatien of anything on the evidence that has been presented," Brafman summed up for the jury. "I'm now transferring his life onto your shoulders."

After seven hours of deliberation, the news came that the verdict was about to be delivered. Every seat was quickly filled with journalists and Gatien supporters. The defendant filed in, and the judge summoned the jury into the courtroom. They did not look at Gatien, who was still woozy from painkillers, following an eye operation he underwent toward the end of the trial.

"Please rise," the judge told the club owner, who stood erect, shoulders squared, hands by his side. The judge asked the jury, "Have you reached a verdict?"

"Yes," said the foreman. "Not guilty."

Jennifer and Alex—once bitter enemies—hugged each other. Gatien punched his fist in the air and leapt over the wooden barrier separating the court from the spectators and into the arms of his supporters. Each time the jury foreman announced, "Not guilty," the courtroom— packed with club kids—erupted into applause.

"I feel elated," said Gatien later, his voice choked with uncharacteristic emotion. "It's as if a million-ton weight has been lifted from my back. It's been a nightmare. My life has been turned upside down. This was an evil, mean-spirited prosecution right from the get-go."

Prosecutor Eric Friedberg was staggered. He felt sick to the stomach. He had spent millions of dollars and thousand of man-hours on an investigation that turned out to be the legal equivalent of one of those big-budget Hollywood blockbusters that flop at the box office. He picked up his papers, put them in his briefcase, hung his head, and walked briskly from the courtroom without comment. Bob Gagne took the not-guilty verdict the hardest: He was clearly bitter and resentful. Matt Germanowski tried to make the best of it. "If I didn't get you today, I'll get you later," he cheerily told Peter Gatien, outside the courtroom.

Friedberg's boss, U.S. Attorney for the Eastern District Zachary Carter, spoke to the assembled journalists: "We had absolute confidence in our case. Testimony of cooperating witnesses indicated that drugs were being sold out of these clubs. We're obviously disappointed. But the jury has spoken."

The feds simply didn't have the goods on Gatien. The club owner beat the dope distribution rap with space to spare. Gatien was acquitted mainly because the government's case relied so heavily on the capricious testimony of thuggish dope peddlers and flaky club kids. One gum-chewing juror explained the verdict, "These witnesses lied so consistently, how could I believe them?" He also revealed that while some jurors initially wanted to convict Gatien, they couldn't rely on the tainted evidence that the government offered as proof.

Brafman not only cleared his client, he also made the government look like a bunch of uptight Fascists. Not for the first time, prosecutorial overreach bred sympathy for the devil. "I tried to make the jury understand," said Brafman, "that you can be the head of an organization without being criminally responsible for everything your employees do, even when they invoke your name."

The overall impression left by the trial was not of a single drug hierarchy headed by kingpin Gatien but of several competing drug crews trying to gain advantage by bribing individual Gatien employees. And in the end, the question of the club owner's guilt was overshadowed by the criminal activities of the witnesses who were supposed to put him behind bars. "Right now, I'm just grateful to God," Gatien said outside the courthouse. "I want to go to church." It wasn't clear whether Gatien was referring to the Limelight or Saint Patrick's Cathedral.

"I proved my case through their witnesses," a triumphant Brafman crowed at the after-verdict party at his client's favorite Italian restaurant, Brunnelli's on York Avenue, where the lawyer was wearing a "Peter Gatien Not Guilty" baseball cap. "When I started this case, I anticipated a long and complicated defense involving as many as twenty-five witnesses," he said.

"From the beginning, there was a mean-spirited quality to this prosecution that I found offensive," added the attorney. "The government adopted a scorched-earth mentality: Let's get Peter Gatien at all costs, the facts be damned."

Surrounded by family, friends, and supporters, Gatien sipped $250 bottles of champagne and toasted his good fortune at beating the feds. "I hope nobody ever has to go through what I just went though," he told the crowd. "Let's get back to making New York nightlife great again."

The party was a sedate affair compared to the wild evenings described during the trial. But the normally reserved Gatien was ebullient, thanking his lawyers, his private eyes, his daughters, and, most of all, his wife Allesandra—who many insiders had predicted would turn on her husband by helping the government and who Gatien, in the initial stages of the investigation, had followed by a private eye—for sticking by him through the most painful period of his life. "The DEA agents, when they interviewed me, made it clear that their goal was to make me leave my husband," Allesandra said. "They said Peter was saying things behind my back."

"The phrase federal justice is an oxymoron," Gatien continued over artichokes and pasta. "It's all part of this hypocritical war on drugs that has gotten to the point where they're looking to create crime. I've become so disillusioned with the justice system in this country that I refuse to stand up for the national anthem anymore."

But what about all the horrible things that went on at his clubs? Legal issues aside, did Gatien not feel morally responsible for fostering a climate that allowed such dubious characters as Michael Alig and Michael Caruso to thrive?

"I did try to send Michael Alig to rehab," Gatien maintained. "But he kept skipping out. As for Lord Michael, I genuinely did not know about all the robberies he commited. Owning a nightclub is like having three thousand children; you can't be responsible for them all."

"Peter does see the disrespect for the value of human life that went on," interrupted Alex. "He completely takes responsibility for what happened. I see the pain in his face all the time."

In the wake of Peter Gatien's federal trial, the slick, behind-the-scenes legal maneuvering needed to secure the "not guilty" verdict became apparent. Michael Alig felt royally screwed, charging that Gerry McMahon, his lawyer on the manslaughter charge, sold him out to Gatien's counsel, Ben Brafman. Prior to the trial, Alig, at the urging of both Brafman and McMahon, signed an affidavit in which he took the blame for drug activities the government was trying to pin on his former boss. The feds were furious. The document he signed was a major blow to their case. They resolved to press the judge to make Alig serve his federal time for running a dope ring at the Limelight after he got out of state prison on the manslaughter rap; in other words, as a punishment, the government wanted the sentences to run consecutively.

Alig accused McMahon of having "conflicted loyalties." "After meeting with Brafman, McMahon suddenly became more interested in Peter's case than mine," said the incarcerated club kid. "Instead of discussing the charges against me, we spent most of the time discussing Peter's case and how to discredit the feds to get them to drop the charges against Peter. All the time, my lawyer was telling me that Brafman would speak to his friends in the DA's office, since he used to work there himself, and get them to reduce the time on the manslaughter charge. McMahon never cautioned that I was engaged on a dangerous course of action. Shortly after, McMahon told me 'not to be surprised,' if I heard he had received a lump payment from Brafman, because he had done a service for Brafman and because the money I was paying him wasn't enough."

Alig went on to say that after he went out on a limb for Gatien and signed the affidavit, he never heard from either Brafman or Gatien again. And the money that the club owner had been depositing in his prison account suddenly dried up for good.

Replying to the complaint filed by Alig with the Disciplinary Committee of the New York Supreme Court's Appellate Division in July 1998, McMahon addressed his former client's accusations in a letter. "With regard to Alig's claims that I persuaded him to sign an affidavit for Peter Gatien, his former employee, because I wanted to curry favor with Mr. Gatien's lawyer, Ben Brafman, that claim is absolutely untrue. I told Mr. Alig on numerous occasions that it was not in his interest to sign the Gatien affidavit. When I mailed Mr. Alig the affidavit which Mr. Brafman had sent me to review, I warned him in the cover letter that 'the federal prosecutors will be extremely angry' if he signs it. Further, I received no money or benefit from Mr. Brafman in connection with the Alig/Gatien case, or any other case for that matter. . . . In truth, Mr. Alig signed the affidavit for Peter Gatien because he loved being in the limelight and seeing his name in the newspaper."

While Gatien was triumphing over the feds, a thousand miles to the south, Chris Paciello was still peeved about his failure to launch Liquid in New York but was determined that his new upscale restaurant in South Beach would be a runaway success. In February 1998, the opening night of Joia electrified the smart set of Miami Beach, where, unlike New York, Paciello could do no wrong. A throng of synthetic beauties sashayed through the front door. In the back room of the nominally Tuscan eatery, Donald Trump, Helena Christensen, Anthony Sabato Junior, Gloria and Emilio Estefan, Rupert Everett, Jennifer Lopez, singer Jon Secada, painter Kenny Scharf and makeup-artist-to-the-stars Kevyn Aucoin mixed and mingled. Madonna couldn't make the date, so she sent a prerelease copy of her latest album, "Ray of Light," which reverberated from the speakers all night. Everett pleaded to sit next to Gloria Estefan, because he was desperate to meet the queen of Latino pop. Trump was spotted having an intimate tête-à-tête with the fashion model Christensen.

Earlier in the day, Ingrid Casares had been so frantic about the restaurant's rapidly approaching debut that her concern clogged up one of the Delano Hotel's lavatories. Her high-powered publicist, Lizzie Grubman, spent the afternoon cleaning up the nervous Casares and soothing her frayed nerves. Paciello, on the other hand, was as cool as a cocktail shaker, happy to mingle with the glitterati, making sure everyone had a drink. Casares need not have fretted. Joia quickly became the Miami Beach equivalent of New York's Moomba, a requisite pit stop for models and celebrities—despite its cardboard food and wretched service.

Famous people felt comfortable at Joia. Madonna picked Paciello's restaurant as the spot for her forty-first birthday party, with a guest list that included such notables as Ricky Martin, Rosie O'Donnell, and Jennifer Tilly. Chris Rock and Daisy Fuentes were regulars at the place, even during the summer off-season. In their wake, gossip mavens flocked to the fancy chow house looking for items. Scandal rags and glossy fan magazines tried to bribe the busboys for dirt. Paparazzi stalked outside.

"If South Beach is the new French Riviera, then Joia is the Hotel du Cap," prattled *Vanity Fair*.

A few days after Joia's star-studded debut, disgraced federal informer Sean Kirkham called Chris Paciello from federal lockup in Brooklyn.

"Liquid," announced the receptionist.

"Can I speak to Chris?" asked Kirkham.

"Who's calling?"

"Just tell him it's a friend who has some information about Lord Michael," replied an irritated Kirkham.

"Hold on."

A few seconds passed, and Paciello came on the line.

"Hello. Who's this?"

"Remember me from our poolside meeting at the Delano Hotel? You gave your brother something for me."

Paciello's tone hardened. "What do you want?" he asked curtly.

"I just wanted to share some information with you. Your name came up repeatedly during the Peter Gatien trial. Your old friend Lord Michael testified and said some shitty things about you."

"Oh really," replied Paciello. "Like what?"

"He said you burned down Risk and that you had something to do with Billy Balanca's murder."

"Caruso is a fuckin' liar and a thief; no one will believe him," Paciello told Kirkham, apparently unconcerned.

"Anyway, I just thought you should know this. You can consider this information on the house."

"Thanks, man. I owe you."

15   COCK OF THE WALK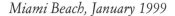

Miami Beach, January 1999

Imagine watching the E! Channel in a Turkish bath populated solely by celebrities you'd read about in *People* magazine. The paint on the walls still sticky with humidity, Ingrid Casares and Chris Paciello's Bar Room debuted amidst a barrage of retina-blinding flashlights. The celebrities paraded into the club in luminous star bursts—a procession of famous faces, many of them fresh from attending the Super Bowl. The locals were abuzz, craning their necks to catch a glimpse of the latest icon influx. Hollywood had come to Florida. Even Miami Beach had rarely seen such a star-studded event nor witnessed a more amazing transformation.

You could have filled a talent agency with the galaxy of actors, musicians, and sports stars in this swanky lounge. Upstairs, Cameron Diaz, Edward Norton, and Ben Stiller huddled together for protection against the suffocating multitude of models, scene-makers, and trendsetters, while downstairs a rainbow-haired Dennis Rodman argued loudly with the bouncer blocking his path to the VIP room. Nearby, Samuel L. Jackson and Tommy Hilfiger swapped fashion tips, while in another corner Chris Rock, Lenny Kravitz, and the Red Hot Chili Peppers' Anthony Kiedes shared a joke.

Gathered in casual groupings under the chandeliers and velvet curtains of the high-ceilinged main room were Spike Lee, Sony Music head

Tommy Mottola, Jason Priestley, baseball player Sammy Sosa, Greg Kinnear, and *South Park* creators Trey Parker and Matt Stone. At the back of the literal hot spot, a harried bouncer, his face beaded with perspiration, barked into a walkie-talkie: "I have the entire cast of *Ally McBeal* entering through the rear."

As he squeezed his way through a crack in the wall of designer humanity, maneuvering carefully toward the packed dance floor, Chris Paciello spotted Jennifer Lopez waving at him. He reflected for a moment on the mutual fascination between celebrities and mobsters. Though he was too unintelligent to fully comprehend the process, he was dimly conscious of being part of this endless to-and-fro between the street and the screen, reality and PR hype, his true self and the façade he presented to others.

Paciello was aware that behind his back, his fabulous friends whispered that he was a movie star gangster come to life. Madonna was rumored to have called him on his last birthday and sung, Marilyn Monroe–style, "Happy birthday, dear mobster" down the phone. The chic and the snooty compared him tellingly not just to the character Ray Liotta played in *Goodfellas* but to Ray Liotta the actor, as well. In the arrogance of the moment, as he slid his thick and perfectly formed arm across Lopez's smooth, slender shoulder and handed her a drink, he wondered who should play him in the film version of his own life? Maybe, Paciello should play Paciello.

His other club, Liquid, had lost its showbiz sheen in recent months, but the sensational debut of Bar Room was another striking achievement for the Staten Island tough guy turned celebrated man-about-town. If anyone still had any doubt, Chris Paciello was the undisputed king of the strip, the most successful nightclub operator in the city, controlling the Beach's hippest destinations. For six short months, Bar Room would be the most fashionable club on the planet.

The exalted existence that Paciello led was one that many young men would have envied. He had squeezed more action, romance, and thrills into his twenty-eight years than most people twice his age. His rise to the top was dramatic, aided, no doubt, by his dual heritage, a combination of German efficiency and Italian clannishness. He lived sumptuously for a boy from the streets, in a sprawling million-dollar stucco and terra-cotta villa on Flamingo Drive, cruised on a fine-looking yacht, and escorted Madonna to premieres and fashion shows. While his pleasure dens prospered, the "hunky impresario," as *Variety* called him, had become a regular fixture in gossip columns and glossy magazines by dating a string of famous and beautiful women, including Lopez, supermodel Niki Taylor, MTV's Daisy Fuentes, and Latina bombshell and former Univision television host Sofia Vergara.

Along the way, Paciello had also managed to seduce an entire social class of well-to-do South Floridians—restaurant owners, real estate developers, well-heeled investors—who helped smooth his path to riches and rub away some of the rough edges he arrived with from New York. He had become so respectable that he even counted the mayor of Miami Beach as a personal friend. In addition, Paciello served on a city committee charged with overseeing clubs in the area, an important source of revenue in this transient town, where the local tourist board claimed that fully a third of the visitors came primarily because of the nightlife. More than just a nightclub operator, he was such a pivotal figure in the resurgence of Miami Beach as an international tourist destination that many locals seriously considered him "a community leader."

Life should have been extra sweet for Paciello. But even in the midst of his luxury lounge's triumphant opening, perched as he was atop the new horizon of hip, something was eating away at the golden boy. And it wasn't just the persistent knot in his stomach nor the strange sensation that he'd felt lately of being constantly followed.

Part of the problem was his punishing schedule, which left him little time to savor his accomplishments. Spoiled and lazy, Ingrid Casares wasn't a partner in any real sense. She certainly didn't shoulder half the workload. Plus, she suffered from attention deficit disorder and couldn't be relied on to remember the everyday details so important to running a profitable disco. She spent most of her time in yoga sessions with Madonna or jetting around the globe. By contrast, friends had to practically force Paciello to go on holiday. "Every day he'd be in the gym by 10:00 A.M. for two hours of boxing with the bag," recalled Michael Capponi, who helped Paciello launch Bar Room. "After which he'd arrive in the office about noon, stay until eight or nine. Then he'd get home from work, go to the gym for another two hours, then go to Joia for a dinner party and then visit four or five different night-clubs, come home about five in the morning with some chick, have two hours with her, and then go to sleep at seven, only to get up again at ten."

Success had also bred boredom. With all Paciello's achievements came not satisfaction but world-weariness. A couple of his close male friends had recently got hitched—real estate mogul Craig Robins to a model named Ivelin and restaurant owner Shareef Malnik to MTV VJ Edith Serrano—and were no longer available to party with him every night. He feared the good life in Miami was turning him into a "pussy." He felt the psycho inside had been hibernating too long. Roping in his wild animal instincts for the sake of public consumption had caused psychic stress. His schizophrenic double life—his two names, his two driving licenses, his two social security numbers, his two distinct per-sonalities—was depressing him to the point where he felt fit to burst.

Despite all the talk that he had risen to the top by using Mafia scare tactics, by this point in his career, his old Italian mob connections were more of a hindrance than a help. The upscale Bar Room, with its strict dress code and tight guest list, was Paciello's way of finally saying good-bye to all the goombahs. "At Bar Room, when these meatheads from Brooklyn turned up, the doormen were given strict instructions that Chris didn't want them in the club," said Michael Capponi.

Liquid doorman Gilbert Stafford confirmed that Paciello was trying to distance himself from his gangster roots: "That whole Italian mob thing, by the end he seemed to hate it. It made him really uncomfort-able. I remember one night, he was sitting at a table with this goon and a tacky girl, who obviously had the meter running, if you catch my drift. Chris leaned over to me at one point, and pleaded, 'Can you come over and get me out of this in a minute? These people are killing me.' He gave orders to the staff that if any tough-looking Italians came to the door and dropped his name, to say he was unavailable or out of the country."

Paciello worried, too, about all the new venues planned for the future that threatened to eclipse his empire, especially Level, a megaclub housed in the old Glam Slam building, and Crobar, a well-financed dance club from Chicago. For a while Paciello had had the field to himself, but now competitors were moving in fast, threatening to cook his personal golden goose. "Ingrid and I created our own competition because everyone saw how successful Liquid was and how much press we got," he bellyached to *Ocean Drive* magazine. "So a lot of people from outside want to come down here to open clubs."

If Paciello was feeling the pressure, it wasn't just from legitimate business rivals. The club owner—"a pawn, a do-boy for others, a really dumb, wanna-be wise guy who, for his whole life, was controlled by people tougher than himself," according to one underworld contact—was constantly being hit up for tributes from the old boys back in Brooklyn. Though never a "made man," only an associate, Paciello still owed allegiance to three organized crime families—the Colombos, the Gambinos, and the Bonnanos. At times, his links to the mob were so convoluted, he didn't even know who to kick up the ladder to; it seemed like everybody wanted a piece of him. To keep up with his financial obligations, he took to skimming money from Liquid's profits to pay off the numerous Italian heavies who regularly journeyed down to South Beach with hands outstretched. One such mobster, feared Gambino capo Jackie "The Nose" D'Amico—the man who helped set up Paciello in business at his first Miami Beach club, Risk—was particularly insistent, believing that his former protégé owed him big time. In addition, according to a veteran local criminal, corrupt local cops were also putting the screws on Paciello.

"In certain circles, it became known that Risk burning down wasn't an accident but a torch job," said the same source. "And when Chris started boasting to the wrong people that he brought in outside talent to do the job, well, that didn't sit well with some folks. The mistake Chris made was that he wanted to be noticed, wanted everyone to know he was a connected bad boy from New York City. But you don't come into this town and start making moves, drawing all sorts of heat and attention, without having to pay the piper. That goes triple for outside Italians. The Good Ol' Boys had been putting big-mouthed Guido gangsters like Mr. Stupid in the swamp for years."

The well-placed source said he was introduced to Paciello by a friend and longtime business associate, who we'll refer to as Mr. Slick. The source asserted that he worked with Mr. Slick in the '70s, when he provided security for "a little import-export business" they had going at the time that involved small twin-engine aircraft, corrupt Cuban government officials, and deserted islands in the Bahamas.

Mr. Slick was Paciello's secret investor in Liquid, claimed the source, who went on to say that, contrary to popular belief, the real backers of Liquid weren't the Italian mob. The real power backstage was Mr. Slick, who appeared to be a respectable businessman. When Paciello hooked up with Mr. Slick, he had no idea about his new investor's alleged criminal past or that he supposedly still kept contacts in that world. Like many locals, Mr. Slick didn't much care for loud and flashy Italian gangsters. He preferred to conduct business in the shadows, away from public scrutiny. But he saw in Paciello a perfect scapegoat. Who better to take the heat if and when the time came, than a high-profile thug like Chris Paciello? "[Mr. Slick] set Chris up to be the fall guy, if anything went wrong," claimed the former associate. "I have to hand it to him, he played Mr. Stupid like Bobby Fisher."

The beginning of the end for Paciello, maintained the source, was when he went behind the Mafia's back and launched Liquid. The Italians back home were mad, but they decided to bide their time. In the meanwhile, with Ingrid Casares's help, Liquid became a goldmine. "So the Italians start wanting a cut," explained the felon. "At about the same time, the Good Ol' Boys also see how successful Paciello had become and they start applying pressure, too.

"But the boys in New York were never satisfied, and they wanted more and more money. Jackie the Nose [the Gambinos' Jackie D'Amico] starts coming down with more and more demands, and Chris starts stealing more and more to keep up. [Mr. Slick] finds out and takes Chris aside and chews him out. Once again, down comes Mr. Nose for one of his regular trips, but this time he's met at the airport by [Mr. Slick's] people and taken out to a fish farm in the Everglades, where he's 'reeducated' by twelve crazy Cubans with chain saws. I don't know exactly what was said, but they put the fear of God in him, so much so that when Mr. Nose left, he was in such a hurry that he forgot his luggage at the airport."

Meanwhile, back in Manhattan, after months of delays and in the face of vocal community opposition, Peter Gatien finally managed to relaunch the Limelight, which had been shuttered by authorities for nearly two years. In the wake of his federal trial, to pay his legal fees, the financially troubled entrepreneur sold the building to a developer who then leased the landmark edifice back to him.

Prior to the reopening, hoping to rehabilitate his scandal-scarred reputation, Gatien bombarded local community board members with mailings about how the new drug-free Limelight was going to be an asset to the community. The club operator told the press that the now neighborhood-friendly disco would be open during the day and would feature puppet shows and a courtyard playground for the local children as well as a juice bar and a "community outreach office," whatever that meant. "We want the neighborhood to feel like this is the kind of place they can come for lunch or a cup of coffee," Gatien told *The New York Times*.

At night, the club was supposed to provide a showcase for the next wave of contemporary young artists. The dance hall was going to be one big art installation. Gatien hired a team of young designers to transform the space from top to bottom. A gallery was created amidst the fluted arches of the chapel area. Avant-garde dance troupes cavorted in the hallways. Ice sculptures displayed in a giant walk-in refrigerator greeted patrons in the lobby. "We want to help new talent, incubate new deejays, artists, and performers," Gatien claimed in the local media.

The controversial Swiss surrealist H. R. Giger, best known to the general populace for creating the monster in Ridley Scott's *Alien*, designed the upstairs VIP room, festooning the exclusive enclave with disturbing aluminum sculptures that were half science fiction/half demonic. The dark and decadent netherworld of H. R. Giger's imagination found a suitable setting at the Limelight, where the artist hoped to install a permanent New York showroom for his work.

"There was a lot of drama surrounding the Giger room," said photographer Jacob Mikkelsen, who helped with the redesign of the club.

"Watching Giger and Gatien hanging out together was like watching two witch doctors sizing each other up. The room was meant to make Gatien legitimate in the art world. But in the end, he screwed Giger on the money, like he screwed everybody else."

The space looked spectacular, but few seemed to care anymore. While business was booming at Chris Paciello's Bar Room a thousand miles south, at the newly renovated Limelight, the dance floor was half-empty most nights. If the old Limelight was a pop culture petri dish that grew some strange organisms, the new Limelight was completely germ free, transformed from a place of illicit pleasures into a yuppie theme park. Gone were the drugged-up club kids, out-of-their-head ravers, and shrieking drag queens on unsteady heels. Here was an older, more conventional crowd—aspiring middle managers and dressed-up bridge-and-tunnel couples on a date who politely lined up outside the club like obedient dogs. The legendary polydrug use and polysexual displays of the past had been replaced by old-fangled pleasures like drinking and necking. Signs throughout the club warned patrons that if they used illegal substances on the premises, they would be ejected and handed over to the police. An undercover team of former law enforcement agents, paid for by Gatien, patrolled the warren of claustrophobic tunnels and dimly lit side rooms. Only one person per stall was allowed in the bathrooms. Such extraordinary security measures ensured that you probably would have died of alcohol poisoning before you scored a line of cocaine at the new Limelight, a granite mausoleum to an epoch of excess, now ancient history.

Barely a month after the Limelight's rededication, on January 8, 1999, Gatien and his teary-eyed wife stood before a state judge and pled guilty to larceny and tax evasion. The nightlife mogul was charged with underreporting millions of dollars in state sales taxes from the liquor sold at the now-defunct Palladium as well as stealing tens of thousands of dollars in city and state income taxes that he and Alex were supposed to pay for their employees. Peter, who could have gotten up to fifteen years, was promptly sentenced to ninety days in jail and ordered to pay nearly $2 million in fines and back taxes. Alex also got off lightly—300 hours of community service.

The settlement hammered out between Ben Brafman and the district attorney's office allowed Gatien, now a convicted felon, to stay in the nightclub business by granting him a "certificate of relief from civil disability," which meant the entrepreneur could keep his liquor licenses for the clubs. Normally, state law forbids convicted felons from holding such permits. Brafman successfully argued that his client would be unable to pay the fines and back taxes if he wasn't allowed to make a living in the field he knew best. Brafman also asked the judge to put Gatien in a facility befitting his celebrity status. The judge, who must have had a sense of humor, sent him to Rikers Island, the same hellhole where Michael Alig went through cold turkey. He did delay the start of Gatien's sentence until later in the year, to permit further surgery on the club owner's eye.

Gatien's troubles continued to mushroom when later in the same month a frail Long Island teenager named Jimmy Lyons died of a suspected Ecstasy overdose at the Canadian's other club, the Tunnel. Convulsing and foaming at the mouth, the five-foot, five-inch, hundred-pound Lyons—called "Shorty" by buddies—expired on the ice-slicked loading dock next to the club's Twenty-seventh Street exit, as bouncers desperately tried to save his life. "He was light as a cork," remembered one of the security guards, who carried his lifeless body back into the club.

Three friends—nineteen-year-old Joseph Grassi and eighteen-year-old Amy Lebrecht, plus her boyfriend—accompanied Lyons to the club that night. Lyons, who had a preexisting heart condition, was celebrating his birthday, and this was his first trip to a big Manhattan disco. Lebrecht told me she worried about Lyons doing drugs because he was so delicate. She also said he was self-conscious about his weight. "He started doing steroids to bulk up," she claimed. "I remember telling my boyfriend four days before we went to the Tunnel that if Shorty wasn't careful, he could kill himself."

Veteran journalist Jack Newfield featured Lyons's grieving mother on the cover of the *New York Post* as part of his ongoing crusade to put the embattled club czar ("the dark prince of nightlife") out of business. Ben Brafman countered that there was no solid evidence that Lyons bought the pill that killed him at the Tunnel. "Our preliminary investigation raises serious questions as to the accuracy of media reports suggesting that this young man purchased drugs at the Tunnel," he claimed. "We hope that responsible city officials will wait until the autopsy and toxicology reports have been completed before seeking to assess responsibility for this tragedy."

Brafman was aware that both Grassi and Lebrecht had told the police they had no knowledge of Lyons buying drugs in the club. But Lebrecht admitted to me that they hadn't told authorities the truth, in order to protect the reputation of their dead pal.

"I didn't want to say anything to the cops that might make Shorty look bad," explained Lebrecht. She went on to say that her boyfriend and Grassi were with Lyons when he purchased two hits of E near the dance floor. "The Tunnel is a big drug house," she said. "It seemed like everybody was tripping their faces off."

While Gatien had largely succeeded in creating a drug-free environment at the Limelight for the purposes of good publicity, in the meantime the narcotics action had quietly moved over to the sister venue, the Tunnel, on the West Side, which now catered to a much younger crowd than the Limelight did. The illegal trade wasn't as structured nor conducted with the same intensity as it had been in the past. But given his track record, this was more than enough for Gatien to lose his livelihood. Drug dealers were clearly visible lined up outside the upstairs unisex bathroom, offering their wares: "Wanna bump. Wanna bump." Or, "E.E.E." I even personally warned Gatien, "You know the drug situation is getting out of control again at the Tunnel." Gatien shrugged and told me in a tone of exasperation, "I'm doing everything I can. It's not fair to expect the Tunnel to be a drug-free oasis, when the surrounding city itself isn't drug free."

At the same time, the DEA was receiving reports from paid stool pigeons who had visited the dance hall that drug activity had started up once again. Indeed, DEA snitches were present the night Jimmy Lyons died. But the agency was reluctant to launch another investigation so soon after the not-guilty verdict in the federal trial, fearing it would look like they were persecuting the club owner. Instead, they passed on the information to NYPD's Manhattan South narcotics squad.

Law enforcement's disinclination to go one more round with Gatien changed with the death of Jimmy Lyons. A team of fifty trained narcotics cops, including more than twenty undercover operatives, targeted the Tunnel over eight consecutive weekends, scoping out the cavernous club and its ad hoc assortment of sometimes underage drug dealers. On a Saturday night in the middle of April, after a two-month investigation, a small army of cops stormed the Tunnel at around three in the morning and arrested fourteen people on charges relating to the sale and use of Ecstasy. Clubgoers were made to stand in line as they were escorted out by cops. Undercover officers pointed out suspects as they were herded out of the disco. The venue was padlocked, and the suspects were taken to the Tenth Precinct, where cops in plastic gloves probed their various bodily cavities.

The next day, I spoke to Gatien on the phone from his Upper East Side town house. He sounded in deep denial and didn't seem to comprehend that this could signal the end of his teetering nocturnal operation. He seemed to think that lawyers, legal loopholes, and special pleading would save his butt once again. Or, perhaps, he could spin his way out of trouble.

"Why are my clubs supposed to be the only nondrug venues in New York?" he asked. He accused the authorities of "highly selective enforcement." "Are you telling me there are no drugs at other clubs? I have my suspicions that someone out there—whether it's Giuliani or the feds—wants to put a major hurt on me," he complained.

"There were ten Ecstasy dealers arrested," he argued. "The cops seized fifty hits of E—that's an average of five hits per dealer. So we're not talking about major traffickers here."

In the wake of Jimmy Lyons's death, Gatien instructed bouncers to be more vigilant in their search for drug use on the premises and to eject anybody caught sleeping in the club. Gatien's private eye, John

Dabrowski—who was in charge of an antidrug squad of a dozen former cops who worked undercover at the Tunnel and Limelight—defended the work he did at Gatien's clubs. He claimed that since the beginning of the year, the Tunnel had ejected 250 people suspected of drug activity. He added that his team met regularly with Tenth Precinct officers, who had assured him he was doing a good job. "They're not giving us a fair chance," he protested. "They don't do this to any other club in New York. This is coming from the mayor's office. The cops have been told to get Peter Gatien at all costs."

Ironically, a few weeks prior to the raid, a spokesperson from the Tenth Precinct's Office of Community Affairs and Crime Prevention assured the *Village Voice* that drugs weren't a major problem at the Tunnel and other major clubs in the precinct. Thanks to "good management" he said, there were only "a few isolated incidents."

Some of Gatien's respectable employees, who were hired in the wake of his not-guilty verdict to burnish his public image, were angry at their boss for not grasping the magnitude of the drug situation. "He sends out mixed messages," said Conyers Thompson, a longtime political activist who was employed to salve the neighborhood anger at Gatien's hot spots. "The promoters are told one thing, the security another. Peter thinks he can finesse his way out of this. He doesn't realize how serious it is."

In the wake of the raid, the cops crowed to the media about the pile of drugs they'd bagged at the Tunnel. They made fun of how amateurish the dealers were. They thought they'd done a bang-up job. But in the end, after the lab reports came back, it was the NYPD that had egg on its face. Most of the E they'd bought or seized was bunk. Instead of a substantial illegal drug haul, the cops mostly ended up with a selection of various over-the-counter medicines available in drugstores nationwide. The final count for all that effort was not the fifty hits of Ecstasy initially reported, but a grand total of four real tablets as well as a packet of cocaine, a small bottle of Special K, and a bag of marijuana— hardly an important victory in the War on Drugs.

That's why New York State Supreme Court judge Paula Omansky overruled the city and allowed the club to reopen. She reasoned in her decision that "wherever you have young people, wherever you have the excitement of music . . . there is going to be drugs. The question here is whether or not the club was operated as a haven for drug use. . . . In my opinion, it seems clear that the Tunnel was what it held itself out to be, namely a nightclub for dancing." Once again, as in the federal racketeering trial, the authorities failed to come up with the real dope to bring down Peter Gatien.

In a strange twist of events, part of the agreement worked out between Gatien and the court required him to hire former city drug-buster Robert Silbering—the man who originally shut down the Limelight in September 1995—to review Gatien's antidrug efforts from top to bottom. Silbering said he'd already sent one of his employees to the Tunnel to check out the venue and declared, "The individual was impressed with the operation. They seem well-trained. They work hard to deal with the issue of drugs in the club."

That didn't stop Mayor Giuliani—who must have seen Gatien as the perfect political bogeyman, a convenient symbol of the old anything-goes New York he was busily eviscerating—from blasting the club owner during a press conference. Referring to the Tunnel, he said, "I think that the club Gatien runs is an abomination. It's disgraceful, and I think he should try and find some other line of work."

In July 1999, yet more turmoil ensued when two troubled teenaged girls alleged that while they were high on Ecstasy and alcohol, two New Jersey men raped them in a crowded restroom at the Tunnel. From the beginning, the story the girls told made little sense. Anyone familiar with the crowded area where they said they were sexually assaulted knew it was nearly impossible for such an attack to take place without someone hearing struggles or screams. Bathroom attendants, club patrons, and bouncers interviewed by the police said they heard nothing. And why would the two men hang around a club for two hours after committing such a serious offense? In addition, security guards claimed they spotted the sixteen-year-old after the rape was supposed to have occurred, sitting on a loading dock outside the club, smiling and swinging her legs, presumably coming down from the Ecstasy.

Subsequently, the girls—who had entered the club with fake IDs—

admitted to detectives that their tale was a hoax, the sex had been consensual, and that they'd lied as a way to explain to their parents why they missed curfew. But not before the two accused—Roddy Caraballo, nineteen, and Orette Fiedtkou, twenty-one—spent most of the week in jail and had their reputations dragged through the mud by the local media. The *New York Post* even reported that the men had confessed to the crime.

"I'm not angry at the girls; I'm angry at the administration," Gatien complained. "Whenever one of his cops gets into trouble for shooting or torturing somebody, Giuliani always says, 'Let's not rush to judgment. Let's wait until all the facts are in.' With me, it's a case of facts be damned."

Even after the story turned out to be a hoax, Deputy Mayor Rudy Washington still told the *The New York Times*, "I'm going to be doubling my effort to close the establishment as soon as possible," he said. "The fact that we have a sixteen-year-old and a nineteen-year-old in a public location, and there are circumstances that would allow consensual or nonconsensual sex, is something we're not going to stand for. We can't allow this as a society to go on."

Baffled by the city's logic, Fiedtkou's attorney, Richard Stoll, scoffed, "If Mayor Giuliani wants to shut down a club because a sixteen-year-old and a nineteen-year-old had consensual sex there, he will also have to shut down every public park and schoolyard in New York State as well as confiscate every car owned by a teenager."

By the early summer of 1999, Chris Paciello was convinced that he needed an extra edge to crush his rivals. The club owner acquired what he believed was a secret weapon to protect his business interests. His name was Andrew Dohler. Paciello made the momentous error of employing Dohler, a Miami Beach police officer, to work part-time as a security consultant. (In Miami Beach, cops are allowed, even encouraged, to work part-time in bars and nightclubs, so they can keep an eye on any illegal goings-on.) In exchange for expensive dinners, VIP passes to local strip joints, and handfuls of cash, the supposedly corrupt policeman supplied Paciello with what looked like classified and confidential deep dish about competing club owners. Dohler also tipped him off about upcoming law enforcement actions to catch underage drinkers and drug dealers. Paciello believed he had an intelligence pipeline straight into the heart of the local police department. He had no idea that Dohler was a plant—an undercover police officer posing as a crooked cop.

Paciello knew the value of dishonest law enforcers. He reckoned Dohler was just one in a long line of bent officials he'd been bribing ever since he first hit town. But Dohler was different from the provincial porkers that Paciello normally paid. The two men shared common roots. Dohler was a refugee from the NYPD whose birth certificate was stamped Queens, USA. He was practically a home slice and knew all the ancient haunts. The macho bond of the streets cemented their relationship. Dohler played on Paciello's sentimental fondness for his home turf. Paciello opened up to Dohler in ways he would never have dreamed of talking to his celebrity chums.

One time, he confessed to Dohler, "Some of my buddies got locked up back in New York. I used to pull a few jobs with them. I hope they don't rat me out. I'm not going to go down like John Gotti, no way." Paciello had heard that some of his former Bath Avenue Crew associates back in Brooklyn—including Tommy Reynolds, Michael Yammine, and Jimmy Calandra, who all participated in the Shemtov robbery—had recently been arrested by the FBI on racketeering charges. As far as Paciello knew, he wasn't a target of the federal investigation, but he was still scared that under interrogation someone might give up his name. He feared that after years in limbo, Judith Shemtov's ghost could reappear.

"You know Sammy the Bull?" Paciello continued, working himself up into a full-tilt rage. "They should kill him and his whole family."

According to the feds, not long after this conversation with Dohler, Paciello paid $10,000 to a Mafia leg-breaker to threaten a family member of an unnamed source who Paciello presumed was snitching on him to the FBI. If the witness continued to cooperate, the family member was told, "Everybody is dead."

Former Port Richmond Crew member Brendan Schlitz charged that Paciello was also paying off a Staten Island neighbor of another cooperating witness, Lord Michael Caruso. The neighbor was passing down information about Caruso's daily schedule and his new career as a manager for the Wu-Tang Clan rap group. Schlitz suspected that Paciello was trying to set up Caruso for a hit or at least a severe beating.

Dohler had single-handedly initiated the dangerous undercover sting. While working the door at Liquid, he noticed a steady stream of dangerous-looking individuals, whom he suspected were mobsters, coming into the club. He told his bosses, and, after warning him to be careful, the Miami Beach Police Department gave him the go-ahead to get up close and personal with the club owner, to investigate his dirty dealings. Cops in ski masks even staged a bogus raid on Liquid—which Paciello was warned about in advance—in order to bolster Dohler's credibility with his unsuspecting target. The stories concerning Paciello's mob links were well known to local law enforcement, as were the string of brutal beat-downs that Paciello had perpetrated on the Beach. Ever since Risk burnt down—which the cops suspected, but couldn't prove was arson—they'd kept a close eye on the club owner.

Over the summer of 1999, Paciello got so warm and friendly with Dohler that he took him for a trip on his fifty-foot yacht, also called Liquid, to meet a VIP even closer to the club owner's heart than Madonna. Paciello introduced him to high-powered don Alphonse "Allie Boy" Persico, the personable but deadly boss of the Colombo crime family. According to the government, Persico had recently ordered the slaying of underboss and archrival William "Wild Bill" Cutolo because of a power struggle within the family. Before Cutolo was killed, Paciello was reportedly paying him $10,000 a week in tribute, money that now went to Persico.

The undercover cop and the don met at a now-defunct waterfront restaurant called Shooters in North Miami Beach. Paciello wanted to impress the cop with a taste of the gangster good life. He was trying to persuade Dohler to quit his job to become Bar Room's manager. He figured that with his police contacts, Dohler would be an invaluable asset to his organization.

The scorching sun baked the back of their necks as they sailed up the Intracoastal. Unbeknownst to the not-so-wise guys, a flotilla of feds bobbed in their wake. By this point, the federal authorities had hooked up with local law enforcement to conduct a joint investigation of the club owner. The government suspected that Paciello and Persico were involved in a money-laundering scheme, using Paciello's flagship club, Liquid, as a front to hide the proceeds from illegal mob activities.

Soon after, Paciello took Dohler to another meeting with Persico, this time at Joia. Paciello drove him there in a stolen Lexus. An unmarked sedan prowled from behind, transporting clean-cut guys with earpieces and binoculars. Dohler's mission—to get close to Paciello and find out if he operated his chic establishments as mob fronts—was going better than his bosses could have hoped. By tooling around town with Paciello, Dohler would obtain detailed dirt about the club owner's businesses, his personal property holdings, and his supposed financial links to the Mafia.

At the end of September, Chris Paciello requested Andrew Dohler's presence at Bar Room for a sit-down. Dohler arrived in full uniform wearing a wire underneath. Paciello wanted to talk about eradicating one of the major stress sources in his life. He asked Dohler to help him put competing club promoter Gerry Kelly out of the picture, permanently if necessary. At an earlier meeting they had discussed having Kelly set up. Paciello wanted something very nasty to happen to Kelly. Kelly, an Irish fashion designer and leading South Beach club personality, had worked for nine months as a marketing director at both Bar Room and Liquid. He regarded Paciello as a good friend. In June, Paciello had even thrown an elaborate masked ball at Bar Room to celebrate Kelly's birthday.

But Kelly soon grew tired of working for Paciello. For some time, the club owner had courted him, at one point offering him $30,000 in cash as a signing bonus, trying to entice the much sought-after party planner to come and work for him. And for some time Kelly turned him down flat. After being made a silent partner in Bar Room, Kelly had finally come onboard. But when he arrived, he was shocked to find Paciello's organization in such disarray. "That company was so improperly run," Kelly claimed. "There were no proper accounting practices. Every five minutes someone was coming in looking for money. It was a mess."

"I can tell you one thing, while I worked for Chris, there was never any money in the bank accounts," continued Kelly. "I don't know where it all went, but the club's bank charges in a year were over $130,000 because Chris would constantly write checks for money that wasn't in the account."

The problem with Paciello's clubs, as Kelly saw the situation, was that Chris and Ingrid only cared about catering to their celebrity friends. "If you weren't a star, Chris and Ingrid didn't want to know," said Kelly. "I tried to make them realize that ninety percent of your business comes not from the stars, but from the general public. If you don't take care of Joe Public as well as Madonna, you won't be in business for very long."

But the thing that really freaked out Kelly was having to share the same office space with a potential madman like Paciello. "He was always a gentleman to me, but I could see the rage in his eyes when he got upset on the phone. That was something I feared. In order to work at peak capacity, I have to feel comfortable with the people I work with. There was never any comfort level there."

As it happened, a fresh opportunity was about to open up for Kelly. Paciello had brokered a deal with a rich young investor named Noah Lazus to open a new club, Liquid 2000, in the old Glam Slam space. For years Paciello had kept his eye on the cavernous former theater, but the Brandt family, who owned the building, wouldn't rent to Paciello on his own. They'd heard the rumors about his mob ties. Now, with the respectable Lazus, the son of a wealthy and prominent Jewish family, as a partner, Paciello was set to open a new version of Liquid that would dwarf the original.

But after he shook hands with Lazus, Paciello started to get cold feet. The original Liquid was still open and, if not exactly booming anymore, was still doing respectable business, and Paciello worried that he would end up competing with himself. Paciello was moving too slow for Lazus's liking, so the investor went behind his back and offered the job of running the new venture to Michael Capponi. Not wanting to betray his buddy, Capponi refused on the spot. Then, in September, Lazus approached the unhappy Gerry Kelly and offered him a partnership in the fledgling dance hall, which was now rechristened Level.

Kelly abruptly resigned and moved over to the competition. "I called my attorney and said I was leaving Chris, but I was scared about what he would do, how he would react," remembered Kelly. "She said, 'I'll type up your resignation and have it hand-delivered to his office, and meanwhile you should get out of town.' So I booked a ticket to Orlando, and just after I left, all hell broke loose."

Kelly's resignation letter said what an honor and a pleasure it had been working with Chris and Ingrid, but according to both Paciello and Capponi, on his way out the door Kelly took mailing lists with all of Capponi's high-society contacts (including Sylvester Stallone's and Madonna's personal cell phone numbers). Capponi found out what had happened when he began getting phone calls from his Palm Beach friends, telling him they'd just received invitations to a new club called Level. Angry already, Paciello went through the roof when he also found out that Lazus and Kelly had poached a big chunk of Liquid's staff, from managers to waitresses.

Paciello threw a tantrum and tossed the resignation letter in the trash. But now that he was a public figure, he knew that he couldn't just go around to Kelly's office, kick the door in, and rearrange his features as he would have in the past. These days, he had to be more subtle. Paciello would ask Dohler to help him set up Kelly by taking his competitor into custody on fraudulent narcotics charges. Kelly had a reputation as a major league party animal. Paciello urged Dohler to transfer to the narcotics division, so that he could use the information to shut down other rival club owners. Pertinent portions of the conversation, secretly taped by Dohler, went like this:

"When we talked about me getting into narcotics, that's got to open some doors for you?"

"Of course, of course. You getting in there could help me a lot. We could put some pressure on those clubs, and also I'll know when there is pressure on me. It works both ways."

"This [Kelly]. What do you want me to do? I know what you're saying. I know exactly what you want. How far do you want me to go? Do you know if the guy is into anything heavy or just personal use?"

"This fuckin' [Kelly] he's got a bad drug problem. He always has drugs on him. People at the club give him drugs. He always drives drunk. You can arrest him, pull his fuckin' car over. They can pull his liquor license for that, right? I really want to hurt this guy good, and I'll take care of you big time."

"Where does he hang out?"

"Not my place. Friday night, we'll ride by his house, see the car, maybe follow him around, and then Saturday or Sunday we'll see what club he goes into, and when he comes out—Boom!—you got him."

Paciello then redirects his bile against Kelly's partner, Noah Lazus, who stole Kelly away from Bar Room.

"I'm telling you the owner of the club [Lazus], we got to get his head fuckin' broken in. We got to get him beat up. We got to get him whacked."

"As long as it's done on the Beach."

"Right, but if something happens to the kid right now, the cops are going to be so far up my ass; but if Kelly is busted for drunk driving or drugs, that's normal shit. He gets beat up, I'm fucked."

"Just remove yourself."

"Yeah, but even if I'm in my office at the time, and someone else walks in and bats him over the head, who are they going to blame? They're gonna know it's me."

A month later, Paciello buzzed Dohler, his pretend buddy, who immediately turned on his tape recorder. He was going to tell Paciello he'd had no luck in scoping out the right situation to entrap Kelly. The cop could tell straight away that Paciello was in a crappy mood. He could hear the stress in his voice crackling over the phone. Paciello bitched about all the new clubs that were about to open on the strip.

"How's everything going? What's happening brother?"

"How you doing? What's going on?"

"Nothing much. I haven't had any luck with that other thing."

"Ah, I figured that, fuck."

"Or else I would have given you a call, but it's just—he don't drive, man. The car sits in the fuckin' driveway almost every night. I don't know what the fuck it is. It's been out there all fuckin' night."

"Is the car in the driveway?"

"It's there now. The driveway's packed."

"So he's doing a party at his house."

"Yeah, I mean, it's a multidwelling place. His place isn't the only one there. There's a bunch of others. I'm still working on it. How's everything else going?"

"Oh, bullshit. All the shit that's going on this year."

"What's the matter?"

"There's fifteen clubs opening. Millions and millions they're putting into these clubs. Warsaw, Cameo, Glam Slam . . . God, I mean nonstop. Ah, fuck everyone . . ."

"At least you got Joia. These clubs come and go."

"That's right. Bar Room ain't going nowhere. Joia is doing well, and Liquid is doing all right as long as I can hang in there. It's rough."

Then Paciello let slip a puzzling phrase, perhaps an allusion to his thug life in Brooklyn.

"To tell you the truth, I feel like putting on my costume and going out trick-or-treatin'. You understand?"

"Yeah, I fuckin' hear you, right. There might be a time and place for that, if things get bad enough. As long as we do it here, I'll take care of the police reports."

"I'm telling ya. I got to come out of fucking retirement. I've become a fuckin big pussy down here, a big sucker."

"I'm getting bored myself, you know. That's what I'm waiting to hear . . . I hope you still got that costume in the closet."

"OK brother, bye."

As it turned out, Paciello was more of a "sucker" than even he imagined. Dohler conned Paciello big time. Instead of waxing Kelly, he arranged for his twenty-four-hour protection. Without notifying the former fashion designer, undercover cops tailed him around the clock.

Kelly finally found out that his former boss was trying to have him hurt from a cover story about Paciello in the *Village Voice*. "After that story came out, my phone was ringing off the hook," said Kelly. "Friends in New York had all read the article and were calling me to ask if I was okay. Within four hours of the article coming out, I got a phone call from a Miami Beach detective, who took me down to the FBI building, where half a dozen detectives were waiting to see me. They showed me transcripts of conversations with Andrew Dohler, where Paciello was proposing to have me killed. Two more detectives came into the room. They looked familiar, so I asked them, 'Don't I know you two guys?' They said, 'Don't you remember us from a few nights ago, when you were standing outside your home, we asked you where Alton Road was. We were just watching you.' I then asked them why, if Chris had been planning to have me whacked for three months, did they wait so long to tell me. They said because Chris was talking to an undercover, they didn't think it would happen. They did inform me that Chris had gone to the club Salvation on a Saturday night and was waiting outside in a car with a baseball bat, until I arrived. . . . Luckily, I decided not to go out that night."

Kelly reflected, "I was blown away. I knew Chris was a tough guy with a really bad temper, but I never thought he was planning to have me killed."

On November 23, 1999, a federal grand jury in Brooklyn returned a sealed indictment against Paciello and eight other defendants, all of them connected to the Bonnano crime family. They were charged with numerous murder, robbery, and racketeering counts. Later that same day, at around seven in the evening, Bonnano captain Anthony Graziano called Paciello. Graziano was the powerful mob boss to whom both the Bath Avenue Crew and the New Springville Boys paid tribute. Neither Paciello nor Graziano knew about the indictment.

"I'm glad I got hold of you; I gotta talk to you," said Graziano. "Could you do me a favor? Could you put a kid on the list?"

"Yeah, sure," replied Paciello. "Who is it? A good kid?"

"Yeah, nice kid. He's a DJ for a friend of ours."

"You should have called me when you were down here."

"Don't be a fuckin' wise guy, I called you yesterday."

"Did ya?"

"I called you and someone said you were in a meeting. I said who the fuck is this guy? The president?"

Graziano complained about his phone calls not being returned. "I called you six times, I said, is this guy avoiding me? I say does he owe me money? Usually when guys avoid me, they owe me money."

"Of course, that's how it always goes."

"Anyway, if you could do me that favor."

"Frankie B will be on the guest list."

"You don't have to go out of your way, just let him in."

"I'll take care of it."

"Now, listen. I'm coming down in like another month. You know what I mean? Maybe we can go for a few drinks, a few laughs."

"Alright, I'd love to. I'd love to go out for dinner."

"Otherwise, how's everything?"

"I'm opening in Palm Beach in two weeks."

"Good luck to ya. Listen to me, there ain't nothing wrong with that."

"Thanks."

"You want to know something? Between me and you, don't even tell too many people. They'll give you the horns."

"Of course."

"I'm gonna label you the Baron. But you know what? It's the other people who think I'm jealous. I'm happy you know."

"Oh, yeah."

"You know why?"

"Why?"

"Because when I need a favor, I can call you."

Paciello laughed nervously. "And that's why I'm always happy to do it for you."

"I know you are, really I do. I'm glad to see that you're doing good, and I'm happy when I hear things. Believe it or not, I am."

"I do believe that, believe me."

"I don't begrudge anybody or anything. Just do me a little favor, just say hello to the kid."

"Of course, of course. Anytime you need anything, just give me a call, it doesn't matter when."

"Alright, you gotta pick up the phone a little faster the next time."

Paciello had tried to leave his past behind and kept his mob contacts at arm's length, but the distance between his two worlds was closing fast.

West Palm Beach, December 1, 1999

Seven days after the federal indictment was handed down in Brooklyn, Chris Paciello was putting the finishing touches to his latest venture—a new club in West Palm Beach called Liquid Lounge, whose debut party was to be hosted by Donald Trump. Paciello's insatiable thirst for social acceptance would reach an apex with Liquid Lounge, "a comfortable stop for important people" as Casares described the venue and a proposed playpen for the rich young things who regarded South Beach as a little louche for their collective tastes. Paciello now fancied himself a figure in high society, and Liquid Lounge would represent his grand entrance into the upper reaches of the American class system. Not bad for a roughneck from Staten Island.

West Palm Beach isn't Palm Beach proper but the funkier mainland cousin that, in recent years, had undergone a renovation similar to that of South Beach. Chic boutiques, antique stores, wine bars, trendy bistros, and jazz clubs had all moved into the formerly dilapidated Mediterranean-style buildings that lined the bustling main thoroughfare, Clematis Street.

"I love West Palm Beach," Paciello told *Florida Travel* magazine prior to the club's debut. "The people are there, but so is a void in the kind of nightlife available. We intend to bring the Palm Beach set across the bridge to West Palm Beach with events, fashion shows, and local charity fund-raisers. We already have an event planned with the Miami City Ballet."

Before Liquid Lounge opened its doors, Paciello sent Michael Capponi from South Beach to West Palm Beach every weekend, where Capponi would network with his upscale pals in the area, handing out business cards and drumming up enthusiasm for the new venture. Capponi's best friend in Palm Beach was German billionaire Felix Sharp. As a promotional device, Capponi threw a 1,200-person gala event at Sharp's lavish waterside mansion. "All young Palm Beach society was there," said Capponi. Every guest received an invitation for Liquid Lounge's upcoming debut.

On the first day of December, Paciello was making last-minute inspections of Liquid Lounge—the sprinkler system worked, there was enough booze, the sound system had been correctly balanced—when he noticed two hulking strangers striding toward him. Paciello realized that they had come to bust him. The club owner turned on his heels, quickly walked out the back door, and fled the scene in his new Range Rover. The agents dialed the suspect's cell phone. "I'm driving to my lawyer's office. I'll talk to you from there," Paciello reportedly told the agents. Later that day, escorted by his lawyer, Roy Black—best known for defending celebrity clients like Marv Albert and William Kennedy Smith—he turned himself in to federal authorities.

The carefully crafted illusion Paciello had constructed for the benefit of his celebrity and socialite friends came crashing to the dance floor. The cosmetic transformation from raging bull to high-society butterfly proved to be exactly that—superficial. Less than a year after the successful debut of Bar Room, and following a two-year joint investigation by the FBI, the DEA, the IRS, the U.S. attorney's office in Brooklyn, the Florida State attorney's office, and the local Miami Beach police, his past finally caught up with him. He was charged with murder and robbery, along with fellow members of the Bath Avenue Crew, after Jimmy Calandra and Michael Yammine cut a deal with the government to rat out the rest of the gang. One of those they informed on was the Binger, fingering him as the wheelman and the mastermind of the botched

Shemtov home invasion. The arrests were part of a federal racketeering indictment that charged over a dozen members and associates of the Bonanno crime family with a host of felonies ranging from drug sales to murder.

Chris Paciello's capacity to span two distinctively different milieus had for a while been a big business asset. Not anymore. His twin worlds had collided; the two cultures had imploded. The It Boy was finally out-ed as a murderer. He'd gotten away with all manner of criminality for years. Now it was time to pay the price.

The South Beach party circuit dived into a state of deep shock. Casares nearly had a nervous breakdown. The frothy flavor of the scene suddenly went sour.

Paciello held his head high and loudly proclaimed his innocence. "I am not a gangster," he insisted. "It doesn't make me a gangster because I hung out with people on the corner when I was growing up." His fashionable chums vowed to stick by his side.

Even Neisen Kasdin, the mayor of Miami Beach, defended his old friend. "A lot of people have rough pasts," he said. A month earlier, Paciello had hosted a reelection party for the mayor at Bar Room.

Paciello's powerful attorney, Roy Black, tried to claim the govern-ment was picking on his client because of his high-profile lifestyle. "He really helped put South Beach on the map," he said. "Unfortunately, anybody who becomes a success in this country becomes an easy target."

"That's ridiculous," scoffed federal prosecutor Jim Walden, the assistant U.S. attorney in charge of the prosecution. "This case is not about celebrity; it's about serious violent crime."

With Paciello under arrest, Liquid Lounge opened without him. "I had to go to the mayor of Palm Beach and convince him we were going to run a clean operation," said Michael Capponi. "It took a lot of very influential members of Palm Beach society to get that club opened. The mayor had publicly said that no way was this gangster going to open a club in his town."

Liquid Lounge lasted for about six weeks, before Paciello sent his thuggish brother George to look after his stake in the club. "George talked bad to me and to some customers, so I quit and walked out," claimed Capponi. "George was basically yelling at me and accusing me of trying to take over his brother's thing. I wanted to just put Ingrid's and my name on the invitations, and keep Chris's interest quiet, so when he came out there'd be a nice chunk of money in the bank for him. With all the bad publicity, with Chris in jail, I was forced to open Liquid Palm Beach with an invitation that read: 'Chris Paciello and Ingrid Casares in association with Michael Capponi invite you to . . . ' It was crazy."

Soon thereafter, George Paciello was himself arrested by the feds for taking part in a string of bank robberies in a dozen states that supposedly netted $1.3 million over a seven-year period.

At the December 15 bail hearing, white limousines pulled up outside the peeling art deco building that houses the Miami federal courthouse, and out poured Paciello's black-clad supporters, who looked like they were in mourning for their fallen comrade. The crème de la crème of the South Beach party circuit—some seventy people in all—had turned out en masse to vouch for the embattled club owner's good character. Yawning and blinking in the blinding sunlight, some of them looked like they hadn't been up this early in years. A-listers like *Ocean Drive* publisher Jason Binn, calendar girl Sofia Vegara, real estate mogul Jerry Robbins, and restaurant owner Shareef Malnik jostled in the hallway, waiting for the proceedings to start. It was more like a VIP opening than a court date. "Much like his clubs, it's standing room only," joked another one of his lawyers, Howard Srebnic, who was standing in for Roy Black. Michael Capponi wanted to testify for his friend, but Black told him to stay away, fearing the party promoter's last name would remind the judge too much of Al Capone. Paciello's mother, Marguerite, was also there, her previously vibrant personality shrouded in worry for her beloved son. She looked like she might collapse at any moment.

"He's innocent, and everybody who's here today knows that," an exhausted and emotional Ingrid Casares told the assembled press from behind a pair of enormous black shades. "Chris is extremely important in my life. Before I met him, I had little direction and goals. He is an extremely hardworking individual who had a vision of what could be done in South Beach. I stand behind Chris one hundred percent."

There was no shortage of glowing testimonials, which flowed into my notebook like overripe Valentines. When I first arrived at the court-house, the reception was chilly. But soon enough, after Casares's publi-cist, Lizzie Grubman (who also briefly worked for Peter Gatien, until he stiffed her on the fee), told them it was permissible to talk to me, members of Paciello's fashion posse stepped forward in their Guccis to deliver fulsome accounts of life with Chris. Sarah Robbins, who designed Joia's interior, informed me that "Chris is not a thug; he's one of the good guys. He's an absolute doll. If I had a daughter, he's exactly the type of guy I would want her to go out with."

I tried to remain polite but wondered why these people couldn't smell the corruption-on-a-rope dangling under their noses. "He has a noble disposition," proffered another former employee. "He has the purest heart of anybody I've ever met," gushed *Ocean Drive* gossip writer Jacquelynn D. Powers. "If Chris Paciello did everything the gov-ernment says he did, he deserves an Oscar," said veteran South Beach publicist Louis Canalis, "because he fooled everybody down here. The Chris Paciello we're reading about in the newspapers is not the person we've come to know and love."

When he entered the courtroom dressed in a blue blazer and gray slacks, Paciello's expression was impassive. He'd lost weight inside. Whether because he wasn't eating, as his publicist claimed, or more likely because he couldn't get hold of any steroids, Paciello looked deflated. But once he spotted Casares and Vegara sitting in the gallery, his face became illuminated, and his old spark returned. After the handcuffs were taken off, he puffed up his chest and blew them both a big kiss.

Assistant U.S. Attorney Jim Walden, a stern stick figure in a drab suit, got up to speak to the court. "The evidence is overwhelming that Mr. Ludwigsen was attempting to bring the violent tactics of La Cosa Nostra to Miami Beach," Walden solemnly told the Miami judge in an effort to deny Paciello bail. His aim was to show Paciello was both a flight risk and a danger to the community. Walden was a formidable adversary. Nicknamed "Tiger Boy" by defense lawyers back in Brook-lyn, this skinny, boyish prosecutor from blue-collar Pennsylvania was known to hold in contempt those who attempted to glamorize the

Mafia lifestyle. He had developed an impressive reputation for putting away wise guys, in the process earning the enmity of many an arrogant street punk like Paciello, whom Walden insisted on referring to by the German birth name under which he was charged, Ludwigsen.

"The case against Mr. Ludwigsen is particularly strong," Walden argued. "It will include testimony from five accomplices. Each of them has information concerning one or more of the racketeering acts. Each of them gives consistent accounts of Mr. Ludwigsen's role in both racketeering acts as well as a series of uncharged crimes.

"Taken together, the evidence will show that, dating from approximately 1987 through 1993, Mr. Ludwigsen was involved in a series of other robberies and burglaries in the Brooklyn and Staten Island areas, including burglaries and robberies of other commercial establishments, such as a pet food store, a hardware store, a pharmacy, multiple video stores, and an armed robbery of drug dealers on Staten Island.

"The Staten Island drug robbery, your honor, is particularly strong, mostly because he boasted about his role in that robbery to several other individuals. Mr. Ludwigsen planned the robbery with others, robbed a large quantity of marijuana, broke it up into portions, resold it to another individual, and then stole it back from one of the pot customers."

After damning Paciello as "an accessory after the fact to murder" because he housed fleeing mob killer, Vinnie Rizzuto, Jr., Walden then went on to bring up the government wiretaps on which Paciello is heard conspiring with the Colombo family's Dominic "Big Dom" Dionisio to beat up club rival Steven Lewis, though Walden didn't mention Lewis's actual name. "The tapes demonstrate, Judge, that Mr. Ludwigsen specifically asked the Colombo associate Dionisio to grab and essentially terrorize the businessman. These tactics, Judge, are the same tactics that members and associates of La Cosa Nostra have used time and again in the New York area. . . . It shows clear and compelling evidence that Mr. Ludwigsen was attempting to do the same thing here in Miami."

Walden also brought up the Dohler tapes. "He asked the undercover agent to run license plates on some of his business rivals, to run criminal history checks on some of his business rivals, so that information could be used to help Mr. Ludwigsen's business interests. . . . Mr. Ludwigsen also asked the undercover to get a transfer to the special narcotics unit so that Mr. Ludwigsen could do two things: one, learn when there was an investigation of his own clubs, and, two, learn when there was evidence of criminal activity in other clubs, so he could use that information to his advantage."

Walden climaxed with the damaging accusation: "Even more chillingly, Mr. Ludwigsen had recent conversations with the undercover officer where he indicated, in no uncertain terms, that all cooperating witnesses should be killed and that a particular cooperating witness had family members that resided in a particular location. And Mr. Ludwigsen expressed the opinion to the undercover officer that the family members of the cooperating witness should be killed as well. We've already had one instance where certain individuals approached family members of one of the witnesses, and, in no uncertain terms, they were threatened with death if their family member decided to cooperate. The government had to spend thousands and thousands of dollars to relocate two families of our cooperating witnesses to stave off the possibility that the defendants and their associates like Mr. Ludwigsen, would successfully undermine the prosecution."

Paciello's bombastic lawyer, Howard Srebnik, countered the government's argument by referring back to the Peter Gatien trial in January 1998 and the testimony given by Paciello's former business partner Lord Michael Caruso.

"Mr. Ludwigsen, for the last two years, has been living under these accusations made by Michael Caruso," said Srebnik. "His testimony was rejected by the jury who acquitted Mr. Gatien. Caruso is an admitted liar, an admitted hustler, an admitted Ecstasy dealer. This is the kind of witness that the government intends to offer in support of the indictment."

Srebnick informed the court that Paciello had donated sums to dozens of charities and held fund-raisers at his club. He said his client had never before been convicted of anything except drunk driving. He entered into evidence fawning Paciello profiles from *Ocean Drive* and *People* magazines. He pointed to doorman Gilbert Stafford in the audience. "The guy was basically on his deathbed, and Chris organized and raised $20,000 [actually $10,000] for Mr. Stafford, who's alive today thanks to the help of Chris Ludwigsen."

Srebnik then addressed the Steve Lewis incident: "Mr. Lewis, as Ms. Casares is prepared to testify today, had approached her to go into business with him. She had asked her business partner, Mr. Ludwigsen, to ask him to stop approaching her because he repeatedly and repeatedly was coming after her to go into business, harassing her, practically stalking her. And she asked Mr. Ludwigsen, 'Tell this guy to get lost.' "

Climaxing his presentation, Srebnik summed up: "Now, Mr. Ludwigsen is going to be faulted because he grew up on Staten Island. Chris didn't choose to grow up where he grew up. He didn't turn his back on the people he grew up with, nor did he commit crimes with them.

"My client is a target because he made something of himself," Srebnick concluded. "Nobody likes to see a guy his age achieve the success he's achieved. He's twenty-eight years old. I daresay that there's nobody else who's invested more money, more time, more effort, more dedication to our community than Christian Ludwigsen."

After the legal arguments finished, wealthy backer after wealthy backer got up and pledged mountains of money to spring Paciello from jail. Ingrid's father, Raul Casares, spoke softly in broken English, tears welling up in his eyes. "I've known Chris for about four years, when Ingrid, my daughter went into the club business with him. Unfortunately, Ingrid, as a child, was doing a lot of drugs. Her favorite drug was cocaine. We sent her to several different places for therapy. She was a total disaster for many years, until she met Chris. Our family thinks that Chris was the one responsible for stopping her from taking drugs. As far as the Casares family is concerned, Ingrid abandoned drugging because of Chris."

Finally, the judge ruled that Paciello could be released on $3 million bond. Walden said he would appeal immediately before another court in Brooklyn. The judge agreed that the club owner should remain behind bars until then. In the meantime, Paciello was flown to New York and locked up in the high-security Metropolitan Detention Center, a windowless complex located in an industrial neighborhood, tucked under the Brooklyn-Queens Expressway, not far from Paciello's old stomping ground.

As soon as he arrived at MDC, Paciello met up with some of his former Bath Avenue cronies, who were also incarcerated in the same forbidding facility, pending trial. "The first day we all met in the holding cells at MDC, he told me and the others he would kill himself before ratting," said the Bath Avenue Crew's Anthony "Gonzo" Gonzalez.

Because of all the publicity surrounding his arrest, Paciello quickly became the star attraction in the Mafia wing, where he was housed. "He's cock of the walk around here," said another inmate, who described the charismatic club king strutting around with a fixed smile on his face, glad-handing fellow prisoners. On Sundays, Paciello went with other members of the Bath Avenue Crew to mass, where they held secret meetings in the back pews to discuss how they were going to defend themselves at their upcoming trial.

One day Paciello was discussing Lord Michael's testimony at the Peter Gatien trial with Brendan "Fats" Schlitz, one of the Port Richmond Crew gangsters, who used to hang out at the Limelight. Paciello asked Schlitz if he could look at the transcripts. When Schlitz came up to the law library with over a thousand pages of documents, Paciello turned white, according to Anthony Gonzalez.

"Lord Michael got Paciello scared," said Gonzalez. "He knew a lot about Chris. The next day, when I saw Fats, I asked him what Chris had said. Fats told me he was unresponsive and that we better have a codefendant meeting to assure Chris he would be alright. I think Lord Michael being a rat put the idea in Chris's mind to do the same thing."

Meanwhile, some of Paciello's glamorous friends, who initially guaranteed financial support for his bail, eventually backed off when they realized that real life is not like in the movies—you can't just turn up in court with a million dollars in a suitcase without the government wondering where the money came from. One of Paciello's closest friends, Shareef Malnick, fell out altogether on the bond deal, possibly fearing his father's alleged Mafia ties would come under scrutiny. But Raul

Casares stuck by Paciello even though the $1 million he came up with was a far cry from the $15 million he originally pledged. And the condominium that Sofia Vergara put up as surety turned out to be worth far less than she first estimated, though she did continue to profess undying love for the club owner. Nonetheless, Paciello was hurt and angry that some of his society friends had abandoned him.

Ingrid Casares pledged the deeds to two luxury condos she co-owned with her dad, but in the end she could only cough up one, because she had her own set of possible legal troubles. Paciello paid his partner large sums in cash from the clubs to finance her jet set lifestyle, and she allegedly failed to pay taxes on most of these monies, although she was never charged with a violation. Despite having a multimillion-aire father who also invested in the businesses, she had to borrow money from a friend to contribute to Paciello's bail package.

In the early months of the new millennium, Sean Kirkham's ongoing battle with the U.S. attorney's office found him once again back at the same Brooklyn courtroom where Peter Gatien was tried and acquitted, this time for a resentencing hearing. The hearing was to determine whether Kirkham, the snitch who tried to sell Gatien evidence of supposed government misconduct, had been excessively screwed: A four-and-a-half-year sentence for lying to a federal agent and failure to appear, when serious criminals like Lord Michael were walking around free, seemed a tad excessive, to say the least. The U.S. attorney's office argued that Kirkham deserved his harsh sentence because of the negative impact his accusations had on the prosecution of the Gatien case, not to mention the careers of DEA agents Matt Germanowski and Bob Gagne.

The Court of Appeals for the Second Circuit had sided with Kirkham's lawyer and overturned the sentence, and Kirkham turned up at the courtroom fully expecting to get time served, which at that point was twenty-nine months, about half his original sentence. He was looking forward to his return to freedom and wasn't prepared for the impolite bombshell that followed.

Minutes before the hearing began, Kirkham got into a row with his court-appointed attorney, who wore an ill-fitting suit and a bright blue tie with pictures of swimming sperm. Kirkham called him a "pathetic bastard" and told him to "rot in hell" for not doing what his client wished. "I thought he was an idiot who had no idea how to argue the finer points of the law," recalled Kirkham. "I knew my ass was cooked when I saw his business card. It was one of those that you print up at a supermarket—$10 for a thousand."

Assistant U.S. Attorney Michelle Adelman—still steamed from losing the Gatien case—arrived wearing a red knit suit, looking like a cross between Chaka from the TV show *Land of the Lost* and a bad copy of Laura Flynn Boyle from *The Practice*.

Kirkham's attorney stammered and stuttered, trying to present the case for his client getting time served. Kirkham groaned inwardly. The judge, Sterling Johnson, looked bored until he spotted the DEA agents in the courtroom and asked them if they wanted to make a victim impact statement.

Germanowski, who wore faded jeans and a blue lumberjack shirt, entered the witness box and said, "Good morning, Your Honor, thank you for allowing me to speak."

He told the judge that Kirkham's accusations had hindered his advancement within the agency. "The allegations made against my partner and I were atrocious and hideous, and I believe Mr. Kirkham went beyond making an allegation and took an additional step to actually manufacture evidence to support his false allegation. The impact is such it is going to follow us throughout our career. Those allegations, even though they were investigated and found to be completely unfounded, will still follow me for the remaining years I have in law enforcement. It has followed me to other trials and it will always be something that I feel I will unjustly have to explain. Our careers are frozen when an allegation like that is made. There are no promotions. There is no lateral movement. No transfers. You are stuck in a holding pattern until that allegation is fully investigated."

Germanowski went on to say that as an agent, unlike civilians charged with a crime, you're not given the benefit of the doubt. "When we are investigated, we don't enjoy the same rights as a typical defendant, who is innocent until proven guilty," he complained. "When those allegations were made, it was almost as if were considered guilty, and if they were unable to prove those allegations false beyond a reasonable doubt, these allegations could have ended our careers immediately, which would, of course, have affected our families greatly."

Then the judge asked the lead prosecutor on the Gatien case, Eric Friedberg, if he would care to add anything. "Mr. Friedberg, do you want to be heard?"

"Yes. Thank you, Your Honor."

Friedberg took the stand dressed in a conservative black suit. He waved his arms in the air and pointed in Kirkham's direction, accusing him of destroying the government's case against Gatien by making false allegations of a personal relationship. Friedberg said he didn't know he was being investigated by the OPR [Office of Professional Responsibility, the ultrasecretive arm of the U.S. Department of Justice that probes allegations of prosecutorial wrongdoing] and was personally and professionally embarrassed.

"When the allegations in the case were made against me, it was in the middle or right before the trial of Mr. Gatien," Friedberg fumed. "Mr. Brafman and Mr. Kirkham were on the phone, and Mr. Brafman essentially milked Mr. Kirkham for over an hour for false details relating to the alleged relationship that Mr. Kirkham alleged that I had with him. So now this tape was taken to the U.S. attorney by Ben Brafman personally. When I found out from the chief of the criminal division that I was the subject of an investigation based on these details, I can't tell you the amount of extra stress that it added to an already highly stressful situation.

"Mr. Brafman leaked the story to the press," continued Friedberg, "as a way of essentially pressuring us during the trial, so I started getting calls from reporters about Mr. Kirkham's story and in the weeks prior to the trial had to be worried about whether there was going to be a front-page story in the *Village Voice* or some other highly esteemed paper, about my alleged relationship with the defendant. And so, in fact, a story did come out. And although it didn't name me by name, anybody familiar with the case could have figured out who he was talking about. So I now, I had to go home and explain this to my wife that I had some informant making up this material about me. That was not a particularly pleasant experience to have to do that."

Friedberg ended by saying, "I would respectfully ask you to upward depart substantially to account for this conduct, Your Honor." The judge obliged the prosecutor, resentencing Kirkham to the same fifty-seven months for failure to appear and thirty-three months on the lying to a federal agent count, both counts to run consecutively.

In April 2000, after much legal wrangling, where even the judge commented, "This is the strictest bail package I've ever seen," Chris Paciello finally left the Mafia wing at the federal lockup in Brooklyn, after a four-month struggle to come up with enough money to make his bond, which in the meantime had been increased to $15 million. The $2.8 million in property that was put up by friends and relatives, among them Ingrid Casares, Sofia Vergara, and Mickey Rourke's mother, Annette, finally secured Paciello's bail deal. To help finance Paciello's legal defense, both Bar Room and Liquid in Palm Beach were sold, along with his yacht and Flamingo Drive home. Paciello's empire was in tatters. Liquid limped on, a pale shadow of its former glory. (The name was eventually sold to another club.) But Joia still remained a major force on South Beach's competitive culinary scene. On the weekends, securing a reservation was still impossible.

As he left the federal courthouse in Brooklyn on his way to his mom's place, a somber Paciello said, "I'm very happy to be seeing my family. It's in God's hands now."

Paciello spent the summer under strict house arrest, under twenty-four-hour guard at his mother's humble house, overlooking the largest rubbish dump in the city. Gone were the glitzy trappings of his former existence, replaced by chili dogs for dinner and an endless season of legal bickering before the trial at the Brooklyn federal courthouse. Visits from his girlfriend Sofia Vergara kept him sane, but, in private, he raged at some of his other glittering friends for dumping him in his hour of need. He nearly got sent back to MDC when during a routine sweep of the house, a bag of stale pot and a case of bullets was found under his mattress—leftovers, as it turned out, from when Paciello's brother Keith bunked there. The deposed club king continued to categorically deny in the strongest terms possible that he had anything to do with the murder of Judith Shemtov.

Just four days before the start of his October trial, Paciello finally dropped the pretense and pled guilty to murder, robbery, and racketeering charges. By this point, he had fired Roy Black and replaced him with Peter Gatien's council, Ben Brafman. Brafman, after a thorough review of the case, explained to Paciello that his situation was basically hopeless. While in public Brafman declared his client entirely innocent and the government's case "razor thin," in private he advised Paciello that, even with his considerable legal gifts and his reputation for getting his clients acquitted in the face of crushing odds, the prosecution would most likely win a conviction. The best thing Paciello could do, Brafman counseled, would be to plead guilty and offer to trade information about Mafia higher-ups in return for a reduced sentence.

Standing in the Brooklyn federal courthouse, flanked by Ben Brafman, Paciello confessed that he was the getaway driver in the botched Shemtov heist. "I participated in the attempted robbery of the Shemtov family," he said, dressed in a sober black suit, reading from a yellow legal pad. His former arrogance crushed, a timid and soft-spoken Paciello took a long pause before revealing, "which resulted in the death of Mrs. Shemtov." He also admitted orchestrating the armed robbery at the Chemical Bank. "I knew these crimes were part of a larger criminal enterprise," he confessed.

"I love Chris, and I always will," said Ingrid Casares in a prepared statement afterward. "Chris has decided to close this chapter in his life by taking responsibility for crimes he participated in many years ago."

"The sad part of this case is the Chris Paciello who is going to be sentenced is not the Chris Paciello who commited these crimes ten years ago," Ben Brafman told reporters outside the courtroom. "He has felt remorse about the tragic death of Judith Shemtov from the moment it happened."

"Look, I never regret where I came from," Paciello informed *Ocean Drive* magazine, a year before his arrest. "I grew up in a certain area where everybody thinks violence is normal. Now, I look back and see that I have come a long way. I was able to leave and see that it's not a normal lifestyle. Everybody can talk about my past, and I'm not ashamed of it at all. As a matter of fact, I'm proud of it. To come from where I came from and to do what I did, I can actually pat myself on the back."

The dramatic downfall of Chris Paciello seemed to match a general slump in fortune on the South Beach nightlife scene. The glamorous milieu that Paciello helped create was fast disappearing. Celebrities like Madonna, Cher, and Sylvester Stallone, who in the '90s had been instrumental in promoting Miami Beach as a desirable destination to the rest of the world, sold their mansions and moved elsewhere. Models still clogged the streets, but they were B-list and C-list girls, not the Kates and Naomis who used to flock here. What was once the sandbox of the stars, by the start of the new millennium seemed more like a freak fest for drunken frat boys. Another chapter in Miami Beach's ongoing history of boom followed by bust appeared to be coming to a close.

Six months after Paciello was arrested, Michael Capponi—who bought Bar Room from Paciello for $1.8 million and turned it into an establishment called 320, only to see the reborn club fail miserably— was at Miami City Hall discussing the problems afflicting the local nightlife scene. The season was a washout. People didn't seem to be going out in the same numbers they used to. "I'll tell you what the problem is," Capponi told the assembled club owners and city officials. He held up a copy of the *Village Voice* and turned to the club listings. "See," he pointed. "In a city ten times the size, they have a third as many clubs as we do. That's the problem—oversaturation."

"The arrest of Chris Paciello killed the vibe and did cap an era," said Capponi afterward. "But it would have happened anyway. In Chris's heyday, when the A-list came to town, they ate at Joia and then had two choices: either go to Bar Room or Living Room. A year later, you had ten hot restaurants and a whole slew of new clubs: Nikki Beach, Opium, Opium Garden, Crobar, Level, Bedroom, you name it."

But what does it say about South Beach, that someone like Paciello could rise to such a position of prominence? "What does it say about all superficial lifestyles?" Michael Capponi shrugged. "How about, party people will forgive anything for a good time. To a lot of us, Chris symbolized the period that was the best time of our lives—South Beach when it was really happening."

Evil—both as a temporary condition and a way of life—
is not too strong a word to describe some of the things that went on at
the Limelight in the 1990s. Certainly not evil on the grand scale we've
lately become accustomed to, but evil enough to warrant a complete
autopsy on what really went wrong: How could a movement supposedly based on the principles of love, peace, and unity turn into the exact
opposite?

Disregard for a moment the corpses and violent crimes that grabbed
all the headlines; after all, criminals have a long history—from the
French revolution to the hippies—of exploiting the liberties opened up
by utopian movements. The damage done could also be measured by
the toxic effects that the lifestyle had on ordinary clubgoers, who had
never committed a serious crime in their lives, except to take too many
drugs. Psychosis beckoned for some. Careers were derailed for others.
Formerly healthy bodies were sapped of vital energies. A number of
young ravers and club kids lapsed into homelessness and prostitution.
For many, even after they'd wiped off the makeup and kicked their various habits, the whole experience left a gaping psychic wound that will
take years to heal. As it turned out, taking copious amounts of Ecstasy
did not abolish greed and violence. Unbridled pleasure seeking without
any ethical boundaries wasn't such a good idea. The path of excess did

not lead, as promised, to disco-heaven-on-earth but instead to a kind of chemical Hades.

"There was beauty but there was also ugliness," recalled Danish photographer Jacob Mikkelsen, who chronicled that period at the Tunnel and the Limelight. "There was love but also madness." And in the end, the madness and ugliness overwhelmed the beauty and love.

But evil deeds usually don't go unpunished. Karma has its own logic, and justice is eventually meted out, though often in unexpected and imperfect forms.

Peter Gatien spent the whole of 2001 trying to salvage what was left of his career. Neck high in debt, his clubs mired in bankruptcy after losing his liquor license, he sold the Limelight to rival club owner David Marvisi and Gay & Lesbian Nightlife Association President John Blair for $1.1 million. Blair planned to close the club down before reopening it, possibly under a new name. In addition, Gatien was evicted from the space that housed the Tunnel for not paying rent for over two years. The landlord wanted to turn the disco into a giant storage facility. Gatien and his family were also kicked out of their sumptuous East Side town house for the same reason. Gatien tried to revive his flagging fortunes by entering into a secret partnership with the men behind Miami's Crobar nightclub to open a new place in the same neighborhood as the Tunnel, in a gargantuan 40,000-foot space that formerly stored the floats from the Macy's Thanksgiving parade. But when the local community board found out, the reaction was so hostile that Gatien was ousted, but the club went ahead anyway.

The last time I saw Gatien was in May 2001, on the steps of the Tunnel, at one of the last of the famous Funkmaster Flex Sunday night rap music parties, just before Gatien lost the space and his precious permit to sell booze was revoked. The club was besieged by an army of cops because the previous month, sixteen-year old Terence Davies of Brooklyn had been stabbed to death under a rusted railway bridge in a deserted parking lot just around the corner from the venue.

The surrounding streets were blocked off by a swarm of cruisers and police vans. An SUV filled with undercover cops who were members of the newly formed NYPD unit charged with gathering information about rappers and their entourages cruised by, stopping every few yards to take down plate numbers. A barrage of blinding police spotlights illuminated the adjacent buildings. Roadblocks were set up across Eleventh Avenue to search cars for illegal handguns. Driver's licenses were scanned through a metal machine before patrons could even get onto the block, after which clubgoers were then herded through a maze of metal barriers. The experience was more like visiting a loved one in a maximum security lockup than going to a hip-hop jam.

Standing on the steps of the Tunnel, surveying the ranks of law enforcement encircling the club, Gatien must have known this was the end of the line. He looked grimmer than I've ever seen him before—a blurry photocopy of the original pale shadow I first met over five years ago.

"It's been rough, these past five years with all these task forces," Gatien groused. "It's getting to the point where we have to violate customer's civil rights with intrusive body searches just to stay in business. You focus so much on security and a prisonlike atmosphere that you no longer have time to be creative. Looking back now, I should have quit the nightclub business after I was acquitted. But I needed the money to pay my legal bills."

The man the BBC jokingly dubbed "the Dr. Evil of Ecstasy" was looking beat to the bone. The flecks of gray that once speckled his hair had turned into thick streaks. He appeared exhausted. He was about to turn fifty, and his world was in a shambles. Fighting a war on three fronts—city, state, and federal—had obviously taken a toll.

"I give up," he sighed. "I've had enough. It's just endless. I can't take the pressure anymore."

All of a sudden, a photographer from the *New York Post*—the tabloid newspaper that led the crusade to put him out of business—appeared from nowhere. "Peter, can I take your picture?" In an instant, the ghostly Canadian—whom the Immigration and Naturalization Service now wanted to deport back home—disappeared back indoors as if in a puff of dry ice.

"Peter Gatien lost his empire and is now indebted to Alex for the rest of his life," summed up archnemesis Steven Lewis, who was sentenced to a year in jail for allowing drug dealers into Gatien's clubs. "That's punishment enough."

For his part, Michael Alig is sitting behind bars in the middle of nowhere, stoned on antidepressants and puffy with jail food fat, as he plans his big comeback. He's writing and rewriting his autobiography, *Alig-ula*, hoping to find a publisher. He's helping out with the film about his life, *Party Monster*, which features former child star Macaulay "Home Alone" Culkin as the club kid turned killer. Alig also spends a lot of his time answering the seventy odd pieces of mail he gets each week, much of it fan letters from around the world from people thrilled to be corresponding with a celebrity criminal. During the holidays, he sends friends hand-drawn Xmas cards, one of which featured Santa holding an axe dripping with blood. Clearly, he enjoys his notoriety.

Alig recalls his time in power as the prince of perversion and wonders what went wrong. "The thought that this lifestyle would end up hurting somebody else, let alone killing him, was the furthest thing from my mind," he now claims. He defends himself against charges that (with the exception of the Angel incident) there was anything innately wicked about the club kids and their antics. "Nihilistic, cynical, defeatist, yes; evil, no," he says. "I don't recall anything intentionally malicious. Even the *Blood Feast* parties were more about camp than anything else. It was more about the absurdity than the nastiness. You have to remember the club kids were all about sensation and media and shock value. If any club kid said he was worshipping the devil, you can be sure it was for the publicity."

Since being incarcerated, Alig has resorted to psychobabble—the last refuge of the scoundrel, if ever there was one—to explain away the killing. He talks about repression and rehabilitation, denial and rationalization, and Freudian defenses. He blames the tragic incident on the twin evils of drugs and the homosexual lifestyle. "I know it's not a politically correct thing to say, but in my opinion the homosexual lifestyle in major cities is all too out of control, and willed by a subconscious desire to self-destruct," Alig wrote me from prison, sounding as crazy as ever. "Homosexuality is by nature counterprocreative. What could be more self-destructive than refusing to replicate yourself?"

I visited him in late January 2002 at upstate New York's Southport Correctional Facility, the proverbial hard place to do hard time, a grim collection of fortified bunkers surrounded by razor wire nestling in otherwise picturesque hills. Alig seemed healthier than I'd ever seen him before, even if he did spend a lot of time complaining about his penis not working, which was kind of ironic given that he had deprived Angel of his genitals. Alig had been sent to Southport from the far comfier Clinton Correctional Facility, after a harebrained scheme he concocted—to smuggle heroin into the prison hidden in legal documents—was discovered. During our visit, Alig was unshackled, unlike other inmates in this high-security facility, an unusual percentage of whom were violent sexual predators. "They put something in the water here," he whispered through a steel cage painted a dirty cream. "I have trouble peeing, and I used to jack off at least once a day, now I'm lucky if it's once a month."

Alig expressed hope that when he was eligible for parole in 2006, he would be released, an unlikely scenario given the botched dope scheme. During our session, he also claimed to be remorseful over Angel's death. As he held his mother Elke's hand through a narrow slot in the cage, he claimed the ghastly reality of what he did nearly drove him to suicide. He also apologized for the negative taint that his deadly antics had on the media image of so-called alternative lifestyles. "I realize that I am the perfect poster boy for the radical right wing to point to and say 'See? Drugs are bad. Being gay is wrong. Look at Alig and what he did.' "

But one former friend believes Alig is crying crocodile tears in preparation for his appearance before the parole board. "It's sad," said childhood chum Ron Alan. "Michael is incapable of normal feelings like empathy. He was born that way: that much is not his fault."

You'd think Alig would have had his fill of horror by now, but just before we split, he asked me to send him a new book he was eager to read: *The Ghastly One—The Sex, Gore Netherworld of Andy Milligan.* He also wanted a subscription to the *Village Voice* so he could keep up with the latest clubland news. He fancies that one day soon he will make a grand return to New York nightlife, his debt paid to society, and everyone will conveniently forget the grisly deed that made him really famous, and once again he will reign in radiant fabulousness, a club king redux. Even more bizarre, he thinks Peter Gatien will be the one to finance this fool's endeavor. A few days later, I got a letter from Alig which read in part, "Do you think Peter was completely lying when he said there was a chance of us working together in the future? I just can't imagine why he'd—oh, I don't know, I guess I just don't want to imagine." In his heart, Alig still thinks he's Peter Gatien's *number one son.*

"Michael is still delusional," said a former colleague. "He should forget about ever coming back to work in clubs because no one will employ him. He is always going to be the guy who chopped up his buddy's body."

As for the artist formerly known as the Binger, in October 2000, just before his sentencing on the murder and robbery charges, Chris Paciello was whisked away from his mother's Staten Island home to "an undisclosed location" after he cut a cooperation deal with the federal government. His mother and brothers were also immediately put in protective custody. The man who once said "all informers and their families should be killed" had turned into that which he most hated—a dirty rat.

The mob turncoat was expected to take the stand, along with other former Bath Avenue Crew killers, to testify against Bonnano crime family boss Anthony Spero. But prosecutors were able to put the seventy-one-year-old don behind bars without calling Paciello to the witness box.

Paciello was next slated to testify against Colombo boss Alphonse "Allie Boy" Persico, the personable mobster whom Paciello had introduced to a slew of his celebrity pals. Paciello was expected to recount any firsthand knowledge he had of the circumstances surrounding the May 1999 slaying of Colombo underboss William "Wild Bill" Cutolo, which the feds allege was ordered by Persico and which happened not long after Paciello had visited Wild Bill at his Brooklyn social club. Cutolo's body has never been found, but his family and the feds believe he is dead. But days before his January 2002 trial on extortion, money-laundering, and loan-sharking charges, in what should have been the biggest trial of a Mafia don since John Gotti was put away, Persico pled guilty and was sentenced to thirteen years in federal prison.

One of the rumors currently circulating is that pretty boy Paciello is to undergo plastic surgery to protect his identity from former colleagues who now want him rubbed out. But even after his guilty plea, Paciello remains a popular figure on South Beach, far more so than his partner Casares, who is widely disliked because of her high-and-mighty attitude. It says something about America's lasting love-hate relationship with outlaws that after his admission that he was involved in the murder of Judith Shemtov, one well-placed observer of the South Beach scene can still say, "Some people wish it was Ingrid behind bars, not Chris."

"Chris will never change his face and never go into hiding," said friend and business partner Michael Capponi. "He'll find some way to make a comeback, even if he has to hire bodyguards. I personally believe that if Chris ever came back to the nightlife industry in South Beach again, he would dominate it instantly. Down here, we have some very fond memories of Chris."

Few had fond memories of Chris Paciello's old business partner, Lord Michael Caruso. Nonetheless, about the time Paciello lost his nocturnal empire, Caruso, in an amazing turnaround of fortune, was forging ahead with a new career as a manager for the Staten Island rap group the Wu-Tang Clan at the same time key members of the notoriously violent collective ("the nearest thing hip-hop has to an organized crime family" according to one writer) were being investigated by the feds for gunrunning and for a deadly feud between Crips and Bloods, which ended with the murders of two Clan associates.

When Caruso sat on the witness stand at Peter Gatien's drug-conspiracy trial two years ago bawling his eyes out, his life seemed effectively over. The big-time rave promoter—the man who turned Staten Island onto Ecstasy and first brought techno music to Manhattan—confessed to a string of vicious crimes: home invasions, extortion schemes, kidnapping attempts, wholesale drug trafficking, and more. These serious infractions should have put him behind bars for twenty years. But in exchange for leniency, he became the centerpiece of the government's case against Gatien. Caruso's testimony about the inner workings of the Limelight's drug network, which he himself created, failed to bag the main target of the probe but did provide a shocking glimpse of the drugged-out underbelly of the New York club world—the corrupt black economy that underpins party people's supposedly innocent pleasures.

Insiders predicted that after turning informant on both Peter Gatien and then Chris Paciello, the double-crossing Caruso would end up dead, in jail, or a permanent guest of the witness protection program. Instead, clubland's version of Sammy "The Bull" Gravano made an extraordinary, if temporary, public comeback as Staten Island's answer to Vanilla Ice, all under the watchful eye of the feds.

Reports kept surfacing that Caruso was seen driving around town in the Wu-Tang Clan's promotional van and club-hopping in the company of group members Ghostface Killa and Cappadonna. Clubland insiders said with a snigger that Caruso's exterior had changed dramatically since the days when he ran his drug ring at the Limelight. Gone were the designer clothes and clean-cut looks, replaced by gold teeth that glinted in the half-light and carefully arranged cornrows. "He dresses like a hood rat," said one bouncer, who had seen Caruso. "He looks ludicrous. I got the strong impression that he's changed his appearance to protect himself from retaliation. He has to try and blend in with a black crowd, because all the Italian kids hate him."

After further enquiries, it emerged that Cappadonna employed Caruso as his personal manager, seemingly unaware of Caruso's status as a federal informer. (Caruso also managed Authorize FAM, featuring Caruso's and Cappadona's respective brothers.) Caruso had just returned from a twenty-five-date national tour with Wu members, even though his government cooperation agreement expressly forbade him from leaving New York state or associating with people who had criminal records—which covered most everybody in the Wu-Tang Clan. This suggested one of two possibilities: Either sloppy government officials weren't supervising their charge, or he was allowed to break his agreement for a specific purpose.

In what may or may not have been an amazing coincidence, at the same time Caruso was in their employ, the rap group was the subject of a federal gunrunning probe, sparked by two murders of Wu-Tang associates involving weapons purchased near the Clan's compound in Steubenville, Ohio, an old-fashioned blue-collar town forty miles west of Pittsburgh and the birthplace of Robert Diggs, the Wu musical mastermind known as RZA. The Clan owned a compound on the outskirts of town, where the self-styled ninja warriors of rap went to relax and practice target shooting, before returning to Shaolin (Wu-speak for Staten Island).

Other than changing his appearance, Caruso made little effort to keep a low profile. He informed colleagues that he was not scared of reprisals from people he'd informed on because the belligerent rap group—formed in the projects of Staten Island, where Caruso first met them—was watching his back. The man who used to be so afraid of reprisals from drug dealers he had robbed that he hired around-the-clock bodyguards, now had his own personal hip-hop Praetorian Guard.

Caruso told the Clan he used to peddle drugs at the Limelight and regaled them with racy tales of drug and sex orgies hosted by Peter Gatien. He forgot to mention he was also working for the government.

"When I first met him, I thought he was a big bullshitter," one member of the Wu-Tang organization said. "You could tell he wasn't really hard-core. He was trying too hard to be down."

"Cappadonna is easily influenced," said the same source. "I'm surprised Caruso was so easily able to get with the group. They're usually very careful about who they let into their inner circle, because they've been burnt before. He just sort of came from nowhere, and all of a sudden, he was a Wu-Tang manager. But just because Cappadonna and Ghostface Killa accept him, doesn't mean the rest of the group does."

The most peculiar thing about the whole story was that the Clan had no idea that Caruso was a federal informer. Despite all the publicity surrounding the Gatien and Paciello cases, Caruso had successfully hidden his snitch past from group members, who were obviously not great newspaper readers. After I started making enquiries about Caruso with the rap outfit's organization, group representatives confronted Caruso about the stories he was a stool pigeon. He not only denied supplying Wu-Tang information to the feds but also insisted that he had never informed on anybody. He told the Clan, "Don't believe anything you've read about me in the newspapers. The *Village Voice* has a vendetta against me. It's all bullshit. Haven't you ever read stuff about yourself that isn't true?" Also, when another of the group's representatives approached Ghostface Killa with court documents and *Voice* articles that conclusively proved that Caruso was a snitch, the rapper threatened to beat up the messenger. "How could you say that about Mike? Mike's a good guy," he fumed. The world-class con man Caruso had managed to sucker even the Wu-Tang Clan, a group defined by its street savvy.

"The Wu-Tang Clan doesn't care if he's a robber or a drug dealer," said another source inside their camp. "That's probably what attracted them to Caruso in the first place. But they would never have worked with him if they knew he was a rat. For obvious reasons, the Wu-Tang Clan is very anti–law enforcement. Having someone like Caruso as part of the organization could seriously lead to the breakup of the group."

After the May 2000 *Voice* cover story hit the stands and numerous other media outlets picked up the story, the Wu-Tang Clan fired Caruso—who was originally expecting to serve some jail time but had yet to spend a single day in prison. The group then went into damage-control mode. Bandmate Raekwon went on a New York radio station the night the article came out and blasted Cappadonna, saying he was never a full-fledged member of the crew to begin with, even though he was always depicted in group photos.

RZA told the press, "As far as the *Village Voice* article, when they're talking about a rat in the Wu-Tang, I mean, Mr. Caruso, he was working as Cappadonna's manager. He was not managing the Wu-Tang Clan. Just because he does something for Wu, that makes him Wu-Tang?"

"Caruso played the Wu-Tang Clan like a violin," said Steven Lewis, who worked with Caruso at the Limelight. "He's a pathological liar and a master manipulator. It's part of a pattern with him. He impresses one group of tough guys with what a big shot he is, betrays them, and then moves on the next group. But eventually even the stupid ones catch on to what a scumbag he really is."

Battle-scarred but fundamentally healthy, having gained if not a whole new outlook on existence, then at least an understanding that life is too precious to waste spending your time lurking around VIP rooms and getting high, I look back over the last six years with decidedly mixed feelings. I am grateful that I didn't end up dead, in jail, or a drug addict, like so many of the people I covered. I feel proud that I wasn't scared off by the numerous threats made against my life.

But I also feel a deep sense of sadness over the harsh truths I uncovered about a milieu I was once so passionately wedded to. Sorrow not just for the many lives lost or ruined, but melancholy at the creative potential squandered, at how club culture had failed to live up to its utopian promises. When I first arrived in America at the end of the '80s, trying to escape the dead weight of Britain's rigid social order, I saw what went on at American clubs and raves as perfect but temporary democracies of desire, an ideal world where racial, sexual, and social divisions were dissolved in the communal abandon of the dance floor. The mass euphoria and emotional solidarity I experienced while dancing at downtown clubs like the World and Sound Factory seemed like a possible model for a future society.

Nowadays, after too many nights seeing club kids' inhumanity to fellow club kids, I'm more likely to view discos as institutions constructed on cruelty. Club culture is supposed to be about community, self-expression, and joyous release through music. Nightclubs are meant to function as laboratories of style where new trends and modes of being are spearheaded. They're not supposed to come with a body count.